T0303138

GUARDIAN

LIFE IN THE CROSSHAIRS
OF THE CIA'S WAR ON TERROR

GUARDIAN

LIFE IN THE CROSSHAIRS OF THE CIA'S WAR ON TERROR

THOMAS PECORA

WITH JON LAND AND LINDSAY PRESTON

Post Hill
PRESS

A POST HILL PRESS BOOK

Guardian:
Life in the Crosshairs of the CIA's War on Terror
© 2019 by Thomas Pecora with Jon Land and Lindsay Preston
All Rights Reserved

ISBN: 978-1-64293-047-4
ISBN (eBook): 978-1-64293-048-1

Cover art by Cody Corcoran
Interior design and composition by Greg Johnson/Textbook Perfect
Author Photo by Mike Krukowski

Per CIA regulations, this book has been reviewed by the CIA's Publication Review Board. This does not constitute an official release of CIA information. All statements of fact, opinion, or analysis expressed are those of the author and do not reflect the official positions or views of the Central Intelligence Agency (CIA) or any other U.S. Government agency. Nothing in the contents should be construed as asserting or implying U.S. Government authentication of information or CIA endorsement of the author's views. This material has been reviewed solely for classification.

Post Hill Press
New York • Nashville
posthillpress.com

Published in the United States of America

To my family, who supported me when I was in harm's way and suffered through the fear. My wrestling coaches who taught me the hard lessons of life—that only by hard work, dedication, sacrifice, and mental toughness can we make a difference. And to the leaders who I was fortunate to have had as my bosses—Tom M., Randy B., and Jim P.—you believed in me and helped me learn how to take care of my people AND get the mission done!

*A hero is someone who has given his or her life
to something bigger than oneself.*

—JOSEPH CAMPBELL

CONTENTS

PROLOGUE

Manila, Philippines ▪ February 1989

"I've been targeted for assassination, sir," Colonel James Nicholas Rowe said, speaking from his desk in Manila.

There was silence on the other end of the line in Washington. Rowe knew that William Taft, Deputy Secretary of Defense, was not equipped to answer swiftly, but at some point he was going to have to say something.

"Sir," Rowe prodded. "Sir?"

Taft cleared his throat. "How sure are we that this source is credible?"

"Very."

"Is he *your* source?" Taft asked.

"No, sir, he's one of my men's. However, this source has informed us many times on New People's Army [NPA] movement. I have no reason to doubt that his intel will be just as credible this time."

Once again, there was no response but silence. Rowe had been doing this long enough to know that the longer the line seemed dead, the higher the probability that he would end up the same way.

"Sir," Rowe prodded, breaking the quiet.

"I find no reason to raise the threat level or to authorize additional protection assets based on the word of a Filipino asset," Taft said, as if he actually understood the NPA and how they operated.

Rowe's voice took on a sterner tone. "Sir, I ask you to reconsider. My name isn't the *only* one on that list. As you can see from the documents I sent you, this threat is very real and they are planning numerous assassinations."

"I read the documents, Colonel," Taft snapped, continuing to brush Rowe off. "My decision is final. I'll reconsider if more information surfaces, but until then this conversation is over."

Click.

So, Rowe thought, there would be no changes to the official threat level and no additional manpower or equipment sent to Manila. He was going to have to regroup, but that was nothing new for him, especially here. If anyone was capable of improvising and overcoming, it was Nick Rowe.

During the Vietnam War, he served as a first lieutenant in the US Army's 5th Special Forces Group, a member of a twelve-man "A-team." After only three months in Tan Phu in An Xuyên Province, on October 29, 1963, Rowe, along with Captain Humberto "Rocky" R. Versace and Sergeant Daniel L. Pitzer, were separated from their team while accompanying a Civilian Irregular Defense Group (CIDG) company on an operation to drive a Viet Cong unit out of the village of Le Coeur.

That morning, Rowe and the team left their camp and followed some canals that led toward the village where intel reports indicated that the enemy was in the process of establishing a small command post. Rowe and his men had a plan on how they were going to deal with the Viet Cong in the village. They all knew their roles, and they also knew the risk. Rowe was ready for battle the moment they crossed into enemy territory. As they passed through some thick brush and trees, the village appeared in a clearing. The only thing Rowe could hear was the beating of his heart. He knew that wasn't right, not at all. He should've heard *something*; the reason why he didn't only dawned on him once he got a closer look at Le Coeur.

The enemy was gone.

Rowe's CIDG company decided to pursue the Viet Cong, tracking them through a thicket of twisted branches, bushes, and thick brush. Suddenly Rowe heard boots crunching the overgrowth—the only warning he got before the Viet Cong viciously attacked the company from three sides, forcing Rowe and his men to run for cover in a direction that left them cut off from their vehicles and any semblance of friendly forces. The CIDG ended up pinned down and mired in a firefight that lasted for over eight hours. Finally, as light bled from the sky amid the stench of gunpowder and scorched foliage, Rowe, Versace, and Pitzer were taken prisoner.

Once they were in the hands of the Viet Cong, the US soldiers were separated, and Rowe was taken to the U Minh Forest in the extreme southern part of Vietnam. He was forced to live in a tiny, filthy bamboo cage but remained determined to keep the Viet Cong from learning that he was an intelligence officer currently in possession of vital information. During his initial interrogation, the Viet Cong questioned him about his background in the Army and Rowe told them he was a draftee engineer charged with building schools and working on civil affairs projects.

The interrogations continued day after day, but the Viet Cong couldn't make Rowe backtrack from his story. His captors gave him engineering problems to solve and Rowe quickly rose to the task, thanks to his basic training years before at West Point. Small consolation, given that his captors had nothing but time and Rowe wasn't going anywhere.

Still, his cover wasn't blown until five years later, when the Viet Cong obtained a list of high-value POWs. That list identified Rowe as an intelligence officer, and the Viet Cong decided to execute him for his lies. On December 31, 1968, he was led deep into the jungle for his planned execution. All he could hear was the pounding of his heart and crackling of the ground brush underfoot, the unnerving silence of his captors taking him back to the day he'd first been captured. That silence, though, was soon broken by the sounds of a Huey helicopter.

It momentarily distracted Rowe from his thoughts of looming death but, more importantly, it distracted his captors.

He knew this was his only chance. With one swift blow he struck his guard and fled into the bush. Rowe was able to get the attention of the chopper that, after initially thinking he was a Viet Cong, landed in a clearing and scooped the colonel up. He ended up being one of only thirty-four men to ever escape from a Vietnam POW camp, where he'd been held for sixty-two months.

Recalling those events from twenty-six years ago, Rowe knew that if he could survive his stint as a prisoner of the Viet Cong, he could survive the threat posed by the NPA in Manila and, on paper, he seemed like the perfect man to do just that.

"I took a different route from most and came into Special Forces," he said in an oral history interview just before leaving for the Philippines. "I had made a decision then that, as far as I was concerned, I had found what I wanted in the military, and I simply had to find a way to stay with it."

Staying with it brought Colonel Rowe to Manila in 1987 to be chief of the Joint US Military Advisory Group (JUSMAG). JUSMAG was the US military element that provided counterinsurgency training for the Armed Forces of the Philippines that were in dire need of improving their combat skill sets, given the strong insurgency threat they were facing. For more than a decade the Philippines had been under attack by the NPA, a communist insurgency not unlike the Viet Cong that was dedicated to overthrowing the government. These insurgents were ruthless and known to specifically target military and police officers, striking fear into the ranks of both as a result. Once an officer or enlisted soldier was targeted for assassination, success was almost guaranteed thanks to the NPA's *Sparrow* hit teams—trained killers known for their ability to go from concealment to dead shot in less than one second flat, which gave their targets no time to react.

The Sparrows operated in small groups, with some members providing surveillance on the target while others functioned as lookouts and backup for the actual assassins. Several of these hit men had been captured and had shared some of their methods with their interrogators. The preferred weapon of Sparrow hit men was a .45-caliber Colt 1911 semiautomatic pistol, which they'd hide in their waistband. They would approach their target empty handed and then, when they were within shooting range, use their nonshooting hand to push up on the end of the barrel to raise the handle of the pistol up and over the waistband of their pants, where they could grasp, draw, and fire it in one single, smooth motion.

Rowe's phone call to Deputy Secretary of Defense William Taft had come in the wake of the discovery that he'd been targeted. Under very real threat, Rowe would have to keep a low profile and stay under the radar as much as possible. He knew that the Sparrow teams would most likely try to take him out while he was moving around Manila, since striking in public places was a part of their modus operandi. He took extreme precautions, taking new routes to and from work as well as trying to travel at odd hours. He began using a light armored vehicle to boot. Rowe, after all, was a master at outthinking his enemies; he was even the creator of one of the most advanced military training courses in the special operations field: the Survival, Evasion, Resistance, and Escape (SERE) course. He felt confident he could survive long enough to find more concrete evidence to push Secretary Taft into supplying the additional security that was desperately needed.

Over the next two months, while staying on the move and continuing to avoid his attackers, Rowe worked to substantiate the informant's claims. Unfortunately, no one had any details about the precise content of the alleged hit list. Finding members of the Sparrow team was equally as tough; these assassins might as well have been ghosts. Every potential lead turned out to be a dead end. Rowe could feel the time ticking away and, with it, his luck ebbing.

Like many career US Army officers, Rowe was a creature of habit, waking every day at 5:00 a.m. sharp. His morning routine never varied, breakfast consisting of coffee and toast, then shower, shave, and a quick kiss on his wife's sleeping head, all before his armored car arrived at 5:45 a.m. to take him to JUSMAG. April 21, 1989 was no different than any other day, as hot and humid as all the others, the fetid air rich with buzzing insects that included a breed of hyperaggressive mosquitos that attacked their prey in waves befitting the best infantry detachment.

Rowe had finished buttoning his finely starched, pressed shirt when he heard his ride pull up in the driveway of the tiny bungalow he had been calling home over the past two years. No matter how hard he tried, he was never able to acclimate to the constant heat in Manila. The air was always as stifling inside his house as outside, sometimes even more so given that the thin walls held the heat like a blast oven. Buttoning up his uniform left a layer of sweat already teasing the fabric, its tightness constricting him and making him almost forget the honor that came with wearing it. Rowe exhaled deeply and then took in a big breath in the hope that the extra oxygen might refresh him, but no luck. He then proceeded to lock the tiny bungalow door and, after instinctively checking the scene around him, made his way to the armored vehicle that would take him to work at JUSMAG headquarters.

"How are you doing today, sir?" his driver, Joaquin Vinua, asked him.

"Very well, Joaquin. How about you?" Rowe responded as he slid into the back seat of the sedan.

Joaquin had been Rowe's regular driver since he had arrived in Manila. Rowe liked Joaquin. He was a nice young man, hard working, and very prompt. He was unfailingly polite and gave Rowe the quiet he needed to do his work on their excursions around town.

"Just fine, sir. Where are we headed this morning?" Joaquin asked once he had taken his place in the driver's seat.

"JUSMAG headquarters, please."

"Yes, sir," Joaquin replied.

He pulled the black armored sedan out of Rowe's gravel driveway and headed across town, leaving Rowe to his work in the back seat. He had a stack of documents a mile high that needed reviewing; at least the considerable drive time allowed for that. JUSMAG was located in Quezon City, a suburb of the capital Manila, and fell within the National Capital Region of the Philippines. Quezon City had a staggering population of more than a million and a half people living within sixty-four square miles. While major parts of Manila were stricken with desperate levels of poverty, Quezon City had been built up over the past decades from a suburb into the beginning of a thriving business district. The roads were wide and paved, in stark opposition to the unpaved, rut-strewn avenues that were common in metro areas.

"I apologize, sir. Traffic is moving slowly today," Joaquin said when their journey had slowed to a maddening crawl of stops and starts.

Rowe looked up from his papers as his armored sedan entered Quezon City limits. His watch read 7:00 a.m., and he was usually at his desk by now.

"It's all right, Joaquin. Nothing we can do about it."

Rowe took a moment, as he always did, to marvel at the sight of the city that was surrounded by the devastation wrought by abject poverty. No wonder there was an active insurgency and frequent acts of terrorism within the country. Quezon City was one of the few places in the capital region where you couldn't see the efforts being made by the NPA to burn the government to the ground. At least, that's what the colonel had always thought.

Not so much today.

"Joaquin, could you speed up, please?" Rowe asked, his voice registering concern, a feeling of dread suddenly coming over him.

"Excuse me, sir?"

Before either could speak another word, a car pulled up next to the sedan and two hooded men brandished M16s and .45-caliber pistols.

BANG! BANG! BANG!

Bullets pelted the car, pockmarking the armored steel and puckering the transparent armor of the windows. Both men instinctively ducked down in their respective seats as bullets continued to impact the vehicle. The ambush happened so quickly that neither

Joaquin nor Rowe himself were able to draw their pistols before a rifle round penetrated the edge of the back door of the sedan and struck Colonel Rowe in the head.

Philippine Army Colonel Eduardo Lachica of the capital's Regional Defense Command was later quoted as saying, "Nothing could have stopped them. This was a precision attack, with every detail planned."

"They [the attackers] just opened the window of their car and started firing," said Rick Austria, a nineteen-year-old cashier at the STP Shell service station near where the attack occurred. "They sprayed him with bullets from the back, then they cut off his car and sprayed it again from the front. You couldn't count how many times they fired."

The lone bullet that had pierced the exterior of the colonel's vehicle was truly Murphy's Law at work, since the only part of the sedan that wasn't armored was a small seam near the top of the rear window. The fatal bullet had managed to sneak through this gap and find Rowe inside the cab. The hooded assassins escaped unimpeded through traffic, leaving Rowe's armored vehicle stalled among the snarl of cars in the traffic circle where the ambush occurred.

Rowe and Vinua were rushed to a nearby military hospital, where Vinua was treated for non-life-threatening wounds. Colonel James Nicholas "Nick" Rowe wasn't as fortunate, dying of his wounds at the age of fifty-one and leaving behind a wife, two sons, and two daughters.

"This act will only strengthen American resolve to stand with the government and the people of the Philippines led by President Aquino," said US Ambassador to the Philippines Nicholas Platt at the time. "We will not be deterred by terrorists. Nick would have it no other way."

Quiapo, Manila • June 1989

"This isn't going to be easy. We're going to have to attack quickly and with force," Captain Andrada of the Philippines National Intelligence

Coordinating Agency (NICA) told his men. Everyone on the six-man team nodded. They had gone over the plan at least a dozen times and now, as they stood before the building where the raid would take place, the men nonetheless felt a deep sense of foreboding about the prospects for the mission's success.

The Sparrow hit team had taken refuge along the Pasig River outside Quezon City, the perfect location for terrorists looking to avoid a sneak attack. Most of the shanty homes in this section of town were joined together with their back sides pressed up against the river, not allowing law enforcement to stage an assault from the sides or rear. That left the front as the only means of access, unless they approached from the river—hardly an inviting proposition at night and even less so during the day, where their movements would be visible to the general public. So today the team was going to take the precarious risk of entering through the front. A dangerous move, but less so than daring the river currents that were running wild from the March rain.

"When we hit the door I want you to move like you got fire ants in your shorts, do you hear me?" Andrada barked, reiterating the urgency for speed.

"Yes, sir!" the men replied in unison.

Andrada exhaled, knowing it was now or never. "GO! GO! GO!"

The seven men ran, guns drawn, toward the middle unit of a four-unit building. Andrada kicked the door in and Tomas, the youngest on his team, entered the home first. The others followed—moving left and right to get out of the "fatal funnel" of the home's entranceway. The team broke up into two-man elements, splitting up the house and following their plan to divide and conquer each room. It was exactly as their American allies had trained them.

"Clear!" yelled Tomas from the back bedroom.

Four more "Clear!" responses echoed through the house as all of the rooms were entered and secured by the team.

"Assemble on me!" Andrada roared as his officers gathered in the living room of the house without encountering a single hostile. "Damn it! The fuckers got away!"

"Now what, sir?" Tomas asked.

"Search the house. See what we can salvage from this mess," Andrada said, doubting that they would find anything useful.

It appeared that everything had been trashed, suggesting someone had tipped off the Sparrow hit team that the forces of NICA were coming. There was no other explanation for why the targets had decided to destroy everything and flee. Andrada was just about to return to NICA headquarters to report on the raid's failure when one of his officers came in, waving a piece of paper.

"What have you got there, Castillo?" he asked the man.

"I'm not sure, but I think it's something important," Castillo said, handing the scrap of paper over to Andrada.

The page contained a list of names. The top name on the list was someone Andrada knew as a senior US government official: James Misleki. Only a very select few people in the country knew that Misleki was actually the CIA's chief of station.

The second name on the list was the late Colonel Nicholas Rowe.

* * *

Andrada sat in the small waiting room outside the office of the head of NICA. Director General Joseph "Vito" Cruz's secretary peeked up from her desk at him, her curiosity almost getting the better of her. Andrada fidgeted nervously, holding a photocopy of the page containing the list of names marked for assassination by the NPA. He didn't know if passing along this information from NICA would make a difference for the chief of station; Colonel Rowe had known of the threat lodged against him, but they'd gotten to him anyway.

"The director general will see you now," said Cruz's secretary, laying the phone back in its cradle.

"Thank you," Andrada said and showed himself into the DG/ NICA's door under her watchful eye.

"Hello, sir," Andrada greeted.

"Good day, Captain. So to what do I owe the privilege of your company?" Director General Cruz asked him.

Andrada handed DG Cruz the piece of paper and explained how it had been discovered in the aftermath of the failed raid. If Colonel Rowe's death wasn't confirmation enough that the threat from the NPA Sparrow teams was real, this list would provide all the evidence needed to raise the threat level and spur CIA chief James Misleki to increase his security resources to the appropriate level, something that was denied Colonel Rowe.

"I will handle this situation personally," Cruz said, "and I appreciate both your service and the fact that you brought this directly to me."

"It's my duty," Andrada replied, "but also my pleasure. We have to show the Americans that we are doing all we can to address these threats."

Cruz showed Andrada to the door, then returned to his desk and dropped into his cushy chair. He knew it would only be a matter of time before another American would fall to a Sparrow bullet if something wasn't done. So he picked up the phone and placed a direct call, specifically to the office of the CIA's chief of station.

"Hello, this is Director General Cruz of NICA and I have an urgent matter to discuss with Mr. Misleki," he told the woman who answered.

Cruz knew that the conversation would be followed by an equally urgent meeting, during which he would share all of NICA's considerable intelligence on the NPA Sparrow teams. What he didn't know was that Jim Misleki wasn't about to run from a fight.

"You think I should pull up stakes and go home," Misleki said, after Cruz had briefed him. "Turn tail and run."

"It's something to consider, until NICA forces can get a handle on things."

"And how would that look to our enemies, never mind our friends? This makes my mission here all the more vital. I'm not going anywhere," Misleki countered.

"With all due respect," Cruz said, his tone measured, "I'm sure Colonel Rowe thought the same thing."

Misleki knew all too well that Rowe had attempted to go through the Defense Department to raise the threat level and had gotten nowhere. Asking for help in-house, from his own people based at the CIA in Langley, would produce far better results. The help had to come fast, though, or he'd be joining Nick Rowe on the long list of Sparrow victims.

Wisconsin, 1989

"Tom, Tom, you have a phone call!!" my stepfather Richard yelled up the stairs, drawing me from the tiny bedroom in the house that I had lived in since I was born. It was just a few weeks after that list had been found outside Quezon City, Philippines.

"Yeah? Who is it?" I yelled back as I slipped into a pair of jeans.

"It sounds important, so get down here!" Richard said, holding the phone on its long extension cord.

I hit the stairs at a run, made the turn into the living room, and gave Richard a rueful grin. "I hope I haven't kept the president waiting!" Then I grabbed the phone and said, "Hello?"

Richard could tell by my facial expression that something was up.

"Are you kidding me?" I asked the person on the other end of the line. "Really, who is this?"

Richard's curiosity was peaked as he watched me.

"If this is a joke, it's not funny!"

Richard looked at me and mouthed silently, "Who is it?"

I put my hand on the phone receiver and said, "It's some guy who says he's with the CIA." I took my hand away. "I really don't like practical jokes!"

Then my stepfather watched my expression turn somber as the conversation continued.

"Yes, sir…. No, sir…. Yes, sir. I am definitely interested…. Thank you, sir. I will be there. Thank you again, sir," I said, hanging up the phone and looking back at my stepfather. "Richard, you'll never guess what just happened. I have an interview with the CIA next week!"

Richard was normally a stoic guy, but this news got even him excited. "Whoa, so that was the CIA?"

"Yes, in the person of Michael Weston, a recruiter."

I had forgotten that, two months before, I'd seen a CIA advertisement in the *Milwaukee Journal* and had sent in an application. I thought the call had been from one of my wrestler buddies giving me the razz. But it was the CIA for real, and now I had an interview.

"Wow, what an opportunity. You have to give it your best shot," Richard said, grinning.

He was ex-Navy and had served a tour teaching engineering classes at the Naval Academy. So the notion that I would be serving my country clearly impressed him, even made him proud.

"Definitely. And then some. Gotta get the suit pressed and shine the shoes."

I met the recruiter at a downtown Milwaukee hotel the following week. He went over my résumé and asked me a bunch of probing questions about whether I had done drugs or had a criminal record. He told me that the next step was to wait for the letter that would let me know if I'd made it past the initial screening and was eligible for the formal set of interviews in Washington, DC. To say I was excited was an understatement. I had always wanted to be in the federal service, having seriously considered the Marines in college and later thinking of applying to the DEA or FBI.

In the meantime, I went back to my normal life as a twenty-six-year-old born and raised in the small suburb of Greenfield on the south side of Milwaukee. I had recently received a master's degree in communications from the University of Wisconsin–Whitewater, and while looking for a "career" job I was doing my thing, which amounted to coaching wrestling and working at a J.C. Penny catalog warehouse.

Several weeks later, I received a letter telling me I'd made the initial cut and giving me instructions on when I was to fly out to Washington, DC, for the next phase of the process. I was nervous. I really had no idea what to expect, because no one I knew had ever worked for the CIA. I didn't even know anyone who knew a CIA employee. I hit the library and did some research on the "Agency," especially its structure and history, to familiarize myself with what I was getting into.

I flew out to Washington on a Monday and went to the hotel they arranged for me in Tysons Corner, Virginia. The next morning a bus came and picked me up from the lobby, along with several other people, and took us to a building only a few miles away where the Agency began to process us. We filled out forms, signed documents, and waited for our interviews. I sat with a whole bunch of people, and no one made eye contact or spoke to each other. A surreal experience, to say the least.

When I was finally called in for my interviews, a really nice lady who I took to be the secretary escorted me up to the third floor and introduced me to my first interviewer. He introduced himself as "Bob," no last name mentioned. I found that strange, but I had no time to consider the anomaly because he jumped in immediately with questions about my background, hobbies, work history—pretty much everything. I was then moved to other offices, where I had several other sessions with more "first name only" interviewers. The last interviewer told me not to tell anyone that I had applied for employment at the CIA, at which point I fessed up to the truth that, as someone from the Midwest, interviewing with the CIA was a big deal, so of course I had told all my friends. He then told me, with a totally serious expression on his face, that I'd have to go back and tell everyone I didn't get the job. He said if I made it through the background investigation and polygraph, that my employment at the CIA was not to be discussed—for my entire career.

"Are we clear?" he asked me.

"Yes, we are," I said, a bit stunned by the fact that if I got the job, I'd have to spend the next twenty or so years living a double life.

The secretary showed up and took me to a small room where I took a personality test and had to provide a writing sample. Once I completed those, I was done for the day. Before I left, I asked the secretary how I could get thank-you letters to the individual interviewers that I had met. She looked surprised and then gave me her name and address. It was a trick I'd learned from a job-hunting book called *What Color Is Your Parachute?* I figured I had nothing to lose and thought the gesture might have some effect. (Sure enough, I was told later that I was the only one of the interviewees from the batch of prospective hires who'd done so and that it had indeed had a strong impact on my getting hired.)

The next morning, I took a polygraph test and then flew back to Milwaukee wondering if the CIA was my future. Keeping with the instructions, I told everyone I'd been rejected. They were disappointed but soon forgot about the whole thing, just as I'd hoped.

Several months later I received a generic letter in the mail saying I had been accepted into "federal service," accompanied by a reporting date. I told people I'd been selected for a different federal job and would soon be moving to the Washington, DC, area. Some of my friends believed me, though others were convinced I was really joining the CIA in spite of my protestations otherwise.

The last week of August 1989, I packed up my 1982 Toyota Tercel hatchback with all my possessions and drove off to start my career in the Central Intelligence Agency, arriving in time for my official "Entrance On Duty" date of September 5, 1989.

So, as the CIA's station chief in Manila, Jim Misleki, feared for his life, I began work at Agency headquarters where plans were already being hatched to keep him and countless other endangered government employees alive.

Author's Note

Methodology

I have chosen to tell this story as a first person narrative account, especially since the majority of this book is about things that I experienced or did firsthand. Once the basic material had been approved by the PRB, I worked with two assistant writers to create a "novelized" approach to the subjects. Although written as a narrative, this is a work of non-fiction. No major events or time lines were altered significantly.

Accuracy

I have included accounts of some events in which I was not directly involved. The information about these events was acquired through personal interviews with participants, and from a review of relevant accounts, reports, articles, and books. In some cases, I have had to use some "poetic license" with certain dates and have consolidated events to provide a better narrative. But in all cases, I have tried to keep the circumstances and events as true to the facts as possible. Any inaccuracies in detail are my fault alone.

PART ONE

THE POC

1

CIA Security Field Office ▪ 1990

"Per your initial CIA orientation, you are not to discuss your CIA affiliation with anyone outside of your immediate family. This is especially important while you are working as a background investigator," Assistant Special Agent in Charge (ASAC) Andrew Connors said to the newly arrived group of security officers as he showed them around the Security Field Office. "You are now an integral part of the Office of Security. Personnel security is a key skill within the multidisciplinary aspects of being a CIA security officer. If you successfully complete this tour you will be well on your way to becoming a Multi-Discipline Security Officer."

The group of recruits nodded in understanding while trying to keep up with Officer Connors, whose fast walk was more like the average individual's jog.

A head popped out of the cubicle next to mine as the fledgling Agency security officers passed by. "Tom…Tom? Hey, Pecora! Calling Investigator Tom Pecora!"

It took a second for me to hear my name being called. I was knee deep in a pile of paperwork that only seemed to grow no matter how fast I worked.

*Entrance On
Duty photograph,
September 5, 1989.*

"What do you need, Brad?" I answered back.

Brad McNickle was the guy in the neighboring cubicle. He was twenty-two years old and fresh out of college, meaning he'd been lucky just to land this job. He had all the right traits to be in the position, along with a slight case of ADD that he'd managed to hide from the review board.

"Did you hear Connors?" Brad asked me.

"Background noise. Kind of like the radio at this point."

"Well, have you ever noticed how he gives the exact same speech to new officers every single time? I mean, he doesn't even change a word. And every time I hear it, I get more confused. Why the hell can't we tell anyone but our parents what we do? It's not like it's some sort of risk to national security, or security of any matter. Don't you find it to be sort of bullshit?"

I'd only been working as a security officer for the CIA for a few months now, but overall I had to disagree with Brad. He was right in the fact that not telling people where we work was a drag, but those were the stipulations with becoming part of the greatest intelligence agency in the world.

"Rules are rules," I said with a shrug.

"Fucking stupid rule if you ask me. I'd be more upset if my girlfriend knew that I worked for the CIA and all I did all day was interview friends and coworkers of current and future engineers, secretaries, and janitors working for defense companies. I wonder if James Bond started out that way? Is there like a *James Bond: The Early Years* book? That's the one I want to read."

I started to laugh. "Nope."

I suppose it shouldn't have been much of a surprise that a lot of us young officers had based our career choice on the lifestyles of our idols from movies and books. We identified with those heroes, and I guess I was really no exception. I'd always been a voracious reader and entertained dreams of saving the world, like James Bond, since I was a kid. But Brad was right: our jobs couldn't be further from that, nothing like the books or movies. It was paperwork. Lots and lots of paperwork. Brad and I spent our days conducting background investigations on current and future government contract workers whose companies worked on classified projects. Besides the engineers and other technical personnel, we also interviewed the support staff who would be working on the sites—the cleaning crew, administrative personnel, and so on. Not very exciting stuff, to say the least, and far from the rarified, adventurous air of James Bond. I felt like a typical grunt working in an equally typical human resources department, going from defense contract site to government contract site, asking the same list of questions and getting the same boring answers.

I didn't realize it at the time, but that was a true test of discipline, gauging who could handle all the mundane drudgery; being a prime reason why it was one of the first jobs the Agency assigned to new security officers. To test our mettle, loyalty, and patience, I guess. As my father used to say, "Success is the management of boredom!" Even so, interviewing references, pulling personnel records, reviewing financial reports, and visiting neighborhoods to learn about the subjects of our investigations was monotonous, especially for a twenty-seven-year-old who thought that working for the CIA was going to be more like a movie than the typical game of life.

Even though I craved adventure, I hadn't originally planned on joining the CIA. I attended Marquette University for my bachelor's degree, then the University of Wisconsin–Whitewater for my master's. Other than the summer I spent bartending in England after I graduated college, I'd rarely traveled from my hometown. Hardly the recipe for a daring life full of intrigue and adventure and, in fact, not really a recipe for anything meaningful at all.

Back in college I'd considered joining the US Marine Corps, but after successfully completing the first six-week segment of USMC Officer Candidate School (OCS), I decided to not attend the required second six-week session of OCS training in order to continue my education. I had certainly never thought of applying to the CIA; it was truly the last thing on my mind. It wasn't until I saw that employment advertisement in the local newspaper that I even considered a career with the CIA. That ad flipped a switch in my head, shining a light onto the calling I'd been looking for. Or so I thought.

As I continued to fixate on the thought that I was no more than a hapless bureaucrat, ASAC Connors smacked a thick file down in front of me.

"Pecora, this case needs to be closed ASAP. Push everything else off your plate. Start with interviews with his neighbors. If you leave now you can get there and be on your way back before dark."

"Sir," I started, "I've got several other cases that need immediate attention. Maybe Brad should take this one."

Officer Connors glanced at Brad, who was leaning back in his seat, chewing on his pen as he listened to his Sony Discman.

"I thought about it, but he's such a smart-ass I'm worried he'll get himself killed in this particular neighborhood," Connors said, knowing full well Brad was listening. "High crime rate, with gangs and such. Don't want to order a man to his death over a background check."

"Fair enough," I said, gathering up what I would need for the interview.

Connors started to walk away, then swung back around. "One more thing, Pecora. Never second-guess my orders again."

I exited the Security Field Office and took the elevator from the third floor down to the garage. The field office was located in a typical office building in the area, innocuous and utterly unremarkable, unless you happened to stroll through the outer door and were confronted by an ultra-secure inner door equipped with state-of-the-art security locking hardware.

My "G-Ride" was a government-provided white Chevy Cavalier. I was required to drive the Cavalier to and from work and to all work-related locations. The snag was that I wasn't allowed to drive the car for any non-work-related matters, which meant that I needed an additional car. This left me with two cars to laboriously find spaces for on the crowded city street on which I lived. It was another example of the CIA being diametrically different from the world I'd envisioned, far more about bureaucracy than adventure and heroism. Everything came with a catch, even a simple work car, and rules and regulations piled atop one another.

What would James Bond have made of this?

I started my thirty-minute drive from downtown to the center of a suburb to meet the subject's neighbors. The subject, one Michael White, had recently applied for a maintenance position at a local government contractor. They were short on maintenance personnel, so this investigation had turned into a rush job and Michael was one of the most skilled candidates on their list. Because of that, I was on my way to interview his neighbors who lived in the middle of the "crime/war zone" suburb, as it was classified.

Because of the rampant drug trafficking, gang activity, and drive-by shootings, the unrelenting violence in the area had continued to escalate. The homicide rate was at an all-time high, and bullets flew through the air like snowflakes on Christmas in my hometown of Milwaukee. So there I was, driving a G-Ride into a war zone, unarmed unless you counted the blue ballpoint pen in my pocket and the old-fashioned tire iron in the trunk. Well, I assumed the tire iron was there, as I had never actually checked.

I parked directly across the street from a house next to the subject's residence. The neighbor's house was a small cottage-style home that was easily the nicest on the block. A chain-link fence surrounded the tiny but well-maintained yard, making it obvious that this resident worked very hard to keep their home up to a higher standard, making the most of what little they had.

The interview was off to a good start before it had even begun.

I grabbed my briefcase, scanned my surroundings, and decided it was safe to head toward the house. I got out of my car and started to walk across the street.

BANG! BANG!

I immediately crouched and looked for cover. I was trying to pin down the origins of the shots when I saw the source of what, for a second, I had been certain was a drive-by shooting with me as the target:

A beat-up Oldsmobile, two driveways down, had backfired. *Seriously? That was just pathetic....*

I laughed to myself, hoping it would calm my nerves and slow my pounding heart. Then I straightened up and walked up to the front door of the residence, keeping my head on a swivel as I scanned the neighborhood for any *real* potential threats.

A few nosy neighbors were staring at me as I knocked on the front door, repeating the process when there was no response.

"Coming, coming," a woman I had listed as a "Mrs. Melville" said from inside the home.

"Take your time," I called back, which sounded strange coming from the same man who'd just mistaken a backfire for a drive-by!

24

Mrs. Melville opened the door. She was an older woman, possibly seventy-five years old, with a pleasant smile and big, deep-set eyes that radiated warmth and kindness. It wasn't hard picturing her taking pride in having the best house and yard on the block, and I had the sense she took similar pride in setting an example for her younger neighbors.

"Yes, how can I help you?" she asked, her voice soft and sweet, no suspicion underscoring it at all.

"Hello, my name is Thomas Pecora and I'm a federal investigator," I replied, launching into my standard spiel. "I'm here to talk to you about your neighbor, Michael White."

"Awfully jumpy for a federal agent, aren't you?" she quipped.

The lady must have been watching when I got out of my G-Ride and seen me react to the backfire. I chuckled, wondering if James Bond enjoyed a similar reaction to the sound of backfiring cars.

"You sure you're in the right line of work, young man?" she asked, still laughing.

I smiled. "Well, maybe not," I said, inwardly wondering what she'd make of the fact that I worked for the CIA. "Your neighbor has applied for a job that requires we conduct a background investigation."

"Well, then come on inside. Happy to help my neighbor in any way I can."

Like many of the neighbors that I had interviewed, Mrs. Melville sang her neighbor's praises, but, unlike many neighbors, she did so spiced with anecdotes and genuine pathos that made me believe she was being both truthful and accurate. I looked in her eyes and saw the high regard she had for Michael. She was no more objective than any of the other neighbors that I'd interviewed, but I had the sense she was more in tune to the goings-on of the neighborhood as exhibited by the care and devotion with which she tended her home and yard. A woman who took great pride in making things the best they could be, both people and places.

The interview was short and sweet, conducted over lemonade and cookies she served on a neat tray embossed with a floral design. I was able to conclude the interview well before dark and made it back to my car for the ride back to the office without any more perceived bullets flying.

Brad, still at his desk, asked me how the interview went.

"Another neighbor who claims the subject is perfect," I replied. "Apparently only saints apply for government work."

2

CIA Security Field Office ▪ May 1991

I wasn't sure what was harder, surviving crime-filled suburbs or the monotony of my day. I knew that there was purpose in the work I was doing, but I wasn't sure if I was going to survive the basic training of paperwork.

To break up the boredom, as a kind of way station before I found what I was really looking for, I decided to spend my free time as an assistant wrestling coach at a local junior college. Wrestling had always been a huge part of my life. I was the first state-champion wrestler from my high school and attended Marquette University on an athletic scholarship. I'd compiled a stellar record in college, competing twice at the Division I National Championships, and in my senior year was ranked eighteenth in the nation. I figured that if the CIA career didn't pan out for me, I could always become a full-time wrestling coach. The assistant coach job at the junior college wasn't action-packed or glamorous, but it was fulfilling and kept me on the mat.

"How's your team doing?" Brad asked me.

"Four and O," I told him proudly.

"Nice!"

"Guys are doing great. They're working really hard."

Wrestled at the US Freestyle National Championships, 1991.

"The coach thing seems to suit you," Brad said sincerely.

"Thanks, man. It does seem to be a good fit. I'm not made for sitting at a desk all day."

Just as I said that, a notice flashed across my computer:

ANY SECURITY OFFICERS INTERESTED IN ATTENDING A SPECIAL PROTECTIVE OPERATIONS COURSE (SPOC) SHOULD APPLY HERE

Intrigued, I continued to read. Those accepted to the course would make up a new elite security team called the *POC*, or Protective Operations Cadre. It sounded like an amazing opportunity to get into the action. At the time, I didn't know the training course was developed to field a new type of security team to respond to attacks like the one that had happened a couple years before in Manila, when Colonel Nick Rowe was assassinated. The POC had been created to make sure the Agency did not lose someone like the Army lost Colonel Rowe. I decided instantly to apply to be part of a team that was going to save lives, the polar opposite of being stuck behind a desk all day running background checks.

I submitted my application for the POC in May of 1991. There was nothing to do but wait to hear back. I was on pins and needles and needed to find a way to occupy my time while I was anxiously waiting, so I decided to ramp up my focus on wrestling, get myself back on the mat as a competitor and not just a coach. I entered a few competitions and after several wins I was invited to compete in, of all things, a US Olympic trials tournament in Las Vegas.

I've heard it said that after wrestling at the high school and collegiate level, everything else you'll ever do in life will be easy. Though I'm not sure about that, I *am* sure that the martial and competitive aspects of the sport brought out the same risk-taking nature in me that made the Protective Operations Cadre so appealing. A wrestling match isn't long, but those brief moments are incredibly intense, and I never felt more alive than during them. In retrospect, I think what drew me first to the CIA, and then the POC, was my desire to continue to experience that intensity and experience off the mat. I craved the challenge that kind of lifestyle would provide. Maybe I would've found that in the Marines if I'd gone that route, because what I really wanted to do was make a difference. And I wanted to find a way to live my life off the mat the same way I had lived my life on it.

I headed straight from work to the gym every day and hit the mat hard. Not a day went by when I didn't do some kind of training. Then the day came. Several other wrestlers and I drove to Las Vegas for the US National Freestyle Championships, an Olympic trials tournament.

I hadn't been to Vegas for a decade, and the changes to the city left me immediately amazed. The hotels, the lights, the people…but I didn't let myself get lost in the distractions. I was there for a purpose and had to focus. I was there to *compete*. I kept my eyes forward and headed straight up to my hotel room. The first matches were scheduled for the next morning.

I headed down to the Las Vegas Convention Center, which was hosting the tournament, to check out the venue and orient myself. It was much larger than I had expected, way bigger than the national tournament venues I'd competed in during college. I had never wrestled in front of so many people before. But I wasn't about to let that distract me. After all, once you're on the mat, it's you and your opponent. All the people watching and cheering no longer mattered, as if they didn't exist at all.

I took off my shoes and walked onto one of the mats and crouched down into position and bounced around. At that moment, John Smith, the most successful American wrestler ever, walked into the venue and over to the mats. Smith had won two NCAA championships at Oklahoma State and the Goodwill Games title in 1986, followed by the Pan-American Championship and the World Championship in 1987. In 1988 and 1992 he was the Olympic champion, and from 1989 to 1991 he won three straight World Championships. He defended his Goodwill Games title in 1990 and his Pan-American gold in 1991. From 1986 through 1990, Smith's international record was 150–3. No other American had ever managed more than three world titles; Smith won four in six years.

"I see I'm not the only one who likes to get to know my surroundings," he said to me in his Oklahoma twang.

I smiled, feeling more than a little awestruck, coming up just short of asking him for his autograph. "Yeah, makes it easier at match time."

"That it does. I'm John Smith."

"Tom Pecora," I greeted, shaking his hand.

"Well, Tom, good luck tomorrow," he said, sincerely.

"Thanks. You too."

I gave John a nod and left the gym.

The competition began at 9:00 a.m. the next day. By a strange twist of fate, I ended up facing John Smith that day. He had destroyed his first three opponents, beating them by fifteen points or more. I was a complete nobody on the national Olympic scene, so I guess John didn't take me all that seriously when he stepped onto the mat. Each match consisted of two three-minute periods and, if Vegas oddsmakers had been consulted, I wouldn't have been expected to last through the first.

I have to say that first period was probably the best three minutes of wrestling in my life, as I attacked and defended every second with the score 0–0. The crowd had begun to pay major attention to our match, given that Smith not scoring a single point was virtually unprecedented. I spotted him in his corner of the mat during the break between periods recalibrating his mind. He had looked past me, a mistake he now had no choice but to acknowledge. In wrestling, you have to focus totally on the match you are in and not think about your next opponent or the matches ahead. But it was too early in the tournament for a match this tough for someone of his level, and Smith was not expecting to meet the big-name competition until the semifinals.

But first he had to get there. I knew he was going to come at me with everything he had, and I was right. By the end of the second period I was down by several points, so with twelve seconds left and nothing to lose, I tried a "Hail Mary" move; a throw. It was glory or disaster—the latter, as it turned out, since the match ended with me on my back pinned during the final two seconds. I gave it my all and knew there was no disgrace in losing to one of the best wrestlers in US wrestling history. I decided to retire from the sport after that match, going out having wrestled the best! John Smith went on to win that tournament and then to the Olympics, where he won his second gold medal.

I returned to the field office a little down from the loss but energized from the excitement of the competition, again hoping the day would arrive when that feeling would be business as usual. And that opportunity finally came less than one month later, when I got word that I had been accepted to attend training for the Protective Operations Cadre.

Washington, DC ▪ July 1991

It was a hot, muggy day in July when I stared out the window of the taxi, trying to see how many landmarks I could spot on the way to CIA Headquarters in Langley, Virginia, knowing it would be my last opportunity for sightseeing during training. I have to admit that I had some butterflies in my stomach, a mix of nerves and excitement. I'd been working at the field office for more than a year, but this was what I wanted, what I craved. Real action, a chance to make a difference.

I was dropped off at the main gate area at the CIA Headquarters complex, where I flashed my identification and was cleared to enter. I walked up the road to the headquarters building, passing through the large glass exterior entryway. As I stepped through the main entrance of the building, I felt proud to find myself before the large CIA seal that was centered on the floor just before the security guard post. After badging in, I walked to the front office area of the Protective Operations Division and stepped up to the receptionist's desk.

"Tom Pecora," I announced. "I'm here for the Special Protective Operations Course."

The receptionist never looked up from her work as she picked up the phone.

"Another one for SPOC training," she said, and placed the receiver back on its hook. "Someone will be with you momentarily," she followed, barely looking up at me. "Have a seat over there, please."

I waited for almost twenty minutes. The reception area where I was sitting had become crowded with other personnel I assumed were there for the SPOC training too. Eventually, a man walked out. He was in his mid-forties, sharply dressed in a well-fitted suit. He stood tall in front of the group of us and cleared his throat.

"Pecora?"

"Yes, sir," I said, standing.

He gave me a quick nod.

"Barclay?"

"Yes, sir," the man who had been sitting next to me said and stood.

"Tyler? Smith? Gonick?"

The other three men from the bench all stood.

"I'm John Gleason, one of the officers who'll be spearheading your SPOC training. Follow me."

We followed Gleason to a large auditorium, where I saw that a number of uniformed personnel as well as plainclothes individuals were already seated. The uniformed personnel were called Security Protective Officers (SPOs), and they were the federal law enforcement–trained uniformed guard force that protected the Agency headquarters, along with any other CIA sites in the Washington, DC, area.

The plainclothes personnel were like myself, Multi-Discipline Security Officers (MDSOs), also known as Security Generalists. The best way to describe MDSOs would be as the "officer" grade of security, since we were required to have a college degree and our career track led directly to the higher-level management positions.

I was one of several officers from Security Field Offices and HQS (headquarters) elements to attend the SPOC training class—the first of its type ever conducted by the CIA in support of the newly created Protective Operations Cadre.

Once we were all settled, Gleason addressed the room.

"Welcome to the first SPOC course. This is going to be a grueling month of training, and we appreciate your willingness to participate. Some of you will find that this is not the right choice for you, while others will find that this is exactly what you've been searching for in your career path. If you successfully complete the training, you'll be eligible to volunteer for temporary deployments from your full-time positions. As of right now, this will not be offered as a full-term assignment. At this point, it's a volunteered paid position, to be filled in conjunction with your full-term assignment. That means you'll need permission to take time off to accept POC assignments, just as you did to come to this training. While this may change in the future, that's the current policy. And now that we've got that piece of business out of the way, it's time to address your training."

Gleason went on to explain that the POC unit was going to specialize in low-profile protection along with elements of standard protective operations, military tactics, and heavy weaponry. The basic core of the training would follow the US Secret Service doctrine, the kind of protective practice that, had it been employed in Manila a few years before, would have likely kept Colonel Nick Rowe alive.

SPOC training was to take place at several locations around Virginia. They were going to cram in a lot of instruction in a short period of time. I'd received some related training upon entering the CIA as a Security Generalist that had included an intensive twelve-week orientation to security covering basic firearms (pistol and shotgun), how to conduct background investigations, and other security-related topics. The SPOs had initially undergone police training at the Federal Law Enforcement Training Center (FLETC) in Glynco, Georgia. Coursework at FLETC included police procedures, police-community relations, criminal law, first aid, laws of arrest, search and seizure, and physical defense techniques.

SPOC training would be different from any previous training the Generalists or SPOs had received. Besides basic protective operations training, the SPOC also focused on antiterrorism driving, surveillance, and countersurveillance. A number of different trainers and training methodologies were utilized to address the complex nature of protective operations support in the foreign field. In addition to the basics of protective operations, we learned a lot about the covert tactics developed by DEA undercover officers as well as traditional special operations techniques and procedures that had been developed by the US military, particularly special operations forces.

Key contributions to the training course came from both official government sources as well as the private sector. One notable private sector company was very involved in training government and US military personnel. It had been founded by experienced US military veterans, and it specialized in training personnel to understand how attackers (terrorists, criminals, and so forth) target their victims, as well as how to use surveillance detection and countersurveillance methodology against them and to fully comprehend the strengths and weaknesses of modern protective operations. Thoroughly dedicated professionals, these instructors brought a civilian mindset to the topic, meaning they were intimately acquainted with dealing with the realities of the field. They knew firsthand the kind of street-level dynamic that had cost Nick Rowe his life and were thus best equipped to help teach us how to prevent another tragedy like that from happening.

We also trained at a commercial driving school with a full-fledged racetrack where we had access to high- and low-speed paved road circuits, unimproved and off-road training areas, skid pads, classrooms, and several firing ranges. The instructors at that school taught us about the diverse disciplines of antiterrorism driving, accident avoidance, and driver proficiency as well as some specialized firearms training.

The training was based on groundbreaking studies of vehicle-related terrorism incidents, feedback and intelligence from client alumni around the world, and the expertise of the highly skilled and experienced training team. The driving course also was where we completed our initial firearms training. The shooting school was staffed by an instructor who was a former Force Recon Marine and world-class competition shooter, as well as a former special operations soldier who'd been on the failed "Desert One" Iranian hostage rescue operation years before during the Carter administration. Besides having expertise in security driving, we were expected to become highly proficient in our firearms skills.

Tough stuff—the real deal, in other words. Just what I'd been hoping for.

During my initial MDSO training, I had received instruction on the standard sidearm of the Officer of Security at the time, a

.357-caliber revolver. During the SPOC course, we were introduced to a new firearm, a 9mm semiautomatic pistol, and trained on the 5.56mm automatic rifle and a pump shotgun. It was a formidable arsenal that nonetheless fell under the "light weaponry" category when compared to what we might end up facing in the field.

To compensate for a lack of heavy weaponry, our intense training regimen included becoming skilled in the art of surveillance detection and countersurveillance methodology, because one of the prime tenets of the new unit was learning how terrorists targeted their victims. Indeed, the POC was going to be operating in hostile environments, mainly outside of the United States and often in war zones, so it was imperative we knew how to operate effectively in stealth mode. We were taught that since the bad guy was always going to have more firepower, it was important to be as invisible as possible.

Because if they can't find you, they can't shoot you! And that meant the men and women we'd be charged with protecting would stay alive.

3

CIA Security Field Office ▪ September 1991

"How was it, man? Tell me everything!" Brad asked me, as if I'd just come back from a dangerous assignment oversees.

"Good, real good. Learned a lot," I replied, turning back to the work on my desk that had piled up in the weeks I'd been gone.

"Good? That's it? Come on! Tell me more!"

I laughed. "You're making it out like I was on a huge adventure. It was all training."

"So when does the adventure begin?"

"We wait for an assignment. Could be a week. Could be a year," I told him, frowning.

"That sucks," Brad said and turned away, suddenly less interested.

Brad was right, it did suck. I had another eight months left in this position to complete my two-year assignment. Those days and weeks passed slowly, and I found myself almost literally counting down the final seconds before I moved on to my next assignment.

Choosing CIA Headquarters as my second posting was the best way to fast-track my career. I'd walked through those glass doors before, of course, but never as a Security Duty Officer (SDO) in the Security Duty Office, my confidence level spiking as a result. I took a moment and gathered my thoughts while standing on the CIA's ornate emblem. As an SDO, I was going to be responsible for all security incidents inside headquarters as well as other buildings around Washington, DC—the eyes and ears of security and an integral part of keeping our people safe.

I was ready for my first day and made my way toward the Security Duty Office just steps from the entrance and the Wall of Stars, a memorial honoring CIA officers who have fallen in the line of duty. I opened the door of the office and was greeted by Officer Dave Dolesh. Dolesh sprung out of his chair as if he was attached to the door by an elastic band.

"You must be Pecora. Welcome!"

He wore horn-rimmed glasses, a gray suit with a white button-down shirt, and a plain tie. He looked more like an accountant than a security officer.

"Thank you," I said, smiling.

"I am a Senior SDO and your training officer," Dolesh said, speaking a mile a minute. "I hope you're a quick learner because everything here happens fast. You have to think, fast, fast, fast," he spat out, snapping his fingers in rhythm with his words.

With that, sure enough my first day began at a breakneck clip. The Security Duty Office was basically like an internal 911 call center for the CIA and several Agency buildings in the Washington, DC, area. It required quick thinking, quick acting, and, most of all, intense documentation. Besides documenting all security events at Agency facilities in the DC area, the Agency telephone operators would flag and transfer telephone calls that didn't meet normal standards—from unknown sources as well as any actual or possible threats, prank calls, and calls from mentally ill people—to our unit to handle.

As SDOs, we paid special attention to calls that involved any threat to the Agency or other government personnel and facilities. Anytime a threat was received that involved the president, the White House, or any other presidential element, we would immediately document the call, create a report, and contact the US Secret Service. The Secret Service would send someone to retrieve the report, anytime, day or night. I soon developed a solid relationship with many of these agents. We were also responsible for all medical incidents on the HQS compound, and we worked extremely closely with the Security Protective Service (SPS) uniformed personnel to document any security incidents or issues.

In the Security Duty Office, I learned so much about the basics of being an SDO and how the guts of the CIA worked. I still hadn't been called for a POC assignment, but I was really enjoying what I was doing. Colleagues were also becoming friends, something that really hadn't happened in the field office. I became very good friends with an SPS officer and former Marine named Bill Stone. I was even given a code name to be used anytime I made a call to an outside (non-CIA) element. At long last, I felt more like James Bond!

Although the days were busy and full of chaos, it was typically manageable chaos; there was some predictability to the day. Until January 25, 1993, anyway.

On that day, I arrived at work at 7:00 a.m. as usual. I got to the office, settled into the seat at my desk, and began sipping my first of several cups of coffee of the day. Mornings were always relatively slow. It seemed those most likely to overtly threaten the national security apparatus liked to sleep in, so I would take advantage of the downtime to get paperwork done. That was my plan for the morning, until the call from the SPS Dispatch Office came in:

"Shots fired at the main gate! We have two down!"

I immediately grabbed my telephone and punched in the button that gave us a direct line to Fairfax County Fire and Rescue and the county police department.

"This is _____ from the CIA," I said, using my code name and speaking as calmly as I could manage. "We have shots fired at the main gate and at least two wounded."

My heart was pounding. This was a game-changing event, utterly unprecedented in Agency annuls. As the events were unfolding before our eyes, it became clear this was some sort of "active shooter" situation, meaning we may not have seen the worst of things yet.

As far as we could gather from witnesses, the shooter was a Caucasian man in his twenties, wearing a dark jacket and dark pants and driving a light brown station wagon. According to reports, he'd gotten out of his car in the middle of rush hour traffic on Route 123, directly outside of the road leading to the CIA HQS building. Route 123 was a busy roadway leading from the capital into Virginia. The shooter had been seen exiting his vehicle with a long gun—a rifle or shotgun. He'd moved quickly and purposefully between the cars that were stuck in traffic, then coolly and methodically began aiming and shooting, shattering windows and claiming victims at point-blank range. He moved between the two lanes of cars lined up to enter the CIA's grounds with a clear mission: indiscriminately kill as many as possible.

My call to the Fairfax County Police Department galvanized the police to respond, but by the time they did it was too late. The shooter was long gone, and two CIA employees were dead and three others wounded. From that moment forward, our office became the center of the storm as the CIA began to execute its response, exacerbated by a combination of the fact that the shooter was still at large and the medical and crime scene preservation activities occurring at the wreckage those fifteen minutes of chaos had left behind.

We immediately began the process of identifying the victims and ensuring that the wounded were being cared for. We also documented information to assist the Fairfax County Police and the FBI with their investigation to the absolute best of our abilities. The next step was notification of appropriate CIA management, along with other US government agencies and leadership. CIA personnel/human resources and our casualty assistance officer were leading all of the efforts when it came to notification of next of kin and other necessary duties for both the wounded and the dead. This included assisting the traumatized survivors who'd just witnessed the murder of their colleagues, knowing that it could have just as easily been them instead.

At one point in the morning, I ended up briefing the acting director of the CIA, Admiral William Studeman. As an SDO, I was part of the team that wrote the official after-action report on the incident. It was one of the longest, most grueling days of my life, one that brought the reality of my job's importance and its inherent dangers home to me in a harsh and irrevocable way.

CIA and FBI began jointly investigating the incident. At the time of the shooting, investigators thought it might have been a disgruntled employee, so we began to look back through our records to see who, from that profile, may have been a potential suspect. We narrowed it down to two names. Investigators were sent out, but both suspects were cleared in rapid fashion. It took several days to discover that the perpetrator, in fact, had no connection to the Agency at all. Mir Aimal Kasi (aka Kansi), a Pakistani national, had bought an AK-47 rifle and then, for no apparent reason, attacked CIA personnel waiting to turn into CIA Headquarters. He was a terrorist, plain and simple, the first of many I'd be encountering over the course of the next twenty years. Kasi ended up fleeing the country before we had the opportunity to capture him and bring him to justice for the massacre.

Kasi lived his life as a free man up until June 15, 1997. That's when, acting on an informant's tip, a joint FBI-CIA task force lured him to the Dera Ghazi Khan District of Punjab, Pakistan. Kasi believed he had been summoned there for a meeting on a business venture to smuggle arms and electronics. He was grabbed at the meeting and brought back to the United States. Kasi later told investigators that he thought he would've been caught immediately at the shooting. He even made a stop at a McDonald's drive-thru, where he got something to eat and sat around waiting to be captured. When no authorities arrived to arrest him, he decided to go home to Pakistan.

This attack happened eight years before 9/11 and is one of the seldom-told stories of one of the first attacks by a radical Islamic terrorist

Rewards for Justice
Stop a terrorist. Save lives.

SUCCESS STORY

Success Story

EXECUTED

Mir Aimal Kansi
Executed

On January 5, 1993, Mir Aimal Kansi murdered two people and permanently injured three others. He attacked without warning or provocation, shooting his AK-47 assault rifle into cars waiting at a stoplight in front of Central Intelligence Agency headquarters.

Kansi fled the United States immediately after the attack and was a fugitive until captured in Pakistan. On November 10, 1997, Kansi was convicted by a jury in Fairfax, Virginia, for the murder of two CIA employees. Kansi was executed on November 14, 2002.

Rewards for Justice—Capture and Execution of Kansi.

on US soil. As a result of those CIA lives being so senselessly lost, I learned many extremely valuable lessons, the first being that personnel accountability is critical and should be the first priority in any crisis. The second thing I learned is that the first bits of information that come in are often erroneous. From that day on, I never took anything at face value again. They were lessons that would ultimately serve me well.

Washington, DC ▪ June 15, 1993

Months later, we were all still trying to recover from the January shooting, still on edge. The casual routine of our day and our duties had been replaced by a keen awareness that we never knew what would be on the other side of the line every time we answered the phone. I tried to tell myself that it was making me better, preparing me to be a more skilled security officer. But the scary part was, I recognized how vulnerable we all were; the Security Duty Office, the CIA, the whole US government. None of these elements, apparently, were prepared for a terrorist attack on United States soil. We'd never seen an attack of this proportion since Pearl Harbor, and it shook us to the core. Sure, the first attack on the World Trade Center had come six months before, in February. But, ultimately, that attack had failed, while the shooting outside headquarters had cost lives that changed all of us forever. It was the beginning of something, a true sea change in the threat environment we were ill prepared to confront at that point.

One morning I was sitting at my desk drinking my first cup of coffee, my mind lost in the past while contemplating what that attack implied for the future.

"Hey Tom?" Bill Stone asked, popping his head in my office door.

I didn't respond.

"Come in, Pecora," Bill said, louder. "Do you read me?"

"Huh?"

"You okay?" Bill asked again.

"Yeah. Just thinking."

"Noticed that. Are you going to come to the bar with us after work?"

"I am. Already thirsty for a cold one, and I'm not even through my first hot one of the day," I said, throwing Bill a half-assed smile.

"Better not bail on us, Pecora," Bill replied, flashing his toothy, jovial grin.

"Never!"

Bill left me to my coffee, thoughts, and paperwork. I was on my third incident report of the morning when Officer Dolesh interrupted me.

"Pecora, line four is for you."

"Pardon?"

"The phone. Line four," Dolesh repeated.

I had never received a personal phone call at my office before. My heart stopped. My parents were the only ones who had my office number, and they knew that they were only to use the number in case of emergency. My grandmother had died two months before and my mother and stepfather hadn't even called to tell me that. I held my breath while I grabbed the phone.

"Hello?" I greeted, my heart pounding.

"Tom?"

"Richard? Is everything okay?"

Richard was my stepdad. He'd been married to my mom since I was eleven years old. He was a great guy and we were really close, but I knew if he was calling something was really, really wrong. My mom had been battling lung cancer, but she'd been doing really well, or so I thought.

I could hear the hesitation in Richard's voice, "I, um, your mom, she, um, she passed away last night, Tom."

Milwaukee, Wisconsin ▪ June 19, 1993

I was able to leave work and immediately caught a flight home to Milwaukee. My mother's funeral arrangements were set for the weekend. My brothers had gathered with their families at my stepdad's house. At thirty years old, I was the fourth child in line.

"Hey, Tom, are you going to be single for the rest of your life?" my oldest brother Peter asked. Laying my mother to rest had sparked thoughts of the life choices all of us had made.

"I don't think Tom will ever get serious," John, the third eldest, chimed in.

My brothers were big on teasing me for not settling down with any of the several ladies I had dated over the years, and for not having the obligatory two or three kids to go with a house in the suburbs.

"Stop, guys. My job keeps me way too busy. I barely have time to sleep, let alone get into a serious relationship."

"Sure, sure. Have you even dated anyone regularly since the lady in England?" my youngest brother Mark asked.

I'd dated an English lass named Allison after I'd graduated from Marquette. I'd spent the summer in London bartending. I wanted to get away and see the world, or at least see England, before I began my graduate studies at the University of Wisconsin. Before that trip, I had never even left the state, believe it or not! Allison was a bartender at the same rustically commercial pub I was working at. She was different, both crazy and fun. We had a whirlwind romance, hot and heavy and over before it even started, because like most summer flings, it ended when the leaves started falling. She hadn't asked me to stay, and I wouldn't have even if I could; I was off to grad school, the next phase of my life. I told her we would stay in touch, but that wasn't the truth. *Uh-uh.* I had no intentions of doing anything of the kind, and I knew it. So I kissed her goodbye and didn't look back.

"Ha-ha, guys. Glad you're all having a good laugh. I'm doing what is expected in my career field."

"Leave him alone, boys," Richard ordered my brothers. "We're real proud of you, Tom," he followed, patting my shoulder. "Keep fighting the good fight."

I had no idea how prophetic that statement would turn out to be, based on where I'd be the following month.

Washington, DC ▪ July 1993

I returned to Washington grief stricken, but I knew I needed to check my feelings at the door.

"Sorry, man, truly. Anything I can do?" Bill asked, poking his head into my office.

"Nah. Thanks, though."

"I'm here for you, if you need a shoulder to cry on," he said, patting his broad shoulders.

"Really, all's well," I said, forcing a smile. "I'm good."

"Come on, man, let it out. Have a good cry!" he said, and pulled me in close for a hug.

"Can't breathe," I squeaked out as he crushed me.

"Doesn't that feel better?" Bill said, finally letting go. "Nothing a good bear hug can't fix."

"Oh yeah, right, nothing better than that," I said, my ribs aching.

"Well, maybe one thing," Bill said, a bit wryly, about to reveal the real reason why he'd come down to my office. "I just received a request to ship out with the POC team to Somalia. And it so happens there's an open spot. Interested?"

PART TWO

MOGADISHU

4

Operation Restore Hope:
Mogadishu, Somalia ▪ July 29, 1993

"You ready to see shit get real?" Bill asked as our British Air flight came to a bumpy landing in Nairobi.

"Sure am!" I said.

It had been nearly two years since my initial POC training, and I'd been ready for my first overseas mission, chomping at the bit really, ever since. But now, as I looked upon the plains surrounding Kenya's Nairobi International Airport, I felt a lump forming in my throat. I knew I had to swallow it and fast. Bill and I were less than a three-hour flight away from Mogadishu, Somalia, where we would be the first members of our POC team to arrive.

The first thing I noticed was the heat. It's one thing to hear about African heat, quite another to experience it firsthand. The air was so hot it felt blasted out of an oven, nothing like regions of America when struck by a summer heat wave. Here the heat came baked into the desktop-flat landscape comprised of plateaus, plains, and occasional highlands. No respite at all, even when the rare storm sprung up, or at night, when swarms of insects seemed to redouble their efforts to make our lives miserable.

In 1993, US military forces in conjunction with United Nations troops entered Somalia to provide security for humanitarian relief operations. The environment was austere and hostile in the extreme, as Somalia had been in the middle of civil war for many years. The landscape in Mogadishu, the capital, was more akin to that of the movie *Mad Max* than the former Italian colony of past glory—utterly lawless, with roving gangs enforcing various versions of law and disorder. The conflict in Somalia had been underway for more than five years, before the UN stepped in and began humanitarian operations. Operation Restore Hope was a multinational coalition of forces from the United States, Italy, Pakistan, Malaysia, and Australia. But there were plenty in the know who had their doubts about how well the operation would succeed, fearing the likelihood even the best intentions would fall into the abyss of corruption and the power vacuum riddling the country.

The Somali Civil War grew out of resistance to the Siad Barre regime during the 1980s. By 1988, the Somali Armed Forces began engaging various armed rebel groups, including the Somali Salvation Democratic Front in the northeast, the Somali National Movement in the northwest, and the United Somali Congress in the south. The rebel forces eventually managed to overthrow the Barre government in 1991. Then the battles between the various rebel groups for influence and power began. In 1992 the laws of the land began to collapse, precipitating the arrival of UNOSOM I UN military observers in July of 1992.

Bill and I had two days in Nairobi before the Agency arranged our transportation to the war-torn piece of hell called Mogadishu. During that time, we explored some of the local markets, negotiating with the Kenyans for last-minute gear such as a safari vest to carry the myriad of tactical gear I was going to need in the course of my deployment. Local craftsmen sold some interesting woodcarvings and a variety of exotic stones that they fashioned into jewelry. On the first night, we visited a famous restaurant called the Carnivore, known as

View of Mogadishu, Somalia Airport.

the "Beast of a Feast." The Carnivore served a variety of exotic meats that included ostrich, crocodile, and camel. I tried all of them and thought most of them tasted like rubbery chicken.

After the Carnivore we headed to a local disco called the Florida 2000, a very dark and crowded place full of drunk expats and locals being served copious amounts of alcohol. The Florida 2000 hardly resembled any of the discos or nightclubs of Milwaukee or the DC area that I'd been to. The music was decidedly African, with the deep bass common to all discos and something else common to them as well: young people grinding on each other in what passed for dancing, after drinking far too much. The nightclub scene in Kenya, like most club scenes in its cities and others in the States, often led to sex—a dangerous mix given the escalation in cases of HIV/AIDS that was approaching virtual epidemic proportions. The main drink offered in the club was *Tusker Lager*, a native African beer. Being a beer drinker from Milwaukee, I had to at least try it. It smelled of grain and grass and tasted the same. Not being one to chomp on the lawn, I quickly changed to more familiar brews.

Despite the disease and poverty, there was fun to be had in Kenya. But our time was short. We had to fly out at 0700 hours on day two, and we arrived at the Nairobi military base at 0600 hours the next morning. Even at that early hour it was nearing one hundred degrees, the air intolerably thick and moist. Strangely, no one on the base seemed to be reacting to the heat, as if they'd somehow adapted to it.

Was I the only one who was cooking from the inside out?

I gave a look to Bill.

"You ain't seen nothing yet," he said wiping the sweat from his wide-grooved brow.

"Awesome," I said, mumbling under my breath. "That's just great."

Given the threat level in Mogadishu, there were no longer commercial flights into the area—only charter planes, UN flights, and military aircraft. Agency operations in the region were supported by a truly unique aircraft, nicknamed the "Gooney Bird." The last year this model was built was in the 1940s, rendering it a collector's item as well as a dinosaur. The Agency had refurbished and refitted the aircraft to support updated specifications and passenger transport requirements. Specifically, it was upgraded with two new engines and all new internal aeronautical equipment, improvements costing millions of dollars. Good ole *Gooney Bird* drew attention wherever she landed, as true aircraft aficionados were immediately attracted to her classic retro beauty. An old dog that didn't need to learn any new tricks.

The pilots of the Gooney Bird had even more character than the chariot herself. Mike and Mike had flown the plane since it had made its way to East Africa. Mike and Mike were both burly country boys with loud laughs and affable natures. They'd been together so long that they'd started to look alike. And if it weren't for the fact that the one Mike wore a cowboy hat every day, there would've been no way to tell them apart when they were wearing their sunglasses. They were the happy limo drivers for Agency personnel and material moving about the region, ferrymen willing to traverse the River Styx to deliver men like us to our appointed tasks and posts. And when they weren't airborne, Mike and Mike spent their time at a five-star hotel in Nairobi, courtesy of the US government.

"Howdy!" Mike the cowboy hollered as we approached the plane.

"Hey," I said, giving a wave.

"You two better move your newbie asses. The temperature ain't getting nothin' but hotter and that air is goin' to feel like a kiss from a blowtorch," Cowboy Mike said, pursing his lips and blowing into the air.

The other Mike laughed hard from his belly. "We ready?"

"Yes, sir," I responded.

"No 'sirs' here," that Mike responded. "Just a couple of good ole boys getting you where you need to be."

We took our seats on the plane. I was always a fan of airplanes, although not a trained aviator, and took it upon myself to ask Mike and Mike question after question about the Gooney Bird.

Finally, Cowboy Mike got out of the cockpit and walked up the aisle to the back of the plane. "Get up there!"

"Huh? What?" I asked.

"Go! Fly the plane."

I didn't move.

"Seriously, man. Go! I need to put my ass in a seat. Get up there!"

I was trying to contain my excitement; this was such a rare opportunity. Alas, it didn't end well. My tenure flying the Gooney Bird ended quickly when I allowed the tail to take an abrupt dip. The other Mike took back the steering yoke and got the plane back under control.

Cowboy Mike, meanwhile, tapped me on the shoulder. "Hope you're better at protecting people than being a pilot."

As we began our approach to Mogadishu International Airport, the pilots took turns stepping out of the cockpit to put on bullet-resistant vests. I realized I was no longer in Kansas, or anywhere in the world that I recognized.

The Gooney Bird bounced down to a halt at the end of the airport that was sandwiched between an aircraft graveyard and hangar area that we nicknamed the "Somali Air Force" and a long stretch of coral beach. As I walked off the plane I was smacked in the face by the smells of sea salt laced with jet fuel. I deeply exhaled in the hopes of pushing the fuel smell from my nostrils in favor of the scent of the beach, but no such luck.

Cowboy Mike was quick to warn us to avoid the derelict Soviet aircraft that sat in and around an old hangar. He called them lethally unsafe, a fact punctuated by a story about how a UN worker had climbed into one of the aircraft and pushed a button, activating the ejection seat and rocketing him to his death on impact with the ceiling of the hangar. Mogadishu, apparently, had other dangers besides Somali warlords and itchy-trigger-fingered UN soldiers. We were also warned about the sand and sea. Most of the coastal area near the city was composed of coral beaches with the surf breaking over razor-sharp coral. One small section south of the runway area of the airport, though, featured a small beach with some tidal pools. Soldiers and UN workers could often be spotted wading into the water to escape the intense heat. Unfortunately, lurking in the water near Mogadishu was the largest unnatural shark population in the world, created by more than a decade of scrap dumping by the meat and fish canning plant located near the port of Mogadishu.

With the civil war having destroyed almost the entire infrastructure of Somalia, especially within Mogadishu, the cannery had been closed for years but the sharks, hungrier than ever, remained. People were warned about them, but such warnings never proved to be enough to thwart dips into waters promising so much relief from the unrelenting heat that regularly stretched into the triple digits. Too bad. Shortly before my arrival, a UN relief worker was killed when she waded in thigh-deep water at the beach. Having been terrified watching the movie *Jaws*, I took these warnings to heart and didn't plop so much as my little toe into the water. Interesting how I was afraid of sharks but eagerly anticipated being part of a POC team driving the streets of Mogadishu dominated by Somali warlords who operated much like sharks themselves.

Upon disembarking from the Gooney Bird, we high-fived the departing POC team members we were replacing on the tarmac, as they hustled into the aircraft. We walked to an unarmored SUV where the remaining POC team guys were waiting to introduce themselves. The one in the driver's seat, Rob, was a big guy pushing six foot five, an odd trait in our field, since most protective ops guys tended to be of average height to better blend in with the crowd. But Rob's skill level more than made up for the fact that he stood out whenever he stood up.

"Don't let Mike frighten you," he advised, grinning. "The mosquitos are plenty scarier than the sharks and those derelict planes."

And with that he spit a gob of chewing tobacco out the window onto the sandy ground.

Don, the other member of the previous POC team, was in the front passenger seat and appeared to be totally ready to leave Mogadishu. He looked tired and a bit worn out. He was all of twenty-five years old, but he carried himself like someone double his age. He was very reserved and would only occasionally join in the conversation. He and Bill had worked together at CIA Headquarters as SPOs.

As Rob drove us to the base, we were given some preliminary information about the threat level and about our operational activities. A looming sense of dread dominated the capital, the rebel groups growing stronger while government forces grew weaker. The players kept changing, the infighting among rebel groups for dominance constant as they struggled for supremacy. People often compared places like Mogadishu to the old American West, but that really isn't accurate; it was really much worse and wilder. By the time we arrived, the government was already struggling to provide even the most basic of services, and the rebel groups continued to seize the opportunity to fill that void, gaining strength. They ruled by fear and terror against an ineffectual system that was helpless to stop the country from dissolving into anarchy.

Our outpost was located along the top of the sand dunes overlooking the airport on one side and the ocean on the other. The main building was a converted trailer outfitted with a communications section and some office space. A large, old military tent served as our food and gear warehouse, and our living quarters consisted of a fifth-wheel trailer, complete with small bathroom equipped with a shower, mini kitchen, and a dual-bed sleeping quarters.

POC members slept in the bedrooms and on sleeper couches in the main trailer area. The trailer toilet was not operational, so an outhouse had been constructed a short distance away on the peak of the hill with seating that provided a wide view of the airport out one window and the ocean out the other. The privacy screen only covered from the waist down, thus anyone looking up the hill had a clear view of the head and shoulders of those using the toilet.

I felt like I'd just been dropped off at summer camp during the hottest summer ever: lots of boys, crappy food, and an outhouse. But the fun and lightheartedness were both going to be short-lived. The next day the real work would start, and Don told Bill and me to settle in and get used to our surroundings.

The sun sunk behind the mountains and darkness swallowed the sky. The guys drifted off to bed, but I couldn't sleep. I needed air. I took a seat in a vinyl lawn chair facing the ocean. The stars were working their magic, shining through the dense clouds. When the waves were fierce enough, I could feel just a thin mist of seawater rising from the ocean onto my face. It reminded me of home. Thoughts of my mom and grandma rushed over me like a ten-foot surf. We used to do family vacations in a place called Point Beach, which was on Lake Michigan. The lake was more like an inland sea, and that place held some of the happiest memories of my childhood, especially since I didn't have to worry about sharks in those waters. Now here I was, just months after my mother's death, listening to the familiar sound of the surf reminding me of Point Beach and the simple days of my youth. At that moment, I felt as if my mother and my grandmother were watching over me, but I didn't know if that would be enough.

5

Mogadishu, Somalia

"Pecora! Pecora! Time to wake up and get to work!" Bill bellowed.

The sun was just starting to breech the deep blue waters of the Indian Ocean, the orange and yellow colors of the sunrise just above the surf. At first, I thought I was dreaming.

"You trying to catch a tan this early in the morning?" Bill asked.

I realized it wasn't a dream. I'd gotten up early and meant to watch the sun come up but must have fallen asleep in my chair and felt stiff as a board. "Wasn't my plan to nod off. I guess it's just the jet lag."

In point of fact, sunbathing grew into a regular pastime among our group, a welcome respite from living and working in a perpetual war zone. Word eventually filtered out among the US military elements that there was a government unit operating from the outpost on the hill. We later heard that they had nicknamed us "the Beach Boys" since between protective assignments and convoy movements we could often be glimpsed laying out and getting a tan. Later in our deployment, after the Navy SEALs began calling themselves "the Jedi," the US troops changed our nickname to "the Dark Side of the Force."

"Lucky some sort of snake or camel spider didn't creep up and kill you," Bill said, making spider fangs out of his fingers.

"A spider didn't kill me, but my back sure as hell is," I said, trying to unkink myself.

"I still say you're lucky. Now go inside and get ready. It's almost zero six hundred hours. Rob is going to take us to meet the outpost chief after we eat breakfast."

I needed a cold shower to wash off the night and wake myself up. The water pressure in the trailer wasn't helping to rush things along. I could spit on myself and have better pressure. *Ugh!* Finally, I was able to rinse off and get dressed. Bill, Don, and Rob were waiting for me in the living room area of the trailer.

Food for the base was brought in on weekly supply runs by our aircraft, until the threat of surface-to-air missiles (SAMs) stopped them. The downside of that was for one or two weeks we were stuck eating spaghetti cooked in the microwave two times a day. A nearby US Army motor pool unit provided breakfast. The only viable alternative was our emergency supplies of military MREs (meals ready-to-eat), but a steady diet of those left you bloated like you had dined on a buffet at a landfill. There was a case of potted meat product, but when a starving Somali cat refused to eat it, the heaping plate got dumped right in the trash. After weeks of the same food every day, I began to experiment with hot sauce and have, ever since, become addicted to spicy food. When supply runs came back, we were treated to some local antelope steaks, which, after so much spaghetti and freeze-dried food in shrink-wrap, might as well have been New York's finest strips.

"You take longer than my wife to get ready," Rob said when I walked in that first morning.

"Ha-ha," I laughed. "The water pressure is for shit."

"My wife always has excuses too. The water. She needs to put her face on. What the hell is that all about? Putting a face on?" Rob wondered.

"Beats the shit out of me," Don, a perpetual bachelor, replied. "This job keeps me safe from ever having to know the answer about makeup and what makes ladies look fat, and I'm okay with that."

"Cheers to that, mate," Bill said, holding up his coffee mug.

Rob took a look at his watch, which read 0630 hours. "Off to see the outpost chief. Come on, ladies. Swallow it down."

We took our final bites and sips of our coffee and headed toward the main building.

We waited patiently outside the office of the outpost chief, Todd Shepley. Shepley was actually a senior support officer whose specialty was finance. I'd heard good things about him, even though his core strength was an oddity for a war zone. Besides the outpost chief, there was also an administrative/communications officer, Chuck Finley. Communications officers usually had significant overseas experience and Chuck was no exception. He had a funny story for every location he had been posted. It was in stark contrast to Shepley, who appeared to be playing the "tourist in the war zone" as he liked to wear military khaki camouflage clothing and a soft cover hat. Strange choice for a man who would rarely leave the office.

Besides the Agency contingent on the base, there were Agency-employed Somali speakers and several members of a US Army intelligence-gathering element that worked with us on targeting the enemy. There were also Fleet Anti-Terrorist Security Team (FAST) Marines on site, who assisted us with perimeter security. All in all, the outpost worked like a well-oiled machine, as it had to in the face of increasing numbers of hostiles who called Mogadishu and the surrounding villages home.

The CIA chief and his deputy worked out of the main office located on the Mogadishu University complex, but still within the walled UN compound. The UN compound was several miles away from the airport, and the road between the two had proven to be hazardous at times. Besides the chief and deputy, the main office staff consisted of a small number of case officers, administrative officers, support/logistics officers, and communications officers. Our core job was to keep the Agency personnel, mainly the chief and deputy, safe, something that was much easier said than done in such a hostile environment.

Mounting up to move our VIP.

When any member of the Agency team needed to move outside of the airport or the UN compound, the POC team would provide secure movement, something Colonel Nick Rowe did not have in Manila. Most of our administrative support movements involved taking the chief, the deputy, or the case officers to and from the UN compound and the airport. Operational movements out into the city were only for the case officers, the deputy, and very rarely the chief. These movements were carefully planned, as they were specifically done to meet with assets and gather intelligence. An asset is a clandestine source (Agent), usually a person, who is in a strategic position within an organization or country that is being spied upon, and who provides information to an Agency officer (Case Officer). In law enforcement parlance, they are called confidential informants.

Any vehicle movements within Mogadishu were dangerous, and it was our job to protect these men with our lives, no matter what. It was similar to what the US Secret Service does for the president, only in our case every non-US person we encountered, every single one, was a potential hostile. You just never knew what to expect with the precarious nature of our mission and the fact that locals were becoming increasingly belligerent toward the UN mission and its personnel. Attacks by rebel Somali warlords were increasing, and their personnel were heavily armed with AK-47s and other ordnance.

Later that day we headed to the UN compound. I drove the lead SUV with Rob providing directions, while Bill and Don followed in another SUV. On the ride Rob told me how to run the roads in "*Mog*." He described how the previous POC team was ambushed and almost hit by a rocket-propelled grenade (RPG) that skipped off the road between the two POC vehicles. The vehicles received some rifle fire that took out a window or two in one of the SUVs, but no one was hurt.

The ride from the airport was uneventful, but negotiating the roads between the airport and the UN compound was like going back in time. If it weren't for the occasional modern vehicle, the foot and animal traffic would have made you believe you were back in the 1800s. We passed a market that sold pigs and chickens that had been recently slaughtered. They dangled from hooks, flies swarming the carcasses. Somalis moved about haggling over this item or that while livestock wandered into the street, making driving much like a game of *Frogger.*

After dodging some seriously beat-up vehicles driven by equally beat-up-looking Somalis, we entered the UN compound. The gate was manned by Pakistani soldiers who were part of the UN contingent. After showing our American flag pendant and a badge, we were allowed into the rabbit warren that was home to a variety of US and European military units as well as two military hospitals, one US Army and the other Belgian.

We zigzagged our way through a dozen camps before we arrived at the US-occupied compound and the area where the main office was located. Like the outpost, there were FAST Marines providing perimeter security for this compound. After dismounting our vehicles, we waited to meet the management team.

It was only a week later that the new chief arrived, not nearly the same caliber as previous officers. Garrett Tibbler was a cop prior to entering the Agency and had previously worked in Africa Division but had never served as a chief. He was an odd duck, on the shorter side and heavyset, with a big, round face and a bushy mustache. He had a habit of speaking about himself in the third person, muttering, "The Chief wants this or that." He would often come into the main office after 1100 hours with bloodshot eyes and hair that looked like he'd stuck his finger in a light socket.

His deputy, John Marcello, on the other hand, was selected for his position based on some specific skills. Marcello was a gregarious Italian American who'd previously worked as a New York City police detective. He had been drafted to support the Somalia mission because he spoke fluent Italian and had a good relationship with the Italians who were part of the UN forces in Somalia, which was something the chief wanted to leverage. Unfortunately, Marcello had no experience in war zone environments, having spent the majority of his career in traditional case officer assignments, but his skill set still seemed much more useful than Tibbler's.

Marcello was well liked by the POC team and proved mostly cooperative with our security protocols. Later, when the pressure to get the warlord Mohamed Farrah Aidid started to take its toll on the office, Marcello began to push harder and harder to try to get actionable intelligence for special operations forces.

When not protecting the chief or the deputy, our primary responsibility was to move about the city mapping out different routes to safely reach the UN compound and to meet assets. We also conducted movements to get security atmospherics and intelligence on the city. We were warned that driving the city was more dangerous than a game of Russian roulette and was fast becoming more hazardous by the day. Aidid's gang of warmongers were out and about ready to attack members of the UN, US military, or us in sneak attacks and with hidden land mines. It had, without question, become a matter of us versus them, with our side providing a last and fleeting bastion of hope for the aggrieved Somalis whose world was on the verge of being turned irrevocably upside down. Think of the myriad crises facing the nation of Syria today and you'll have a notion of what we saw unfolding before our eyes in Somalia, up to and including civilians turned refugees by the civil war.

Mohamed Farrah Hassan Aidid was born in 1934 in Beledweyne, a city in Italian Somaliland. He was educated in Rome and Moscow and served in the Italian colonial police force in the 1950s before later joining the Somali National Army. For advanced military training, Aidid studied at the Frunze Military Academy in the former Soviet Union, an elite institution reserved for the most qualified officers of the Warsaw Pact armies and their allies.

In 1969, a few days after the assassination of Somalia's second president, Abdirashid Ali Sharmarke, a military junta led by Major General Mohamed Siad Barre staged a bloodless coup d'état. Aidid was one of many officers serving at the central command of the army at the time of the *putsch*. He quickly fell out of favor with the new regime's leaders and was subsequently detained. Aidid was eventually released from prison six years later and went on to serve as President Barre's advisor and as Somalia's ambassador to India before finally being appointed intelligence chief, the position from which he laid the foundation for his own eventual rise to power.

By the late 1980s, Barre's regime had become increasingly unpopular, leading to the formation of various resistance movements that led in 1991 to the outbreak of all-out civil war, the toppling of Barre's government, and the disbandment of the Somali National Army. Aidid had already established his power base from his position as intelligence chief and was one of the officials to take charge of the United Somali Congress (USC), strongest of the many opposition groups that had sprouted to fill the power vacuum that followed the ouster of Barre's regime. But the groups were riddled with infighting. Armed factions led by the USC (commanders Aidid and Ali Mahdi Muhammad, for example) clashed as each sought to exert authority over the capital. And while Aidid was not immediately successful in attracting waves of followers to his cause, he had built the foundation from which to ultimately position himself to rise to the top of the warring factions, en route to uniting as many of them as he could under a single umbrella under his charge. And, similarly, he saw that by offering a resolute challenge to the presence of US-led United Nations troops, he would gain the swiftest and surest means to secure his power throughout Mogadishu and, thus, Somalia as a whole.

Aidid, interestingly enough, hadn't always been out to get us. Up until June 5, 1993, he was considered a friend to the UN, but on that day, during an inspection of a Somali weapons storage site, twenty-four Pakistani soldiers were ambushed and massacred. As General Thomas Montgomery, commander of the US forces and deputy UN force commander in Somalia from March 1993 through March 1994, put it, "There was this awful attack at a feeding site, with Pakistani soldiers. We had soldiers at each feeding site to help the organizations that actually did the feeding. At one of those sites, Pakistanis, an officer and seven men, were overwhelmed by women and kids, which was a typical way the Somali militia operated. They put women and children at the front and just sort of let the crowd press in, and they pressed in around them and then disarmed them and then there were shooters in the crowd and they shot a couple of them. A couple of them were literally taken apart by hand. This is the kind of viciousness we saw. It was a very awful day."

The next day, the UN Security Council issued an emergency resolution calling for the apprehension of those responsible for the massacre. Though Aidid was not specifically named in the resolution, it was, in effect, a call to apprehend him. Twelve days later, Admiral Jonathan Howe ordered Aidid's arrest, offering a $25,000 reward for information leading to his capture.

After Aidid became *persona non grata* and the UN put him on its most wanted list, the US military began putting a lot of pressure on the Agency to come up with a plan to capture him. Several strategies were considered, including an operation in which the Agency inserted a beacon into an ornate cane and provided the cane to an asset in the hopes that Aidid would accept it as a gift and carry it, allowing US forces to track him. Unfortunately, the cane operation didn't work and Aidid, a very cagey and clever operator, went underground, limiting his movements and never staying in a single location for more than a night or two. A moving target, in other words.

But Aidid wasn't happy simply going on the defensive. Knowing how the Agency, and specifically the POC teams, operated in Mogadishu, Aidid went on the offensive, targeting us even as we were chasing him. He had demolitions teams place command-detonated land mines in potholes on major routes, subjecting us to potential assassination every time we left the confines of the base. They'd already successfully used this methodology on four US Army military police personnel and that, from their perspective, made it tried and true. At one point, we learned that Aidid's men were especially interested in the large white armored SUV we used, which the Somalis had nick-named the "White Whale." As it was the only white vehicle of its kind in country, we began to strictly avoid using it on our movements into town. Really unfortunate, since it was the only fully armored vehicle available to us. Our only other armored vehicle had been moved up to North Mogadishu for use as an emergency evacuation vehicle for our personnel who, accompanied by a SEAL sniper team, were currently hiding out in a safe house.

After years of civil war and a total absence of anything resembling a government, Mogadishu was run by warlords supported by their militia members. They controlled the pothole-marred, mainly unfinished streets of the city in trucks converted into "technicals" distinguished by having heavy machine guns, .50 calibers mostly, mounted in their beds. The lawless bands of gunmen wreaked havoc on the more stationary-positioned UN forces, who were like sitting ducks when compared to what was fast becoming a full-scale guerrilla army.

The city power station sat in ruin; all of the piping, wiring, and circuits of any value stripped from the building. There were no restaurants, stores, or other established businesses open anymore; things had reverted back to tribal conditions and laws, with the Mogadishu residents acquiring their food and other goods in traditional markets. Many of the buildings had been rendered uninhabitable, their walls pockmarked with bullet holes and gaping, jagged fissures carved out of rooftops by either errant mortar fire or collateral damage from larger explosions that had gone off in the vicinity. The streets were littered with makeshift checkpoints set up between rival clans in a continual pissing contest for dominance, as if the clan that stoked the most fear and intimidation in the locals won top prize.

Vehicles of all types moved over the wrecked streets. Buses with no windows, loaded to the max inside and carrying the overflow on the roof, careened about trying to avoid piles of trash, abandoned cars, and the refuse of blown-out buildings. This, in addition to displaced people spending their days in the streets and the odd wandering mule, camel, or goat. People scattered whenever the heavily armed technical units roared through an area, guns swiveling toward any potential hostile intent and opening fire sometimes even when not encountering any.

The animal population in the city was bewildering, as we'd encounter herds of camels and goats that seemed to find some strength and safety in numbers, unlike the residents whose movements were normally made solo or in very small groups so as not to attract undue attention to themselves. But on the highways, where you could actually build up some speed outside of the city, you had to be watchful of the kids who liked to play a version of chicken, waiting until the very last moment before crossing in front of your vehicle and laughing hysterically when they survived the moment. I guess living in a war zone among the hail of bullets wasn't enough for them and, in a world absent of normal activities, that passed for recreation.

It didn't take long for Bill and me to learn the ropes and get the lay of the land. We quickly realized that our only real defense was stealth. We worked very hard to make it difficult for Aidid's people to track us, as we knew they were committed to doing. We continuously developed new routes to move around the city, changed our vehicles, and even tinted the windows to make target identification problematic. We salvaged some surplus armor plating in the form of floor plates from a US military helicopter found in the airport graveyard that we rigged into one of our vehicles, a small Isuzu Trooper. The plates would only cover part of the front and back areas of the vehicle, but it was as close to armor as we could get. We also acquired some pistol-rated ballistic (bullet-resistant) vests that we strapped to the front bucket seats of the vehicle. While it wasn't much, it was better than nothing, maybe even enough to save our lives someday.

Bill and I decided it was best that we commit our driving routes to memory, since the maps had been rendered useless by the rampant destruction and roadblocks, except for on some of the main drags. Over time, roads, specific routes, and even landmarks would be given nicknames so that we would remember them. Someone named a road outside the UN compound "Dead Cow Road," for instance, for a poor cow that was killed in a traffic mishap and had lay rotting on the pockmarked pavement for weeks.

But it wasn't just cows that ended up dead on the roads in Mogadishu, as we were soon to find out.

6

Mogadishu, Somalia ▪ August 1993

The day came for Rob and Don to high-five out of Mogadishu.

Their replacements on our POC team showed up on the base just as the threat level was increasing to its all-time high. It was more than just the rebels who were out to get us; the civilians were also attacking now. Aidid had been spreading rumors that the UN and CIA were the enemy of all Somalis, that this was an *us-versus-them* thing, and many unwittingly became part of his army against us, creating an even more precarious environment in which to operate.

One of the two new members of our team was Jimmy Dogan, a true joker with a dry, zany wit. As a sergeant in SPS, Jimmy was an experienced leader and a wise team member. Like Bill, he was a former Marine and retained just enough of his military mannerisms to leave no doubt about his prior enlistment. He was a professional, no matter how his casual appearance and colorful language might have otherwise suggested. That's the thing about true field operators—they may not have the button-down shirts, creased pants, spit-shined boots, and high and tight haircuts, but they are all men with whom you're comfortable going into combat.

Chris Petrie, the other new member, was the only married man and father on the team. He was formerly US Air Force, then an SPS officer and an opinionated wise cracker. You may have noticed that one of the common denominators of the operators who inhabit my world is a sense of humor. It's kind of a given, a necessity as either a defense or coping mechanism, and a godsend when it comes to deployments in foreign war zones. I imagine a guy like Chris had to laugh or he would find himself distracted by thoughts of the family he left behind in the States.

There is a mindset you have to have when you deploy to a dangerous location. You have to both materially and emotionally prepare prior to the trip. Before I left I got my will done, all my beneficiaries accurately noted, and tied up all the loose ends with contingency plans in the event I never made it home. This ensured I could concentrate on my mission.

As for emotions, you have to compartmentalize your feelings for the family and friends you leave behind. You cannot allow yourself to dwell on them or else you risk being distracted from your mission. That is more important than you might think, given that a distracting thought at the wrong moment might well cause you to miss something in the environment—a movement, an action, a clue about a potential threat.

You can only open the emotional vault when you're in a safe place. For me, that place was on the top of the dunes behind some sand bags that made up our observation point. With the constant breeze coming off the ocean and the low murmur of the waves, I would allow myself to think of home and the recent loss of my mother and grandmother, both taken in the same year, a tough pill to swallow and a source of ongoing grief. The fact that my grandmother was a survivor of the *Titanic* gave me a sense of pride in our family and a tradition to uphold. I came from tough stock on both sides of my family, all of whom faced adversity head-on when they arrived in America in the early 1900s. I knew I had to live up to this family trait, and Somalia

POC Team member Bill Stone.

was another test. I would not let my teammates down, and I would be ready to do what needed to be done to protect our personnel.

These two new men had joined our team and would have our backs if and when things went south. I appreciated their senses of humor, and they fit right in. That was important because, believe it or not, if someone is wound too tight he can pop like a cork at any time. And if they're wound that tight in a noncombat situation, imagine how they'd likely respond when bullets start flying. Knowing that someone can still laugh in high-stress situations tells me they've managed to strike a balance between who they are and what they do, keeping things in the proper perspective.

We made it a habit to always wave to anyone, especially Somalis, who had their hands on a machine gun; that way they would have to pull their finger off the trigger to wave back. I can't say I enjoyed the danger inherent in those "death runs," as we came to call them, but I did miss the adrenaline charge when we had downtime on the base awaiting our next mission.

Speaking of downtime, when we did not have operational movements we spent time jogging along the airport runways or taking turns on the small weight set that we used religiously to stay in shape and keep our physical edge intact. Other times, when we were exhausted from multiple runs through the city, we'd all crash out in front of the VHS player and watch one of the few videos we had. One day, as a steady ocean breeze pushed its way in through the open windows of the trailer, we were watching *Ace Ventura: Pet Detective* for maybe the twentieth time when I heard a squeak and shot straight up. I knew that squeak.

That damn squeak.

"That little fucker is back, isn't he?" Bill asked.

"Yep," I said, listening for him.

"I say it is time we teach the little shit a lesson!" Jimmy said.

Crouching down, I cautiously looked for the rat that had become our arch nemesis within the trailer walls. With lightning speed, he zipped across the floor. This particular Somali rat was five inches long and enjoyed scampering around the trailer and occasionally would run right over the top of our feet, not caring whether they were booted or bare. For our part, the three of us—hardened operators used to patrolling streets laden with heavily armed enemies—took to scrambling atop chairs, tables, and counters to avoid possibly getting bit by a rat infected with God only knows what.

Finally, Jimmy had had enough and whipped out his pistol, readying it for the rat if it showed its face again.

"What the hell are you doing?" I screamed before he was able to pull the trigger.

"I'm going shoot the damn thing. What does it look like I'm doing?" Jimmy replied.

"You'll fucking blow a hole in the floor!" I said.

Wham! Wham! Wham! I heard before Jimmy could reply.

We both turned toward Chris, who had grabbed a baseball bat and smashed the rat until nothing was left but a pile of fur, bones, and blood.

Our trailer, at long last, was safe again. If only the same thing could be said for the rest of the country.

On July 12, weeks prior to Jimmy and Chris's arrival, there had been a major escalation when US military Cobra helicopter gunships attacked a residence in South Mogadishu where a group of clan leaders were meeting, destroying the building with TOW missiles and cannon fire and killing a number of Somalis. Soon after the incident, four Western journalists who'd gone to investigate were beaten to death by an angry mob near one of the main markets. The tragedy was emblematic of the growing tensions and an atmosphere increasingly fraught with strife and the likelihood of violence. Casualties among media and journalists were not unusual. What was striking here, though, was the degree to which Somali society was dissolving and the accompanying increased levels of violence that wrought.

Indeed, even the UN was no longer able to get supplies to the Somali people because of the inherent dangers to their personnel charged with transporting them. And this had a ripple effect with the Somali warlords, who relied on stealing a measure of those supplies and selling them on the black market to fuel their continued rebellion. Humanitarian supplies made up a substantial part of their profits and with UN shipments drastically reduced, they grew more desperate and violent in seeking alternative means of revenue.

The warlords were also losing their ability to move about the city freely, so they decided to fight back in a new way. They began holding gatherings where they preached the evil of the UN forces, contending that the foreign soldiers would ban their religion, rape their women, and spread AIDS throughout the populace. With a population averaging less than a grade-school education, it was easy to turn them against just about anyone without challenge, the UN being an especially easy and savory target. As the gatherings increased in occurrence, we began to notice the locals becoming more and more hostile. And it seemed only a matter of time before the mean looks, rock throwing, and general civil disobedience escalated. Instead of shooting us the finger, they'd soon be curling it around an assault rifle slung from their shoulders.

By the time August rolled around, it was clear we were sitting on a powder keg, and sure enough, all hell broke loose on the first day of the month. The US Army intelligence personnel working on our base were asked to assist an American military unit by providing blocking force support during a raid on a rebel compound in Mogadishu. It was normally a low-risk proposition, providing perimeter security to prevent any fleeing Somalis from escaping. House raids in Mogadishu had become a regular occurrence so it should have been, by definition, a by-the-book situation.

Wrong!

The Army was in place to raid the house, with intel personnel part of the team surrounding the perimeter. The soldiers stormed the house as planned. This time, though, the Somalis in the neighborhood didn't react as had been anticipated. Once the firefight broke out, local Somalis outside of the raid area decided to join in the action, forcing the intel personnel and their US Army companions to defend themselves and, just like that, the "by-the-book" mission flipped to a new page. The blocking force had to change positions to defend themselves, facing outward from the raid component, as enemy fighters descended in waves on the area. Bullets whizzed everywhere, smashing windows and digging divots out of the exterior walls of the surrounding buildings. During the chaos, several of the targeted rebels, the ones who'd survived the battle anyway, were able to escape. Not a single American soldier was lost on our end, but the damage had been done because the incident seemed to embolden and encourage more

Somalis to do the same. It was a true game changer, especially in view of what was to come just a few months later.

Eight days later, four US Army military police officers were scheduled to travel down 21 October Road, one of the busier roads in the area. Army intel personnel had provided them with threat reporting on the area and, coincidentally, our POC team had been doing countersurveillance and atmospherics while on runs there. The MPs had been given the absolute latest intelligence. The ride should have gone smoothly.

But it didn't.

KABOOM!

In a split second, the entire unit was killed by a command-detonated land mine, eerily similar to the deadly IEDs (improvised explosive devices) we'd encounter a decade later in Iraq. There was nothing anyone could have done to anticipate the new and more sophisticated attack by Aidid's forces.

The Army was only able to recover three of the bodies. The fourth was later found hanging in a tree, having rotted to mere scraps before soldiers were able to reach it. CNN and other networks would have reported on the incident, but a week prior an angry crowd of Somalis had massacred several journalists by stoning them to death so they were too afraid to venture into the area.

In retrospect, it's easy to see how things were spiraling out of our control, beyond any reasonable capacity on our part to hold even the status quo. When you're tactically adjusting day by day, though, you don't often get the bigger picture, at least not at that time. From ground level, we knew things were getting far more dangerous, but we had a job to do and couldn't simply cash in our chips because we didn't like the hand we'd been dealt.

Tensions continued to escalate. Nightly attacks on the UN compound and the airport, as well as daytime attacks on convoys, became a regular occurrence. Many of the UN personnel were getting burned out from the constant threat level, even some of the more hardened military personnel. Being dropped into a war zone with clear mission parameters to clear or hold an area was one thing. But we'd found ourselves in this dark netherworld where our enemies could be smiling and waving at us an instant before they whipped out a gun or grenade launcher. The rules of engagement had changed inalterably because we didn't really know who we were engaging. And, in that respect, our experience in Somalia became both a harbinger and blueprint for our future encounters and entanglements in the Middle East. Good intentions were rendered meaningless in the face of the hatred Aidid and his cadre had stoked up with the masses.

On August 13, 1993, US Army intel personnel had to make a movement with our team from the airport compound to the UN compound. They were nervous about the move, especially the senior NCO who'd been in country for months and had lost several of his friends to the escalation and increased murkiness of our situation.

Two soldiers jumped into the back of one of our SUVs and one of them, with a totally serious look on his face, said to his teammate, "See you in hell!"

Bill and I burst out laughing.

"Who you think you're riding with, the National Guard?" Bill asked.

"Not sure who you guys think you are. But those crazy-ass Somalis have targets on all our backs, so what the hell's the difference?"

It wasn't a matter of who we thought we were but what we, as POC team members, had been taught and how we applied it when working in hostile environments. The POC had learned to utilize some specific skills to avoid an ambush or, if an ambush could not be avoided, how to survive it. These were specialized skills taught to a variety of US government and private sector personnel who attend training at both civilian schools and official classes given by specific US government agencies. In the protective operations world, they are sometimes referred to as protective intelligence (PI) skills, while in other security disciplines they are referred to as situational and tactical awareness skills. POC members were taught to be proficient in route analysis, surveillance detection and countersurveillance, attack recognition, countering the "surprise factor," and evasive action.

Route analysis, for example, is the tactical examination of the environment from the point of view of a potential attacker. Specifically, we examine the routes we plan to use looking for potential attack sites, chokepoints, and any hazards that might cause us harm or impair our ability to move from one location to another securely. Potential attack sites are locations that provide the enemy with the ability to control our movements, while providing them cover and concealment and leaving them potential escape routes. The actual location where the attacker stages or initiates the attack, where the most firepower is focused, is called the "X." Chokepoints are areas with limited ability to maneuver but that we are required to travel through when moving from one location to the other. These could be the result of geographic features (bridges, parks), traffic patterns (the only road between two points), or architectural features (buildings and structures) that restrict movements. Historically, if an attack did take place it would most likely occur at one of the chokepoints. Route analysis, done correctly, showed us where our primary chokepoints were and helped us determine likely attack sites along the route.

In order to target us, the attacker had to know where we were going and when we would be there. Although much of that data could be gathered electronically, at some point our potential attackers needed to employ "eyes on" the target. Thinking like the attacker, putting ourselves in their mind, we would look for the most likely surveillance points near our work, our residence, along our routes, in chokepoints, and near potential ambush sites. We would then analyze those places and the possible methods they might use to blend into the specific environments.

Once we located likely surveillance points, we began to look for correlation (movement by people or vehicles that corresponded to or was concurrent with our movements). Additionally, we needed to look for some common mistakes made by the surveillants. Once we discovered a correlation or an unusual activity, we needed to immediately investigate: this could be done covertly (using countersurveillance) or overtly (using interviews, arrests, site inspections, and so on).

If there was enough evidence to warrant concern, we would respond by changing our routes and times or by posting obvious security at the chokepoints. To effectively employ the above elements, we practiced surveillance detection on all movements, especially those involving chokepoints and potential ambush sites. Surveillance detection is most effective against the initial surveillance phase in the "attack cycle," since untrained personnel are frequently employed and such surveillance takes place over a longer period of time. It is less effective against the final surveillance phase when trained personnel are utilized, bringing a more operational and experienced mindset to the game.

We were also taught to anticipate the likelihood of an attack or ambush. To do this, we utilized the same skills when we did surveillance detection. This was especially critical when it came to chokepoints and potential ambush sites. Specifically, we were looking for unusual interest in our vehicle movement, anything that could slow or stop our movement, and any unusual activities by pedestrians or vehicles. And, of course, we were perpetually scanning the area for any visibly deployed attack team and/or vehicles.

In a nutshell, we were constantly on the lookout for anything that caused us to feel that something was wrong or, at least, not quite right. If anything anomalous, unusual, or potentially threatening was observed, we immediately raised our awareness level in order to pin down the anomaly and mentally prepare ourselves, working out potential options within a potentially hostile environment. We had to be intrinsically aware of the whole of our environment, kind of seeing things in three dimensions instead of just two in order to anticipate what might be coming next. It was pretty clear at that point that attacks were likely going to happen; it was the surprise ones, the ambushes you did not see coming, that we were really trying to avoid.

Everything seizes up when you're subjected to a surprise attack, the inevitable shock you feel freezing your reactions for the seconds or even milliseconds that could also cost you your life. Shock is a condition when the body reacts to great stress, releasing chemicals into the muscles at such a rate that the muscles are overloaded, interfering with their normal functioning, to include possibly freezing. This reaction can last three seconds or more, and in combat three seconds may be all the time we have to act and save ourselves.

My confidence in our team and our ability to do our mission came from my knowledge of our protective operations methodology. We relied upon our ability to fly under the radar. We never were on the offensive; in fact, the complete opposite. If a group of Somalis came running toward us, we would avoid them and move in another direction. Our secret to success was being covert. That was how we stayed safe on all our runs. And that was how Bill and I were planning on keeping ourselves and the soldiers safe during our foray outside the base on that August 13 of 1993.

That was why we were laughing at the intel personnel, because our plan was to be a ghost. You can't successfully attack what you do not see! Stealth mode wins every time. And, as a result, the day's movements proved uneventful and both soldiers were returned to base safely.

Our protective skills and our ability to move about the city undetected became increasingly well-known among our US military counterparts. So when the predeployment unit for Task Force RANGER arrived in Mogadishu without any transport or firsthand knowledge of the lay of the land, the chief offered our services to move them safely between the UN compound and the airport. The task force of special operations personnel included the best of the best, from operators to support personnel, all of whom were trained and ready to deploy in ten days.

The predeployment element was led by Colonel Daniel McKnight, commander of the 3rd Ranger Battalion. McKnight was the same officer who'd later become famous during the Battle of Mogadishu and was played by Tom Sizemore in the *Black Hawk Down* movie. Colonel McKnight and his officers didn't have any means to move between their airport compound, UN headquarters, and the CIA's base of operations. But they had us, and we were thrilled to be able to assist and protect Task Force RANGER operators as they prepared for the arrival of their main unit. These additional movements in and around the city, though, increased our risk level and eroded our ability to stay low profile, threatening to render moot many of the very precautions we'd set in place. Although we had to break our normal protocol, we were able to keep the Task Force RANGER team safe. That was our goal, while the task force's main objective was to attack and destroy the enemy, specifically to get Aidid, but it's hard to do that from the shadows in an unfamiliar, continually evolving landscape.

On August 28, 1993, as noted in Mark Bowden's superb book *Black Hawk Down*, the day before Task Force RANGER and the special operations forces landed in Mogadishu, the CIA's main asset in the hunt to get the renegade warlord Aidid killed himself while playing a drunken game of Russian roulette. He left a "not quite" grieving widow who was the sole heir to his considerable fortune acquired as a local warlord and for his well-paid service to the Agency. Initial examination of his head wound did not indicate that the shot was at close range, leaving us with some doubt about the Russian roulette story. The POC team ended up visiting his compound just after he died to collect some gear and for the deputy to personally convey his condolences to the widow. You can imagine how dangerous it was to be locked in the compound, not knowing if one of his minions had killed him and was possibly going to turn on us. It was with a huge sense of relief when we left the compound and headed back to our own. Later, an autopsy revealed that the wound was indeed created at contact distance, indicating a possible self-inflicted gunshot.

After Task Force RANGER arrived, we were kept very busy shuttling the CIA chief and his deputy to meetings in their operations office adjacent to the hangar they occupied on the airport compound.

We ended up sitting for hours within the task force compound. Photography and video recording anywhere near the task force, especially near the special operations forces area, was forbidden. Reporters who flaunted the rule and ran afoul of task force soldiers would be forced to relinquish their cameras and watch in horror as the soldiers pulled out the film and strung it around the barbwire surrounding their area as a warning to others. (This was long before the days of digital cameras and smartphones.)

But there we were with August finally coming to a close and the threat level continuing to escalate. We had hoped that once the wretched summer heat died down, maybe the itchy fingers of the Somali fighters would too. *Perchance to dream,* as Shakespeare might say.

One night, after a long, hot day of movements to and from the UN compound, I was more than ready to collapse on my bed in my trailer. I was dead tired. It was after 2200 hours and I was just about to nod off when a huge explosion rocked the trailer, blowing out the back window. I curled into a ball to limit my exposure as the glass shot across the trailer and rained down on top of me. The blast shocked all of the camp out of their beds with the exception of a soldier taking an outdoor shower next to his trailer. I stood up and brushed the glass off my back and out of my hair.

What the hell just happened?

I walked outside of the trailer, cautious and still on edge. I was primed for whatever was coming next, certain there would be something. When I scanned the base, it seemed everyone was as confused as I was. From first look, it appeared that no one was injured from the blast or any debris or shrapnel, which was truly amazing. Post-blast investigation revealed that a lone 60mm mortar round had detonated directly behind our trailer. Most mortar attacks came in pairs. Since we hadn't heard a second detonation, we performed a thorough search of the area in case a dud mortar round remained in our compound but found nothing. The next morning, we learned that a Somali rebel commander had ordered his mortar team to fire, even though they did not really have their mortars sighted in on a target.

That represented a turning point for us to the extent that the danger we felt on movements outside the base was amplified by the new dangers we faced within our encampment. Not only were we still targets, the Somali rebel attacks were clearly escalating. They weren't backing down, they were not giving up, and they appeared to no longer be content to wait for us to come and get them.

Instead, they were coming for us.

7

Mogadishu, Somalia ▪ September 4, 1993

The sun had not yet cut through the darkness and my eyes were still shut when the static crackling of my radio cut into my dreams. My bed was the closest to the radio charger where we kept the radios when we were all asleep.

"RATTLER, RATTLER, this is PUMA. Do you copy?" PUMA was the radio call sign for the deputy, John Marcello.

"PUMA, PUMA, this is RATTLER TWO, go ahead," I said, trying to hide the sleep from my voice.

"Roger, RATTLER TWO. I hope I didn't wake you."

"Of course not, sir," I said, moving the mic away from my mouth so the deputy wouldn't hear me yawn.

"RATTLER TWO, I need to make a move up to North Mogadishu tomorrow. Over."

I wasn't quick to say "yes, sir," as was my custom. And I'm not sure whether that was because I was still half asleep or because I knew that it was a problem, since it would be the second time in less than two weeks we'd be seeing the same asset, a man we normally met only once a month. The sudden request for a movement to North Mogadishu was unusual and broke the established pattern of meetings.

POC teams knew changes like that often increased the risk as people tended to do less planning and get caught up in the urgency of the issue, forgetting the required security threat assessments that needed to be made. A divergence from routine, though harmless in the civilian world, often resulted in disaster in ours.

There was actually a specific reason for us to be wary. The previous evening, just before we hit the rack, we learned that one of the two remaining routes we used to get to North Mogadishu had been mined by Aidid's men in anticipation of our using it again. This left us with only one route we'd have to use to get there and back. Such time and place predictability was the surest recipe for disaster and would leave us vulnerable to an attack. I couldn't just tell Marcello "yes, sir" whether he was the deputy or not. My job was to protect him, not just do as he said.

"PUMA," I said, "advise against traveling to North Mogadishu, as we have just received new threat information that one of the two routes we use has been mined. Suggest we hold off until we can find alternative routes. The threat level is extremely high. Over."

"RATTLER TWO, report to the office at zero nine hundred hours to plan the movement. Over."

"Roger, PUMA, will be there. Over and out."

It was obvious from the radio conversation that Marcello wasn't listening to the warning. I woke up the rest of the team.

"What's he thinking?" Jimmy asked.

"This movement could get us all killed!" Chris chimed in.

"It's our job to assess the threat and figure out a way around it," I countered, trying to calm everyone down in spite of my own reservations.

"Like trying to find a way around ants in an ant hill," Bill said, chewing on the end of his coffee straw.

"Well, we better find some bug spray and fast!" I said, unrolling a map.

At 0900 hours, our team made the movement over to the main office from the airport outpost. Bill and I provided Marcello with a complete threat briefing. We explained the serious risk involved in only having one route in and out of North Mogadishu in terms of predictability and a lack of available options. After more than an hour discussing the risks associated with the movement, the deputy grew even more insistent, stating that the meeting with his asset was vital and worth the risk.

"If you have a problem doing your job, then I will go myself!" Marcello said, his face red with anger.

He had us over a barrel, knowing that our job was to protect him with our lives. It was at that point that SHEPARD II, the US Army intelligence officer recently assigned to serve as liaison with the main office, spoke up.

"There may be one more option."

We all turned to look at him.

"Any suggestion is welcome," I said. "Keep talking."

"I've been on leave for six months and just returned to Somalia. But prior to my departure, we used to travel 21 October Road to Checkpoint Pasta, which is manned by the Italian military."

SHEPARD II provided us with all the information he had on the run. Despite the fact that his intel was rather dated, we decided to take a look at the route, since there wasn't enough time to reconnoiter any alternative routes. At minimum, though, we insisted that we needed a helicopter overflight of the proposed route to acquire actual roadway atmospherics about the area we would be traveling through.

The US military provided a Black Hawk helicopter, and the deputy and SHEPARD II accompanied Bill and me on the overflight. The new proposed route began with a long, straight run north by northeast up 21 October Road. From there, the route would have us enter Checkpoint Pasta and then turn immediately south down Mogadishu Road, moving through a densely populated area with a market that served the Somali people. At the point we passed the market, we'd be several blocks from the asset's residence. After the meeting, the convoy would continue south along the un-mined route, passing adjacent to the port, and then into the area controlled by the Pakistani UN contingent guarding the north end of the Mogadishu airport.

We observed that 21 October Road was relatively clear of debris, that there were no burning tires, overturned vehicles, or any other obstacles that would either stop, slow, or hinder our movement. There was a small crowd in the market area south of Checkpoint Pasta, a normal occurrence since, without refrigeration or electricity, the Somali people were inclined to visit the market on a daily basis. The pedestrian traffic in the market area there did not appear to be anything out of the ordinary and didn't seem as if it would affect our movement. The final stretch of the route to the asset's residence and then straight down to the airport was unremarkable.

After the helicopter flight, the deputy made the decision that we would go through with the movement to North Mogadishu. My team and I were flabbergasted. Although we hadn't spotted any obvious threats, it was apparent that there were no backup routes in the event something went wrong. Also, there were no accurate maps of the areas on either side of 21 October Road, so if we had to deviate off the main road into these unmapped streets, we'd end up lost, precisely what would happen to the US Army Rangers the following month during the Battle of Mogadishu that became known, tragically, as *Black Hawk Down*.

That afternoon, the POC team held a private meeting about the increasingly reckless attitude adopted by our leadership and how the number of movements we were making were too numerous and dangerous. Our repeated attempts to warn them about the worsening environment had fallen on deaf ears. The number of movements being made was bordering on foolhardy. No one else was on the road in Mogadishu other than heavily-armed UN military convoys and crazy media people, and both groups were taking casualties. We knew how much pressure our special operations forces and the US government as a whole was putting on us to find Aidid, but getting us killed was not going to help matters. It was as if they had convinced themselves that nothing was going to happen, as if we were bulletproof, victims of our exemplary record in country so far. We all felt that continuing with the new "status quo" meant we were certain to get hit.

"We've got to change our ways. Job or no job, these are our lives they're playing with," Jimmy said, pacing the trailer. "They created the POC to do the job. They should just let us do it."

"Fuck this! If HQS knew the threat level, they would shut these guys down!" Chris added, chewing on his thumbnail.

One of the things I admired about Chris was the fact that he never mentioned his family situation during planning sessions, never played that trump card, willing to take the same risks we did with more to lose.

I nodded, weighing their comments, searching for a diplomatic solution. "Let's make it through the next run, and then we'll talk to the chief," I suggested. "It's only one more run."

We all agreed that after the North Mogadishu movement the team would hold a meeting with the CIA management to discuss the elevated threat level and the extraordinary risks we were being forced to take against the spirit of our mission parameters. But for now, for tomorrow, it was the POC team's job to keep Deputy Marcello from following in Colonel Nick Rowe's footsteps.

The next morning, on September 5, 1993, at 0700 hours, after breakfast and as much coffee as I could swallow, my teammates and I prepped our vehicles for the morning's movement to North Mogadishu. We reviewed the local maps as well as the sketches we had drawn from our helicopter ride the day before, then ensured our radios were charged and that we had spare batteries. Since the run would be longer and farther than the movements we typically made, we also loaded up several bags with additional ammunition. And, as an additional precaution, we decided to radically adjust our movement protocols in several ways. First, we chose a very unlikely follow vehicle in the form of a pea-green pickup truck with a roof rack. (We later found out that Aidid's security group was using an identical vehicle, an incredible coincidence!) We also decided to begin our movement earlier and run the motorcade differently. This would make us more inconspicuous to any hostiles watching for our presence by appearing more like two random vehicles that happened to be on the road.

Bill and I would be driving the deputy in our four-door Isuzu Trooper. As I mentioned, we'd already "up-armored" the car with two steel plates that previously had been used in a US Army helicopter to cover part of the front and rear door areas below the window line, supplemented by those ballistic vests covering the front bucket seats. The Agency had only been able to get two armored vehicles into country: the large white SUV known as the *White Whale* that was already on Aidid's target list, and a small SUV that was unavailable to us since it had been deployed elsewhere. Thus, our "enhanced" Isuzu Trooper was the best vehicle for the run and the most viable choice for survival.

It was just after 0700 hours amid a slightly overcast morning when our POC team—armed with 9mm pistols and 5.56mm automatic rifles—drove off the airport and made our way to the UN compound to pick up the deputy. Our route took us through a market that, at this early hour, was mostly deserted.

The Pakistani guards at the main gate to the UN compound were prepared for us. They passed us through and we arrived at the office moments later. We greeted the FAST Marines on duty, and the deputy jumped into the back left rear seat of the Isuzu. I was sitting in the left front seat, with Bill doing the driving. Jimmy and Chris, meanwhile, were riding in the pickup truck, ready to come to our aid at a second's notice if the shit hit the fan.

I radioed to the communications officer in the main office, "RAT-TLERs and PUMA are on the road!"

As we drove out of the UN compound, I had to shut out any fear, doubt, or distractions and totally focus on the task at hand. The only thing that mattered was doing my job of protecting the deputy and

POC Vehicle—Isuzu Trooper in Mogadishu, Somalia, 1993.

completing our mission. No more "Nick Rowe" tragedies remained our unspoken mantra. This was what the Protective Operations Cadre had been created to prevent, and I'd be damned if we were going to lose anybody on my watch.

We made our turn onto 21 October Road and the convoy immediately assumed the nonconventional configuration with the pickup truck leading at a slight distance and the Isuzu at the rear. That should have fooled any Somalis observing the movement into thinking that we were just two separate vehicles cruising along the road. Anything to avoid confirming any suspicions on the part of hostiles that it was, in fact, a protective detail.

There wasn't much traffic as we moved up 21 October Road, but we quickly noticed that the environment had changed since we'd flown over it the day before. We started to see remnants of burning tires along the side of the road, normally an indication that there had been some type of incident in the area. My awareness level ticked up a notch. Bill and I shot each other a look that held an unspoken message: we needed to be ready for anything.

At the midpoint of our run up 21 October Road, we came up on some traffic that had slowed in reaction to what appeared to be a vehicle accident. As we moved closer to the "accident," we could see that an overturned bus had been deliberately placed across the road to force all vehicular traffic to move around it by using the shoulder.

"I have never heard of the Somalis using this type of obstacle before," Bill said, almost in a whisper to me.

He slowed the Isuzu to a stop a hundred feet away to observe the area and to see if any type of attack would occur when the other vehicles snaked their way around the bus. We could see that one of the vehicles in line was a CNN media truck. We watched intently as the vehicles swung around the obstruction and then moved back onto the road without incident. Once the CNN truck sped away up the road, we cautiously began to make our way around the bus, but we deliberately kept a slow pace to create some distance from the CNN truck, since reporters had been the target of several attacks in recent weeks.

We knew that just a short distance farther down the road we would reach Checkpoint Pasta. Per the intel briefing we had received from SHEPARD II, the area along 21 October Road up to Checkpoint Pasta was under Aidid's control. We knew that along this section of road we needed to be hypervigilant of our environment, keying on anyone who might appear even the least bit hostile.

Prior to reaching the Italian checkpoint we encountered several more smoldering tires, further convincing us that something serious had happened in the area. It was at that point that Bill moved the Isuzu Trooper ahead of the pickup truck to assume a more traditional convoy configuration. Just before we entered the checkpoint, I prominently displayed our US flag placard in the front windshield of the car and I made sure my weapon was out of sight.

The Italians manning the post seemed disinterested in our presence, barely giving us a look before waving us through. We circumvented their barriers and turned hard right heading southbound around the traffic circle toward the local market area on Mogadishu Road, placing us squarely into what we were told by SHEPARD II was Ali Mahdi Muhammad territory. Ali Mahdi was a Somali warlord who had been recognized as the president of Somalia by the United States and several European countries but who only controlled a small section of the capital. Even though he was on good terms with the UN forces and a sworn enemy of Aidid, we still needed to be cautious in this area, given that his followers were young, heavily armed, and trigger-happy.

We traveled the first few blocks without much traffic, but as we drew closer to the market the number of pedestrians substantially increased. At the entrance to the market there was a solid crowd of local Somalis whose attention appeared to be directed to the south, along the route we were about to travel down.

"What are they all looking at?" Deputy Marcello asked.

"Not sure," Bill responded.

I was trying to concentrate, hoping I could get a glimpse down the road, but I couldn't see a thing through the crowd.

Most of the crowd was facing south, toward the city center, and their facial expressions appeared to be a mix of surprise and hostility when they noticed our motorcade. Bill and I knew we were at a decision point. *Do we reverse course and retrace our route back along the very dangerous 21 October Road, violating one of our security practices of not traveling on the same road twice in a day, or continue farther into what we'd been told was the less hostile Ali Mahdi clan territory?*

"Maybe we need to turn back," Marcello commented halfheartedly from the back seat.

Neither Bill nor I answered the deputy, as we knew we were responsible and therefore in charge. At that stage, he was just a passenger. Bill and I exchanged glances, confirming the fact that we both knew the strategic move was to continue toward safer territory rather than retreat the way we had come.

We crept on through the crowd at a snail's pace, the people around us on both sides parting reluctantly. I had my rifle on the dashboard in a position to fire through the windshield if any hostiles appeared. Until that time came, I was doing my friendly American act, waving with my left hand while my right hand was ready to flip the safety selector switch on my rifle from SAFE to FIRE. We ended up moving through the crowd like a big fish parting a large school of smaller fish, hardly a reason to breathe easier yet.

As we passed the market area a few minutes later, the crowd seemed to have thinned out measurably, allowing us to resume a faster clip absent all the stops and starts. A hundred yards farther along the route, though, we noticed that the road had been narrowed to a single car width by a number of concrete blocks on either side of the street, something else that hadn't been there the day before either.

Oh, man....

Without saying a word, Bill and I quickly scanned our sectors, mine being from the center of the vehicle to the left for ninety degrees and Bill's from the center to the right side. Seeing no other obstructions or any people in the area who might pose a threat, we moved through the chokepoint.

Less than a block away, a wave of black tire smoke completely engulfed the road, slowing us to a crawl again and denying us view of what lay ahead. By chance, a wisp of breeze cleared the smoke just below knee level and we saw that the Somalis had pulled a gray freight container across the road, completely blocking our route.

My heart skipped a beat, since this could be nothing else but a hostile action. An ambush!

Bill immediately whipped the Isuzu into a hard left U-turn and floored the gas pedal. In the one to two seconds it took for the Isuzu to complete the U-turn and straighten out, enemy bullets started impacting the right side of our vehicle.

Under extreme moments of stress like that, the mind can react in a variety of ways. One common effect of extreme survival stress is auditory exclusion, a temporary form of partial or full loss of hearing. Other effects may include tunnel vision and tachypsychia, which is an altered perception of time. Also known as the "tachy psyche" effect, it is when time as perceived by the individual appears to slow down, making events and objects seem to move in slow motion. The opposite has also been described, where time appears to speed up, sometimes moving so fast that things appear blurred. In my case, I didn't hear the rifle shots but registered with crystal clarity the sounds of the rounds piercing the right side of the vehicle.

While part of my mind was counting the bullet impacts, the active part had me yelling, "Get down!" to the deputy and then "Go! Go! Go!" to Bill.

At about the fourth impact, I heard Marcello yell out, "I'm hit!"

The Isuzu's engine was screaming as Bill redlined it, gathering as much speed as possible. There was a one- to two-second cessation of gunfire and I had a momentary thought that we were out of danger when we began taking rifle fire from our left flank. Time froze for me as I came to grips with just how bad things were, a true "oh shit!" moment that we might not make it out alive.

Bill's lightning quick U-turn had allowed us to avoid the main ambush point, and picking up speed again made us a more difficult target for the hostiles. Bill's fast thinking and even faster driving got us off the "X" and out of danger and, in another two seconds, we were rocketing back toward the market. Due to the small cabin of the Isuzu, all of the gear, and the restrictiveness of my vest, I wasn't able to climb into the back seat to attend to the deputy. I was able, though, to turn around and lean over toward him.

Marcello was slumped over on his right side, facing forward, his head leaning against the right door. There was a bullet hole in the glass of the right rear door window, as well as one in the right rear door near the handle. I knew he had to have been hit high in his body. At first glance I couldn't see any wounds to his neck or head, but I could see blood on the seat.

"Is he alive?" Bill asked, almost yelling.

I didn't respond. If the deputy was breathing, it was so slight I couldn't tell.

"Where was he hit?" Bill asked.

"Trying to find the entry point," I responded.

I grabbed the deputy's flak vest and began to pat him down in the hope of finding the wound from which he was bleeding. The entry wound was near his collarbone, between his neck and shoulder. The bullet had just missed the collar of his flak vest and had entered his body at a horizontal angle. I opened the vest enough to see the heavy arterial bleeding and began trying to apply pressure while simultaneously fighting to keep him from sliding off the seat and onto the floor area as the Isuzu thumped down the potholed streets.

"He was hit near the neck and we need to get him to a hospital," I managed, still fighting to stanch the bleeding. "I need to keep him conscious. John, John, stay with me! Stay with me!"

8

Mogadishu, Somalia ▪ September 5, 1993

Marcello was losing blood faster than Bill could drive or I could think. I held pressure on his neck as tight as I could.

"Stay with me, John!" I yelled.

"Our follow-up vehicle is gone," Bill said, sounding frantic. "We've lost radio contact!"

My heart sank. Chris and Jimmy, in the pickup truck behind us, had been caught up in the ambush point much longer than we had. At that point we had no way of knowing what had happened to the rest of our team, to our friends. But I couldn't think about that now. I had Marcello to worry about. I could feel his life ebbing further and further away.

Bill was pushing for more speed. "Should we stop and work on him or keep going?"

He was asking if we should pull out our FAT (first aid trauma) medical kit and do emergency care ourselves or try to get to the nearest medical facilities.

"Keep moving and fast! Maybe we can get some help at Checkpoint Pasta," I told him.

I suspected that Marcello's condition was beyond any lifesaving care that either Bill or I could administer in the car. All we could hope for was that we would make it to the Italian checkpoint in time.

Bill kept on the gas until the concrete block obstruction of the checkpoint became visible. He expertly raced our now bloodied Isuzu toward it, and I felt relief wash over me as we zipped up toward the Italian soldiers, who must have heard the rifle fire but hardly looked up from their post upon our return.

"We need help!" Bill screamed out the window before he even stopped the car.

The Italian soldiers either did not understand English or pretended not to.

"Do you understand? We need *help!* We have *wounded!*"

"Go! Go! Just keep going!" I yelled to Bill.

The Italians weren't going to help. We had no time to get them to understand.

"Where now?" Bill asked.

"We need to get him to the hospital on the UN compound!"

Bill hit the gas while I began, as calmly as I could, to alert command over the radio that we were heading to the US Army hospital on the UN compound.

As we were pulling out of Checkpoint Pasta, we still had not heard from Chris or Jimmy. Since the follow vehicle was in a much more vulnerable position then we had been when the ambush struck, it was hard to believe that it hadn't taken more fire than we had, meaning Chris and Jimmy might've been in even worse shape than Marcello.

"John, stay with me," I pleaded, continuing to apply pressure to his wound. "Can you hear me, John?"

"I can't breathe," he sputtered.

I tried sitting him up more. His eyes fluttered, rolled back, and closed. My heart sank. I laid him back down and yelled, "John, John, wake up! Do you hear me, goddammit, wake up!"

The blood-soaked seat in the Isuzu Trooper.

Bill, fighting to keep the Isuzu on the road at a breakneck clip, risked a glance toward us. "What's happening? How is he?"

I had to choke out the words. "I think we're losing him."

Then I went back to calling Marcello's name to no avail. He still had a pulse, but it was weak and failing.

I hardly saw the road from that point forward, doing everything I could to keep Marcello conscious while repeatedly radioing the main office that we had wounded and were heading to the Army hospital. I only turned forward as we neared the UN compound, when I needed to pull out the US flag identification card and my UN badge to flash to the Pakistani guards manning the gate. Fortunately, the Pakistanis had been manning this guard post for so long that they recognized our faces and didn't slow us down. We flew through the gate and worked our way into the maze of streets leading to the guard post and drop-arm barrier fronting the US Army hospital.

A female US soldier stepped out of the booth as we pulled up. I rolled down the window and flashed my UN badge with my blood-covered hand.

"Let us in!" Bill demanded. "We've got a seriously wounded man here!"

The guard glimpsed Marcello's blood covering me. "I can't let you in until I clear it with my supervisor," she said, clearly frazzled as she fumbled with her radio.

Bill and I weren't about to let some bureaucratic bumbling lead to our protectee's death. Every second counted, none to spare. Bill shot me a look and I gave him an acknowledging nod. With that, he hit the gas and smashed through the PVC pipe drop arm and sped straight to the hospital entrance.

The field hospital consisted of one large, sprawling tent connected to a network of smaller tents housing other medical units. Once the car stopped, I immediately moved the metal plate from the bottom section of the door and stepped out, fully expecting that someone from the main office had already alerted the medical staff to be ready for our arrival, but no one had.

Fuck!

I ran to the hospital door and threw it open. "I've got a dying man here! I need help *now!*"

Doctors and nurses came running and rushed outside to our vehicle, going to work on Marcello immediately. He was barely conscious but, somehow, still alive. After about twenty seconds, he tried to sit up.

"Get me out of this fucking car!" he cried out in a wheezy, crackling voice before collapsing.

The medical personnel slid him out from the back seat and onto a stretcher, then rushed it inside the tent. For some reason I remember the wheels squeaking as a doctor came running back out to ask me what had happened. He had a grave expression on his face as I reported the details. He then sprinted back toward the hospital entrance.

I swung back around to find SHEPARD II standing with Bill and two other figures who looked like apparitions silhouetted by the harsh sunlight: Jimmy and Chris! To say I was relieved to see them safe and sound would be a tremendous understatement. From the moment Marcello was hit, Bill and I had to concentrate on our primary duty, which was getting our protectee to medical care. We had no idea what condition the other POC team members were in, and I'd feared the worst until that very moment.

A nurse came out to the car and gently took me by the arm, asking if she could help me get cleaned up. I had forgotten about all of the blood on my hands, arm, and vest. After I had gotten cleaned, several US Embassy Regional Security Officers (RSOs) arrived and began their investigation. It was standard operating procedure for the RSOs when US citizens were wounded or killed in that type of joint environment. After answering the questions of the RSOs, our POC team went to the office where we met with the admin officer to file our report on the incident.

Our vehicle was evidence under RSO purview, so we would have to find another ride. Our admin officer arranged for us to catch a US military helicopter that would shuttle us from the UN compound to the airport. After a traumatic situation, the human body produces an enormous amount of adrenaline and other chemicals, so technically our team was as high as kites. While we waited for the US Army Black Hawk to take us back to the airport, I walked over to one of the door gunners and asked if he could ask the pilot to give us a fun ride as I made a swooping motion with my hand.

"You sure about that?" the gunner asked, lifting his tinted glass visor on his helmet. I could tell he was staring at my bloodstained vest.

"You bet," I said.

"Then get on in."

He walked over to the cockpit area of the helicopter. He spoke to the pilot, who gave me a questioning once-over, then nodded.

The ride back to the airport was like nothing I ever experienced before. I sat in the outer seat area exposed to the rotor wash coming through the open side of the helicopter. The tremendous noise and the rush of air were sensory overload, and during the flight I lost track of where I was and flashed back to being in the Isuzu during the attack. That happened several times during the flight as the pilot dove and swooped through the air. When the Black Hawk touched ground, I landed smack dab back in reality, needing to somehow shake off the experience.

Unfortunately, one of the hazards of working in life-threatening environments is the psychological effect it has on you, especially afterward. Having a "flashback" was not an abnormal thing when you have come so close to death. The tough part is coming to grips with the fact that there are mental dangers as well as the physical ones, and that there is always a "payment plan"—we just don't always know what currency we will be paying in.

For me, the flashbacks were just the start of several issues I would face that I now know as post-traumatic stress disorder (PTSD). At the time, the CIA, like other federal agencies, did not have a clear understanding of the psychological effects of critical-incident response so the services they offered for people like me were rudimentary at best. We were just expected to be able to "deal with it," because we were professionals and that's what professionals did. I am happy to say that the CIA has come a long way since then and has made it a priority to help their personnel, first through education and then with mental health services, after a critical incident.

I spent the rest of my day staring at the ocean from a chair on the beach, replaying the scenes from the morning over and over in my head.

Was there anything we could have done differently? If we'd gone another way would Marcello be okay right now? What if we'd just refused to make the move to North Mogadishu?

No answers came and none would be coming. All that mattered was that Marcello needed to pull through. That would make everything else pale by comparison, lending purpose to the whole experience since it would've meant I did my job and saved my protectee.

Eight hours passed and the sun had already gone down when Bill walked over from the communications office.

"Tom, get the rest of the team together."

I ran down to the trailer and got everyone outside.

"Marcello pulled through, guys," Bill said. "You hear me? He pulled through!"

An enormous sense of relief washed over me like nothing I'd ever felt before. The guilt, remorse, uncertainty, and fear I had been alternatively feeling all day was instantly vanquished. *Maybe this was what I was supposed to be doing; maybe this was where I was supposed to be.* It was as if it was our destiny to be in Somalia. I realized at that moment that all the adventure books I'd read as a child had helped prepare me for that situation and that just maybe I'd found my calling. I had no idea how much of a profound effect the incident would have on my life. But I did know that it was great to be alive, that we had saved Marcello, and that for all intents and purposes we were done running the streets of Mogadishu. It hadn't been our time to check out. We had "seen the elephant," a phrase used by my protective operations instructors that meant we had faced a life-threatening event and lived to tell the tale.

We later found out that the deputy was hit by a jacketed 7.62mm rifle round that fragmented on impact. The jacketed part of the round had torn a hole in his brachial plexus nerve bundle and the core of the round had almost severed his subclavian artery. The arterial wound explained the heavy blood loss that had almost killed him. Upon his arrival at the hospital, Marcello was immediately given almost eleven units of blood, which indicated that he was minutes or maybe even seconds from bleeding out when we got him there. It made me wonder what would've happened if we hadn't crashed through the barrier. The shock trauma surgeons at the US Army hospital were some of the best and had been able to quickly stabilize his condition, replace a section of the subclavian artery with a piece taken from his leg, and do a nerve graph from his leg to try and repair some of the damage to the brachial plexus. Marcello would most likely end up with some serious disability in his left arm, since the nerve wasn't completely repairable, but otherwise he'd have a full life. Our actions had probably bought him another thirty years, enough to watch his kids grow up and get to know his grandkids too. This was what we were supposed to do, what our unit was created to do.

The *Washington Post* later reported that a Somali ambush killed seven Nigerian UN soldiers and seven others were wounded in a predawn ambush believed to have been carried out by the forces of fugitive Somali warlord Mohamed Farrah Aidid. On Sunday, the Nigerians came under heavy fire from both sides of the street as they were arriving at Checkpoint Pasta to replace Italian peacekeepers who were being reassigned to the Somali countryside. UN officials subsequently accused the Italians of making separate agreements with Aidid partisans as a means of forestalling militia attacks on Italian troops.

There were reports that the Somalis skinned alive several of the Nigerians while one Nigerian soldier was taken captive. Clearly, we'd been caught in the tail end of the attack on the Nigerians, and all of us would have suffered the same fate had we not managed to escape their ambush by doing what we were trained to do. Doing for Marcello what nobody had done for Colonel Nick Rowe.

Given that report and the events that occurred, the threat level was deemed too high for further movement around the city, so we spent our last days in Somalia confined to the airport compound. There wasn't much to do, and it felt like a pretty decent respite after what we'd just been through. The team and I spent the days on the beach, working out, watching movies, or catching up on sleep. And, of course, discussing the ambush and our actions.

The dissection served us for several reasons, the first being that it gave us a chance to really examine our facts and determine how we ended up in an ambush—the good, the bad, and the ugly. What we did right, what we could have done better, and what advice we would give to the POC training staff on how to use the event to better the POC and further our institutional knowledge.

The second reason to dissect the incident was equally if not more important: it gave us a chance to discuss the life-threatening event among a supportive group, something that is now done as a matter of normal recovery procedures among law enforcement and other personnel who experience a critical incident. The third reason for the in-depth examination of the facts was to help us mentally prepare for any "second-guessing/Monday morning quarterbacking" we might encounter back in Washington.

But the second-guessing, in point of fact, is an unfortunate part of the job, and you have to be prepared for it. If you can't handle it, you should not do protective work. The only way to avoid second-guessing is if nothing happens on your watch, which in war zones is unlikely at best. We weren't working with the right equipment (no armor, no real maps), and our management was under tremendous pressure to get a lead on Aidid's location so Task Force RANGER could "find, fix, and finish" him. Intelligence gathering, especially amid the chaos of a place like Somalia, is a high-risk scenario and, while we did everything we could to prevent being caught in that ambush, sometimes life conspires against you. Or, as we would later learn, Aidid did!

On September 16, we found out that Aidid had previously acquired physical descriptions of three of our POC team members, along with the make and model information for most of our vehicles, and had put out a contract of $20,000 for anyone who got one of us, a veritable fortune in Mogadishu. That same day, Bill and I were asked to go to the main office to go over the damage to the Isuzu. Thanks to the stand-down on land movements we had to use an alternative method to get to the UN compound, and arrangements were made for us to get a lift from a recently arrived Agency helicopter. It picked us up from the airport and flew us to the main office, where we met with the logistics officer, Marcus Harvey. In order to confirm documentation of the damage to the vehicle and to assist with any subsequent reports, we needed to be present for Marcus's examination of the Isuzu. We knew Marcus from our many visits to the main office but never had any significant interaction with him before the review.

"Thank you both for your assistance today. I can see from the condition of the vehicle that this must've been quite the ordeal," Marcus said, sounding genuinely compassionate.

"Just tell us how we can be of assistance," I said, grateful that he got the picture.

"Let's just get through this as quickly as possible. The last thing I want to do is make you relive this," Marcus said.

"We appreciate that," Bill told him.

Marcus began his inspection of the Isuzu, specifically noting where each of the bullets hit the vehicle. In all, we estimated thirty to forty rounds had been fired at the motorcade, with seven striking our vehicle. Examination of the bullet holes showed that most of the rifle fire had entered the vehicle at an angle from the rear. This led us to believe that the majority of the attackers must have been positioned near the road obstruction and that they'd thus been forced to initiate their attack before the motorcade had reached the dreaded "X," the exact spot where the bad guys want you to be so that you take maximum impact from their weapons. This theory also accounted for the fact that the attackers had fired on us while we fled the area.

As we continued our inspection, Marcus pointed out that a bullet had pierced the left rear window of the Isuzu and had struck the side of my seat. The trajectory of this bullet should have taken it straight into the middle of my back, a fatal wound. Somehow, by some miracle, the bullet had made a sharp right turn upon impacting the seat. It then skipped along the back of my seat, striking one of the head rest's metal struts, and then lost velocity and ended up lodging somewhere in the bottom of the back seat's foot area. It was at that moment that I realized how close I had come to losing my life in that ambush, and how that would have, by consequence, cost Marcello his life too.

The rear seat area of the Isuzu absorbed the rest of the bullets, making it clear that the deputy was indeed lucky to be alive, helping erase some of the survivor's guilt I had felt over him being seriously wounded on my watch. As hard as we had tried to protect and armor up the Isuzu, not a single bullet had struck the plates we'd installed. I was sure this review would influence the Agency to make it a priority in the future to supply the POC with the proper equipment, such as armored cars, to protect our people.

But that was all moot for Bill and me, at least in Mogadishu. The fact that the threat level was so high and that we knew Aidid was actively targeting us would effectively render the POC team unable to resume land movements. That meant the time had come for us to be rotated out of the hellhole, so we were scheduled to fly out in the back of a US military C-130 transport aircraft that same evening.

There wasn't much time for us to do anything but say our good-byes to the base personnel and our remaining POC team members who would soon follow us back to the States. Before we knew it, we were walking up the ramp into the C-130. I dropped my gear and picked a web seat for the flight to Nairobi. Settling back, I watched out the tiny windows as the chaos that was Somalia faded into the distance. While neither I nor anyone else could predict the looming disaster that would later become known as Black Hawk Down, it was clear the country was disintegrating into utter lawlessness. We took off from the airfield where the special operations forces and the Rangers were based, none of them having any idea what was coming.

We'd completed our tour, while US military forces remained to face the fate for which our experience served as a harbinger. The writing was on the wall, but, as was the case all too often, nobody bothered to read it until it was too late.

PART THREE

HOTBEDS

9

Washington, DC ▪ October 1993

"In September [of 1993], Secretary of Defense Les Aspin turned down a request from [General Colin] Powell for tanks and gunships to aid U.S. forces on a peacekeeping mission in Somalia," according to the news website Politico.

Requests from professional operators and cadre on the ground continued to go unheeded, even after our departure from Somalia in the wake of the brutal attack on the Nigerians, the wounding of our deputy, and the threat of a price on our heads. For someone in my position, who'd been charged with completing a mission only to realize that we didn't have the tools we needed to contend with the escalating threat situation in Mogadishu, that pattern was especially disconcerting. Lives were being threatened and lost, and those charged with missions similar to the protective responsibilities of the POC weren't being provided with what they needed to succeed.

A mere ten days had passed since Bill and I had left Mogadishu, since I'd looked over the Somali countryside knowing something terrible was going to happen. But I never could have predicted how bad it was going to get; no one could. Underestimating and misjudging enemy capabilities had, unfortunately, reared its ugly head all too often

CIA Intelligence Star Medal, 1994.

during the Vietnam War, as had a lack of knowledge about the geographical logistics. In Vietnam, those logistics had involved a jungle environment. In Mogadishu, it was quite the opposite—an urban landscape that negated the vast technical and ordnance advantages enjoyed by our battle-hardened troops. As it has happened throughout millennia, when we miscalculate the enemy's intimate knowledge of his terrain, his experience in the battle space, and his will to fight, we lose lives. That had been proven in Mogadishu, and it has come to pass in the newer conflict areas of Iraq and Afghanistan.

The so-called Battle of Mogadishu, part of Operation Gothic Serpent, was fought for two furious days on the third and fourth of October between the United States forces, supported by UNSOM II, and Somali militiamen loyal to Aidid and other armed civilian fighters. US forces encountered the same obstacles and urban logistics I had when I was moving my protectees around the city. The rebels successfully shot down three US helicopters in the Somali capital and killed eighteen US troops in what became known, infamously, as *Black Hawk Down*. Both Mark Bowden's superb book of that title and the film version that followed did an excellent job of tracing those days in heartrending, blow-by-blow fashion. Hardly a surprise to someone like me who witnessed the downward spiral of the security situation in Mogadishu and whose warnings to leadership had gone unheeded. I wasn't the only one, as General Colin Powell's warnings had been ignored as well.

"In the face of harsh congressional and media criticism, Aspin admitted that, in view of what happened, he had erred," that same Politico article related, going on to detail the secretary of defense's resignation over his handling or, better stated, *mis*handling of the situation.

My team got lucky, so to speak, in Mogadishu, but that wasn't the case for those Rangers and special operations forces ten days later. Nor was it the case for Ambassador Chris Stevens and his protectors nearly twenty years later in Benghazi, Libya.

When, exactly, was Washington going to learn?

* * *

Upon returning home from Mogadishu, I'd decided there was no way I could go back to my job at headquarters. I couldn't be chained to a desk again. I needed something more exciting, where I could feel I was making a discernible difference, as I felt I had in Somalia.

Beyond that, there's a mentality about serving in a forward position, on the front lines, that sets in. You feel you have a chance to affect things, make a definable contribution. I'd fought to save American lives in Mogadishu. I also had learned firsthand that there was a payment plan when you rolled the dice with your life. My first night back from Somalia also marked my first anxiety attack. I didn't know what they called it; all I knew was that I was so tired that it felt like if I laid down I would stop breathing. The horrible fear and sickening adrenaline rush that came with that feeling took me hours to get over.

At the time, the Agency only required a one-time visit to an Office of Medical Services (OMS) psychologist after a deployment.

Several days after we got back to DC, Bill and I swung by for our appointment. We told the psychologist what had happened to us in Mogadishu and he offered to see us "off the record," but we knew that was not possible, by regulations, and without even discussing it we both knew we wouldn't be taking him up on his offer. In a sincere effort to help us with any residual effects from our life-threatening event, the psychologist described about ten different things that we could experience as our bodies and minds tried to process the critical incident. The symptoms included sleeplessness, loss of appetite, anxiety attacks, disrupted short-term memory, mood swings, irritability, and more. Bill appeared to take our "adventure" in stride, but I suffered with about half of the symptoms. The short-term memory degradation grew into a serious problem over the next two weeks. My colleagues on the Director of Central Intelligence protective security staff could not understand why I was having so much trouble concentrating on my duties while I was on their protective detail.

Eventually I acclimated, and the symptoms mostly disappeared… except one—a newfound sense of claustrophobia, or at least that was what it appeared to be. I found that elevators, traffic jams, and small spaces where I could not easily move sometimes caused me severe angst. I began to understand that it wasn't really small spaces that bothered me; it was, more accurately, situations where I was not in control or could not do what I wanted to do when I wanted to do it. I hid these symptoms very successfully over the next twenty years, but I was motivated by my suffering to learn as much as I could about PTSD so that I could not only help myself but also others specifically in their desire to avoid it or, at minimum, assist people who were beginning to show symptoms.

As for myself, after Mogadishu I just wanted to climb back up on that bull and ride it. I had learned what it was like to come face-to-face with the enemy when he was just across the street or through a windshield. As Winston Churchill aptly stated, "Nothing in life is so exhilarating as to be shot at without result!" Once I "saw the elephant," I knew that my life would never be the same. Indeed, I wanted to have the kind of impact on missions that I couldn't possibly have from behind a desk or through a computer screen.

So I applied for a position in the Counterterrorism Center as a Counterterrorism Unit (CTU) officer. CTU officers were tasked with providing specialized countersurveillance, surveillance detection, and operational tradecraft support for Agency operations. It was a perfect transition from my time in the POC. The closest comparison to the unit would be the British 14th Intelligence Company, sometimes referred to as 14 INT, 14 Company, 14th Intelligence Detachment, or "the Det," a British Army Special Forces unit established during *The Troubles* to conduct surveillance operations in Northern Ireland.

Even with all the security and POC experience under my belt, I had a lot to learn, so off I went to undergo several months of highly specialized training. I thought I knew everything I needed about the enemy, but this training was going to take me to new depths. I was going to have to immerse myself in the world of the terrorist; learn their thought processes, their motivations, and how they react. Specifically, their "modus operandi," a.k.a. mode of operation. I was going to have to learn how to think and act like a terrorist and when I mastered that, I'd then have to reverse engineer the process to learn how to beat them at their own game. Counterterrorism at the "big boy" level, in other words.

We started out learning about terrorism philosophy and then moved on to case studies about the major terrorist groups: who they were, how they were formed, and where they operated. We then began a deep dive into their activities. While we were doing this, we were also learning some basic "tradecraft" skills, the nuts and bolts of clandestine operations. How to operate under the radar, how to move, how to conduct surveillance, how to avoid surveillance, how to set up on a target, gather information, organize it into a useable plan, and then how to act on that plan. Instead of assassinating or kidnapping a target, our mission was to prevent those types of things from happening to those we were responsible for.

Two months into my training, in the spring of 1994, I received an official invitation to a private award ceremony for John Marcello. The ceremony was to be held in the Director of Central Intelligence (DCI) conference room. The invitation had such a formal look you would've thought I was being invited to a grand ball. I must've read the four-line invite over a hundred times at work. I thought about the event while sitting on the couch in the small living room of my apartment. I hadn't spoken to any of my POC teammates from Mogadishu since I'd started my CTU training, and none of those guys had picked up the phone to catch up with me either. As I thought about the ceremony, my mind shot back to the ambush, the desperate race to the hospital, and how we'd later narrowly escaped the bounty Aidid had put on our heads.

As I sat there, the lock on my apartment door clicked and the handle turned. I was so distracted by my thoughts that when the door started to open, I jumped up from the couch.

The door swung open and I heard a female voice call out, "Tom, I'm home."

My heart started to slow down as the young woman who walked in shot me a look.

"Jesus, Tom, did I startle you?" she asked, shaking her head and maybe wondering why I was always so jumpy when she came in unexpectedly.

"I'm not used to having someone else living in this apartment with me, that's all," I replied as I walked toward her to give her a hug.

I had started dating Luna before I left for Somalia. Luna was a beautiful young Filipino woman who I'd met out at a nightclub in Tysons Corner, Virginia. She was five foot one and barely a hundred pounds, but she was full of fire. She had thick, long black hair that stretched to her waist, tied into a tight bun atop her head when she had walked into the club. Her complexion was perfect, and she had caught my eye from the moment she entered. As she walked toward the bar to grab a drink, she pulled out a bobby pin and her hair released like an animal set loose from a cage. It tumbled down her back and bounced several times before settling in its place.

She must have caught me staring at her, because she walked up next to me and said, "Buy me a drink?"

I wasn't able to speak. I think I gurgled something out and nodded to both her and the bartender. The guy walked over to us.

"What can I get you folks?"

Luna laughed. "I'll have a Bud Light in a bottle," she said.

With that I was totally in love. A beer-drinking beauty? What more can you ask for?

"Luna," she said, sticking out her hand to greet me.

"Tom, Tom Pecora."

"So you do speak."

"I do. Just had something caught in my throat there for a moment," I said, which was sort of true.

Luna and I spent that first night talking about everything. She was working on her business undergraduate degree at George Washington University. She liked apple pie but hated fish. She was afraid of dogs, and she had an almost identical twin sister. She was born in the Philippines but had lived in Europe until she was a teenager because her father was a Filipino diplomat. As we talked, I realized that I could tell her many things about my life before the Agency, but my work life was off limits, no one outside of my immediate family allowed to know the truth of my profession. Unfortunately, when so much of your life is your work, not being able to talk about it can be a serious strain. With Luna, I told her only what I was allowed to say, lies of omission forced upon me by Agency procedure.

I kept it vague and boring. Maybe she wasn't one of those ladies looking for someone with the high-paying job and she would settle for someone like me.

I got lucky. We started dating and our relationship quickly blossomed. The good thing about being in training was that I wasn't traveling, which gave us plenty of time to be together. Luna gave me a sense of being grounded, almost of being settled. She helped to take my mind off of things to the point that, when she stayed over, I actually felt like a regular citizen.

I always loved watching her when she came home. The moment she crossed the threshold, she'd perform what became known as the "pull the pin" gesture to release her flowing hair. But I wasn't watching for it today, because I couldn't get the invitation to Marcello's ceremony out of my head. Did I really want to live that experience in Mogadishu again?

"Tom?...Tom?...Tom?" Luna called out, getting louder each time, as my mind remained in a kind of fog.

"Yeah."

"Is something wrong?"

"No, just thinking about something from work," I said.

"What?" she asked.

"An invitation."

"For what?" she asked as she came and sat beside me on the couch.

"Honoring someone I worked with."

"What did he do?"

Luna rarely asked about my job; she had come to respect the fact I was vastly limited in what I could say. In point of fact, I wasn't really allowed to say anything, because if I did, I'd be breaching national security. I knew several guys who definitely crossed the line by telling their wives or parents too much information about their work, but I was a stickler for the rules. Also, Luna was just my girlfriend, not my wife. And, even if she had been at this point, I wouldn't have told her a thing. Following the rules, procedure, is how my team survived that day in Mogadishu. That kind of experience tends to stick with you. As far as my personal situation went, there were two kinds of people in the world: those with the proper security clearance to hear anything and those without it. Luna plainly belonged to the latter category.

"He headed up a project I worked on," I said, keeping it brief.

Luna knew not to push the matter and snuggled in next to me on the couch. "Any chance there's an 'and guest' on that invite?"

"Sorry, babe. Not to this one. Must be a small event."

"Maybe next time," she said, sounding disappointed.

"Doesn't matter. I may not even go," I said.

I was serious about that and wasn't at all sure if I was ready to relive the event, especially in the wake of the disastrous Battle of Mogadishu. The last thing I needed was the stark reminder that I could have been killed as easily as those eighteen soldiers, even if it meant missing out on the chance to help honor Marcello.

But Luna had other ideas.

"Go, my love," she whispered in my ear.

DCI Conference Room, CIA Headquarters ▪ June 29, 1994

I decided to attend the event and soon found myself pacing nervously around headquarters in Langley, where the ceremony honoring John Marcello would be held and the same building in which I'd spent some very memorable moments as a Security Duty Officer. Then I spotted Bill and the other two POC team members, Jimmy and Chris, coming around the corner and, in that moment, all felt right in the world.

"Hey, buddy!" Bill yelled out, his voice jovial as always.

"Hey, man, it's good to see you."

We gave each other the traditional one-armed hug. We chatted for a couple of minutes as we waited for the conference room door to be opened. Marcello and his family were already inside waiting for our arrival.

Marcello, the man whose life we'd saved the previous year, still had his arm in a sling. I'd heard that he was contemplating taking a medical disability retirement due to paralysis in his arm, but he was alive and with his family because of our team. The private ceremony for Marcello with the DCI was a huge honor to be a part of, and I found myself slightly overwhelmed with emotion. John's family made it a point to thank Bill and me personally for saving his life.

I guess attending the event was the exact thing that I needed to pick me up and get my mojo back. I hadn't realized how much time I'd spent rehashing everything that had happened in Mogadishu, asking myself what we could have done different. But none of that mattered. We'd succeeded in our mission, and our actions had saved the life of our protectee.

After the ceremony, the DCI, Jim Woolsey, approached the POC team to let us know that we would be receiving the Intelligence Star, a rare award given by the Central Intelligence Agency to its officers for "voluntary acts of courage performed under hazardous conditions or for outstanding achievements or services rendered with distinction under conditions of grave risk."

"Thank you, sir. That's a huge honor," I replied, my voice cracking.

"Yes, sir," Bill chimed in. "It truly is."

"The honor is mine, men," the DCI replied.

After the DCI walked away, Bill, Jimmy, Chris, and I had big shit-eating grins on our faces as the news sunk in.

"Guess I'll see you all at the award ceremony," Bill said, beaming.

* * *

"How was it?" Luna asked when I walked in the door.

"Better than I expected," I replied.

"That's good."

I could tell she was waiting for more of a response, but that was all I could give her. I couldn't even tell her about the medal I was going to receive, which would be given its due at a big ceremony for all of the personnel who had served in Mogadishu. It was such a huge honor, and yet I had to keep it to myself. Due to the limited seating I was only able to invite one family member to the event, so I invited my father. It would be the first time he'd see proof that I actually worked for the CIA. I would've really liked to have had Luna at the award ceremony, but at least my father would be there.

Africa Division Award Ceremony, CIA Headquarters Auditorium ▪ October 1994

Two days prior to the award ceremony, the protocol office realized that they had not invited Marcello, a serious faux pas considering the severe injuries he'd sustained in Somalia. The protocol office scrambled to get him an invitation, but he still felt slighted and rightfully so.

I went out and purchased a really nice suit so I'd look good upon receiving my award. I had it tailored and everything. It was hard to keep such a big thing from Luna but, believe it or not, I managed to.

The real highlight for me was being able to show my father what I did. To remove all the mystery and stories I'd been employing for so long. I'd kept the scary stuff from him and the rest of the family, but now he was going to hear that I had saved someone's life. My father was going to find out who I really was, all I'd done, kind of like Batman taking off his mask. He and my stepmother had driven all the way from Milwaukee for the event. Luna had decided to stay with a friend for the weekend while my dad was in town. It was sort of nice. It was the first time in quite a while that I would have one-on-one time with my father.

The ceremony was held in the "Bubble," the nickname we had for the large auditorium that sat next to the main headquarters building. The last time a security officer had received the Intelligence Star was all the way back in 1963, so it was no small feat. The Intelligence Star is the second-highest honor for valor in the Central Intelligence Agency, second only to the Distinguished Intelligence Cross, and is analogous to the US military's Silver Star, the award for extraordinary heroism in combat.

When I heard my name called, I stepped onto the stage and DCI Woolsey handed me the felt-covered box with the "Star" inside it and shook my hand. We paused for a photo and I walked back to my seat. After the ceremony, I handed the award to my father to look at.

My father was beaming.

"Oh, my boy," he said, "I'm so proud of you. I don't say it enough, but I am so proud of you. Standing there, I can't believe you're a hero. My son, an American hero."

It was one of the most glorious moments in my life, as well as my father's. At the same time it further reinforced my desire to continue working the adventurous side of my career in the Agency. To do that I needed to complete the training that would allow me to enter the world of counterterrorism, where I'd be pitted against some of the greatest enemies this nation has ever faced.

10

Southeast Asia ▪ July 1994

Receiving the "Intel Star" was more than enough motivation to see me through the remainder of my training. The CT training course flew by, not because we were having so much fun so much as because we were so damn busy trying to pack in as much information as possible before we would go out on our first deployment. We had to master hard skills associated with counterterrorism work, such as high-speed driving and evasive maneuvers, and vehicle as well as foot surveillance. We trained on a variety of weapons, learned the most effective ways to carry our weapons concealed, and how to tactically operate alone and in teams. We also studied photography: the old-school use of film, multiple lenses, and how to develop our own photographs. We learned how to surreptitiously take photos while in static positions, on foot, and in vehicles.

It was finally time for my first overseas deployment as a CTU officer. I greeted the return to a travel lifestyle with no small degree of excitement, especially when I learned I was heading to a country in Southeast Asia. Luna was from that region of the world, as her family was from the Philippines. It was a big bummer that I couldn't tell her where I was going or what I would be doing! In fact I couldn't tell anyone. My activity was strictly "need to know," and Luna along with my colleagues didn't have a need to know. Any slip in that area could put lives and the mission at risk.

When Luna walked into the apartment on the evening before I left, we should've been celebrating, but I couldn't even muster a smile.

"Why so serious?" she asked playfully, trying to coax one out of me.

"Nothing."

Luna did what I like to call her "sexy cat walk" over to where I was sitting on the couch.

"Something?" she purred.

"Nothing, work stuff," I replied.

"More 'I can't talk about it' stuff?" she asked, making her voice deep.

"Yes," I said, pulling her down onto my lap.

Luna kissed me hard, sticking her tongue deep into my mouth. I began to slowly unbutton her top. The whole time we made love right there on the couch, though, my emotions were a jumble, torn by my inability to tell her where I was going or what I would be doing. The lying by omission was already starting to be a real bitch. Little did I know then how much of an impact it would have on my life.

A Major City in Southeast Asia

My first assignment with the CTU was providing countersurveillance for CIA personnel and some other civilians working in one of the major Southeast Asian countries. My critical mission was to determine if terrorist or insurgent groups were targeting any of those individuals, given that the CIA was determined there would be no repeat of the attacks already launched against our people based in Athens and Germany, two places where incidents had already occurred.

I lived with my team in a residence in one of the wealthier neighborhoods of the city. The house we were living in was a small villa in a walled compound. It had five bedrooms, a large kitchen, and an even larger living room. It was on the older side but still well maintained.

*Counter-terrorism
Unit (CTU) "Terrorist
Buster" Pin.*

We parked the various vehicles we would be using to move about the city in the circular driveway within the compound. The residence was in a gated community with a guard force standing watch twenty-four hours a day at posts at each of the street entrances. We were in that neighborhood because some of the people we were responsible for protecting lived there. Residing in close proximity to my protectees allowed me relatively unrestricted access to them: what we call "Cover for Action" (why I was doing what I was doing) and/or "Cover for Status" (why I was in the area). It also provided me with added layers of security certain to make it more difficult for the bad guys, of which there were plenty, to acquire the location of our team. If they learned we were in country, we'd almost certainly be targeted, similar to what had happened in Mogadishu forcing our evacuation from Somalia.

When I first arrived in country, I not only had to learn the routines of every single one of my protectees, I also had to learn my way around a new city, a teeming metropolis of more than 1.6 million people crowded into about fourteen square miles. When you added the suburbs, there were almost ten million people inhabiting the metro region. I drove the city's main street and into the suburbs more than eight hours a day for almost ten straight days, on my own or with team members, before I felt confident in my capabilities to negotiate the city to conduct operations. This area familiarization was also critical in the event I had to face a crisis situation similar to what I faced in Mogadishu. In addition to prowling the city on four wheels, I also did so on foot, hitting the pavement during the day and at night. I covered the same streets over and over again, memorizing the layout as a grid in my mind. This was pre-GPS days, so half-assed paper maps were all we had to go on. The city streets, much like their counterparts in Mogadishu, were a warren of crisscrossing avenues and alleyways, many of which were dead ends, something to be avoided at all costs for obvious reasons.

Knowing the area intimately was paramount to me being able to do the job I'd been sent there to do. I needed to be able to predict the most likely place where a terrorist would sit to surveil my protectee. I carefully documented the potential surveillance points and began a systematic, regular review of all the locations, keenly scanning for the surveillant's telltale characteristics that I had been schooled on.

My team and I also conducted more aggressive operations by following our protectees during even their most routine movements, such as taking their kids to school, going to work, or going out to a club and the like. One area of particular concern was the International School, as a sizeable number of US children attended the institution. I spent a considerable amount of my time making sure there were no surveillance teams watching the school, its buses, or the bus stops where a large number of children waited on school days. That was much more difficult than it sounds, because the school was in the heart of the business district and the major streets in the area were subject to some of the most horrific traffic snarls I have ever seen. Additionally, there were limited places where we could set up, so being creative was a necessity. I learned the rhythms of the area, when the traffic was at its worst and when I could mingle with the population as they left their jobs to grab lunch at some of the street food vendors that lived off of the office crowds.

At one point, we became concerned about possible assassination teams stalking some of the roadways beneath one of the major streets in the area. This street was a limited-access freeway circling the city in continuous use by regular traffic as well as mass transit vehicles. The large buses, indigenous vans, cars, motorcycles, and scooters moved around the center section of the city along the route. Under the freeway, between one of the main expatriate neighborhoods and the business district where the International School was located, there were several "squatter" areas, places where the most destitute of the population lived. Their dwellings varied from cardboard shacks to derelict wooden structures. Some of the older residences were actually small brick structures with one or two rooms. Insurgent groups and their armed elements maintained their strongholds in just these sorts of areas, and the new threat from the insurgents was focused on high-value targets moving on and off the freeway. Normally, high-value targets for the insurgents were crooked police and military personnel, rich local citizens of Chinese descent, and US military personnel. In this case, though, they appeared to be targeting foreign expats as they transited to and from the freeway from their residences within the suburbs. We began to make more frequent trips through the areas, disguising our movements by changing up vehicles.

My time in the country was far less intense than my time in Somalia—or, more accurately, it came with less of a sense of immediate danger that was a part of every movement in Mogadishu. That could easily cause you to get complacent, the absolute most dangerous mindset an operator can have in any Southeast Asian country. The consistency of my mission in Mogadishu made my first posting with the POC easier in some respects than my CTU work. But I brought the same mentality and skill set of the POC to my work in counterterrorism, an advantage I had over some of my CTU colleagues. The CT work required a tenfold increase in my time on the streets, as well as more creative use of my imagination to remain low profile in a sea of Asians. We were out day and night, and the stress level was different.

We had to keep our eyes and ears open for a variety of threats, not the least of which was the traffic and ever-present crime. This city was a great training ground to build up skills I would need in much less hospitable places, places where my ability to blend in would be tested to the limit.

During that posting, I learned the true art of counterterrorist methods and tactics, knowledge I'd be forced to employ numerous times in my postings to come. My six-week tour flashed by. I was excited to go home, to see Luna. Before I knew it I was on my way back to the US.

My Apartment ▪ August 1994

"Right here," I said to the cab driver as we approached my apartment building in a suburb of Washington, DC. I handed him the fare and got out of the car, mumbling, "Home sweet home."

Luna knew I would be coming back that day, as I was able to call her before I left. As I turned the key and twisted the door handle to the apartment, I heard whispering. Faint at first, but someone besides Luna was definitely in the apartment.

Damn it! What was going on?

I hated the idea of my homecoming being spoiled.

"*Surprise!!!!*" Fifteen voices yelled in unison as I came through the door.

Ugh! I appreciated the fact that she'd invited people to welcome me home, but it was the last thing I expected or wanted. I wanted—needed—sleep, rest, comfort. That's the thing about a CTU-type deployment. When you're in the field, there are extraordinarily few moments when you aren't working or at least on call. You really don't have any downtime, because the enemy doesn't take time off. It was a constant threat environment for my team and me, as well as to the people we were charged with protecting. Something bad could really happen at any moment, which weighs heavily on you, resulting in a level of stress that's impossible to describe to someone who hasn't experienced it. At that point, a surprise, *any* surprise, was the last thing I needed.

"Oh, wow!" was all I could say. "Wow, you guys, thank you! So nice of you all to come."

I knew what was coming. A round of questions about where I'd been, what I'd done, and requests to see photos, as if I'd been on vacation instead of surrounded by insurgents who could have staged an attack at any moment during my deployment. I couldn't tell them the truth, and I certainly did not have any pictures to share.

"Are you surprised?" Luna asked, jumping into my arms.

"To say the least," I replied, forcing a grin.

I tried my best to say a quick round of hellos before ducking into my bedroom, where I closed the door behind me. My apartment may have been taken over, but in that moment my mind was still back in Asia, not having adjusted to the sea change yet. I dropped my stuff in the corner and fell onto the bed.

Just as I shut my eyes, the door flew open.

"Seriously?" Luna blared, hands planted firmly on her hips. "I throw you this great party and you come in here to hide out? Are you kidding me?"

I couldn't tell if she was angry or hurt. Part of me was too tired to even care.

"I'm really tired. It was a long couple of flights," I said. "I'm numb. I can't even think, but I'll make it up to you, I promise."

"You can make it up to me now," she said, and stormed out of the room.

I mustered every bit of strength I could find and rejoined the crowd of people packed into my living room. Just as I feared, I was instantly bombarded with questions and did my best to bore them with generic descriptions of a typically dull government trip. I got them talking about what they had been doing while I was gone, knowing that everyone likes to be the center of attention, something

I was ducking at all costs. Luckily, the guests who'd come to welcome me home weren't shy about talking about themselves, especially with a little or, for some, a lot of alcohol in them.

I was so tired, I don't even remember going to bed that night. My sleep was dreamless and when I woke up the next morning I initially had no idea where I was.

11

Khartoum, Sudan ▪ September 1994

I waved goodbye to Luna as the taxi took me to Dulles International Airport. She had barely spoken to me for days. It was pretty obvious she was mad at me for being so antisocial during the time I was home. She didn't understand what I'd gone through while I was traveling and the toll it continued to take on me during the two weeks I was home. I just needed to unwind.

I really couldn't blame her. It was bad enough I couldn't share where I had been, much less what I'd experienced while I was there. And I'm not alone there. Talk to any professional operator, from Marine Force Recon, Army Special Forces, or the Navy SEALs, and they'll tell you the same thing. The stress of the job, the time away, and the need to recuperate puts an incredible strain on any relationship. Add secrecy to the mix, and instead of a relationship based on openness and honesty you start to become someone they don't recognize. This explains why relationships in my line of work often don't last, the divorce rate is so high, and, tragically, why some veterans end up homeless and suicidal. You can lose your wife, your kids…sometimes you can even lose yourself.

I couldn't explain to Luna the intensity of the job. When people are trusting you to protect them, you literally hold their lives, and their families' lives, in the palm of your hand. A slipup, even for a second, could result in a disaster. How could she understand this, much less the fact that I was leaving for one of the most dangerous places in the world: Khartoum, Sudan, the terrorist's version of Club Med. I was heading for a land where Hezbollah, Hamas, Abu Nidal, and Osama bin Laden (and his group that was the precursor to Al-Qaeda) all pretty much had free reign. Sudan was where these terrorist groups trained and, generally, ran amuck, the government too weak and intimidated to stand up to them. Luna thought I was going to France and ripped into me to no end. I had no choice but to let her. What else could I do? Prior to departing for the airport the last thing I wanted was to have a no-holds-barred fight. So, I grinned and beared it—well, beared it, anyway.

"Luna," I said, as warmly and calmly as I could muster, "I'm sorry you're upset. I truly am. I hate leaving you like this. I know it might not mean much now, but I want you to know how much I'll miss you."

She sighed. She knew there wasn't time to push the issue any further, and we waited for the last possible minute to part.

"Will I be able to talk to you while you are gone?" she asked.

"I'm not sure what my schedule will be," I said, even though I had a pretty good idea things would be even more intense than my time in Southeast Asia. "But I'll try to call. I promise."

She nodded grudgingly, and I could tell that assurance didn't satisfy her.

"Be safe," she said anyway, wrapping her arms around my neck. "I love you."

"I love you too," I said.

Then I grabbed my large suitcase and my carry-on duffel bag and went out to the taxi that was waiting to take me to the airport and my Air France flight, the first leg of my journey to Sudan.

After making my way through security at Dulles and the obligatory two hours waiting in the departure lounge, I finally took my seat on the aircraft. I wasn't looking to converse with the person next to me on the flight so I closed my eyes, figuring it was best to get as much rest as I could during my last hours as a "civilian."

* * *

My flight landed in Khartoum early in the morning almost twenty hours later. I knew that I would be met outside of the baggage claim area of the airport by "Rob," one of the guys on the CTU team. He quickly, and pretty much wordlessly, ushered me out of the airport and into a slightly beat-up late-model sedan he was driving. Once we were in the car and on the road, he lightened up.

"Sorry, man, for being so quiet, but the Sudanese security services are always looking for an excuse to rifle through a bag to collect their bribe. Just best to spend as little time in the airport as possible," Rob explained.

We pulled out of the airport into the ruins of Sudan, which made most of the places in Asia and even some parts of Mogadishu look like Paris.

"Welcome to Khartoum," Rob said, smiling at me, as if reading my thoughts.

Rob was on his second tour in Sudan. He was a former police officer from Detroit who'd somehow found his way into the Counter-Terrorism Unit. He later told me that after police work, this was "a better way to play the game." He was only a few years older than I was but looked plenty more than that. He had those serious eyes you see on people who've seen life's seedier side and were no longer surprised by the capacity of humans to do harm to each other.

Was this what was in store for me?

Rob drove me straight to my new home away from home. It was a house in the middle of a decent Khartoum neighborhood that

CTU Deployment to Khartoum, Sudan.

was rented for us. There were other CTU team members staying in houses in other neighborhoods, the idea being to keep us as spread out as possible. For security around my house, I had a wall and serious locks on all the doors and windows. You really could not count on the Sudanese "security" guards who sat in front of the place and whose only real job was to start the house's generator when the local power went out, something that happened on a daily basis. Since the temperatures in Khartoum could reach as high as 140 degrees, air-conditioning was beyond a necessity.

The house was old, dirty, and sparsely finished. The CIA station often used it to stock supplies and equipment since it had several bedrooms but was normally occupied by only one person at a time. Being spread out in the southern section of the city meant we could quickly respond to the office or to support activities that were normally carried out in the desert on the outskirts of the city. The majority of US personnel lived in a housing development with a number of condo-like buildings within a fortified, walled compound. We had very limited food options due to the totally unhygienic conditions of the few local restaurants. Thankfully, the US Embassy Club, located along the White Nile River, provided us with the only "civilized" activities in country. There was a swimming pool, billiards, a small bar, and a restaurant. It also had a small commissary that was a real lifeline, providing the only source for buying food, bottled water, and other supplies. Due to the horrific living conditions in Sudan, we could only drink bottled water, since anything from the tap or in the bathroom would make us deathly ill. When I showered, I had to close my eyes and mouth and be very careful not to swallow or even taste the water for fear of dysentery or worse. Khartoum was also known for having the "highest level of airborne fecal particulate of any city in the world," which was a fancy way of saying that there was a lot of shit in the air, literally. Just breathing was often enough to get you very sick.

As if being surrounded by terrorists, along with polluted air and water, wasn't dangerous enough, we had to contend with parasites too. So many people were infested that many of the men looked like they were pregnant from all the parasites in their bellies. The entire country was out to kill us—literally!

The topography of Sudan was similar to Somalia. It was a desert city, and the buildings looked like they had just risen up out of the sand. Most were made of mud bricks, with some more modern construction found only in the so-called "business district."

I was given an old brown sedan to drive that smelled like body odor and stale cigarettes. The upholstery was fraying and sullied. It was obvious that past officers who'd driven it had spent most of their time closeted inside, each leaving behind stains of their existence I couldn't erase.

I started each morning at 0545 hours brushing my teeth with bottled water and then carefully taking a quick shower. I then ensured all the windows and doors were securely locked while taking the opportunity to look outside, checking the perimeter of my residence. I was looking for static surveillance and/or a staged attack team. Specifically, that meant pre-attack cues, personnel, or vehicles that were sitting in a position to watch my departure and hit me when I left the residence or when I drove away.

If the coast was clear, I would exit my residence and conduct an inspection of my vehicle looking for any signs that someone had tampered with it or had left me a present in the form of an improvised explosive device (IED). I had a small dental mirror that I used to look in the wheel wells, under the fenders, in the engine compartment, and behind the bumpers. If the vehicle was clear I would climb in, wave to whatever old Sudanese "security" guard was on duty, none of whom spoke English, and head into the office. Given what we were facing in Khartoum, I never felt safe while I was in Sudan, not for a single moment.

The US Embassy was located in a converted apartment building with almost no setback on several sides. Locals could drive along one side of the building and reach out and touch it from their open windows. This meant that there would be no preventing a terrorist from placing a car or truck bomb close enough to the building to obliterate it. For protection, the embassy was relying on the Sudanese government's intelligence service and some local Sudanese police who stood post across the street from the embassy. If it had been post-9/11, the

United States government would never have allowed US personnel to work out of a location like that, but, in this case, they were part of a skeletal crew maintaining diplomatic ties with Sudan so that the US could maintain some influence. A calculated risk, given that the Sudanese government wanted the legitimacy of having a "United States Embassy" in country.

Once at the office, I would gather with the rest of the CTU personnel to receive our assignments. I was lucky to be part of a very diverse and talented team. Besides Rob, I was working with Sasha Dzeltov, a guy from my initial CTU training course. Sasha was of Eastern European descent and was fluent in several languages in that region. (I would later work with him in Eastern Europe as well.) There were also several former US military personnel on the team—one from the US Marines and another, a true living legend from the US Army Special Forces, William "Billy" Waugh. Billy was a crass sixty-year-old fitness fanatic and insomniac who slept four hours on a good night. He was a master planner, organizer, and report writer. His exploits in Vietnam as a Special Forces operator, a Green Beret, were the stuff of legends, as he worked behind enemy lines in Laos and Cambodia. In Vietnam he became acquainted with the CIA after being assigned to the joint Army/CIA Military Assistance Command, Vietnam—Studies and Observations Group (MACV/SOG). After retiring from the Army, Billy joined the CIA, where he worked a variety of jobs that included overseeing the Agency's paramilitary personnel. When you combine his time with the US Army's Green Berets and the CIA, he had served more than *fifty years*. A true patriot who'd been kicking ass and taking names almost since I'd been in diapers.

Prior to my arrival in Khartoum, Billy was in country when Ilich Ramírez Sánchez, a.k.a., Carlos the Jackal, one of the most elusive and notorious terrorists of all time, was discovered hiding in Sudan. Carlos had moved from Venezuela to Khartoum, but he had never left any clues as to where he was hiding over the years and was rumored to never stay in the same place for more than a few consecutive nights.

His wife was found to be moving through the Middle East and had made a stop in Khartoum. This small slipup led to the discovery that Carlos was actually living there under the name "Abdullah Barakat" and masquerading as a Greek merchant. The French were alerted to his presence due to the fact they had an official warrant for his arrest. After some hemming and hawing, the French finally swooped in and made the actual arrest.

The work never stopped in Khartoum. After a morning situation report, the CTU team members would receive their assignments. Typically, I was assigned to target an area where embassy personnel had reported possible terrorist surveillance activity. I would also support operational activities by running routes, doing surveys, and providing protection/countersurveillance for operations. Many of the operations took place at night, which wasn't unusual at all and something I was trained for. However, Sudan made everything more difficult. Large drainage and sewage ditches barely covered by large concrete slabs ran alongside the roads, making the driving exceptionally hazardous. If you inadvertently drifted onto the concrete covers they'd often crumble, dropping your car into a two- to four-foot hole, breaking your axle and leaving you stranded. Few areas had power, so there were no streetlights and there was very little ambient light from the city, which left the streets incredibly dark, especially when there was little or no moonlight.

Moving around the city at night made for quite a challenge indeed. The stray dogs, camels, and people were part of the obstacle course that was the night driving experience of Khartoum. Outside the city there were a few paved roads, and the majority of drivers used the many unpaved sand trails, speeding along with reckless disregard to any semblance of traffic laws. One of our station officers appeared to be either slightly night blind or very unlucky, as he took the record for hitting the most number of stray dogs in a tour, leaving a front bumper with a dent for every impact.

I'd never operated in an environment so austere and so hostile. The Sudanese government ruled with an iron hand and was incredibly aggressive in protecting itself, which explained the large concentration of troops guarding their government buildings, airfields, and security offices. They also prohibited any photography in the city, making our job yet more challenging and difficult.

* * *

From the movie *A Few Good Men:*

Lieutenant Weinberg: Why do you like them so much?

Lieutenant Commander Galloway: Because they stand on a wall and say, "Nothing's going to hurt you tonight, not on my watch."

Operation Gummy Worm ▪ "The Bake Out Stakeout"

One of my first strange adventures in Khartoum involved a two-week assignment to provide countersurveillance support for some personnel staying in a multistory house near the edge of the city. I spent six to eight hours a day in a small shack on the roof of their residence with my eye glued to the eyepiece of a camera with a two-foot-long telescopic lens observing and photographing anyone coming and going from a nearby restaurant run by Iranians believed to have terrorist ties. We had learned that there were people working or living in the restaurant that may have some bad intentions toward the people living in the house, thus the surveillance activity. Unfortunately, the only spot that offered a direct view into the restaurant for the camera was the rooftop utility shed. Lucky for me this shed had an air-conditioning unit, such as it was. Without the air conditioner, the shed could have easily topped the 140-degree heat radiating off the roof. Sweat would collect in pools at my feet and I had trouble concentrating, not a good thing when you are doing surveillance. I resorted to eating Gummy

Worms for constant sugar intake while on that job, bags and bags of sticky, melting Gummy Worms. Gooey and gross, they nonetheless kept my blood sugar level at the red line.

During the course of my surveillance of the restaurant, I noted that there were people in the building who we would only see moving around at night. Given their behavior and manner of activity, it appeared that, indeed, there were nefarious activities afoot in the establishment. It was not atypical strategy for groups in Sudan, as the country had become a sanctuary for terrorist groups from all over the world.

I was glad when that particularly unsettling assignment ended. I never found out whatever happened to whoever was hiding at the restaurant, but I can only hope that it ended up being good for us and bad for them.

Near the end of my tour in Sudan, the terrorists operating in the area began to harass US citizens. We started to see more aggressive activity by possible terrorist groups, specifically more surveillance of our facilities and personnel. From my optic the local government, corrupt as it undoubtedly was, appeared to be trying to put pressure on the terrorist groups to not take any lethal actions against us. It seemed that the Sudanese government was probably afraid the US government would respond militarily to any attack on its citizens, but it appeared their efforts to curb the terrorists did little to deter those more aggressive actions.

As the terrorists became bolder and more aggressive, we realized that countersurveillance wasn't going to be enough to protect our people. Station management decided that the CTU team would provide protection movements for the office employees, escorting them from their housing complex to and from their work locations. We had to rely on changing routes and times as much as possible to try to limit their ability to set up ambushes. It was not typical work for the CTU team and, other than myself, there was only one other team member trained to do that sort of work: Billy Waugh. Luckily for us, he was very experienced and, given the severity of the situation in Sudan, it was great having him on the team. Putting to good use some of the lessons we'd learned from the assassination of Colonel Nick Rowe, I began to use every trick in the book from my days with the POC to disrupt the rehearsal runs the terrorists performed in an effort to prevent the real thing. Our strategy centered on being time and place unpredictable, varying routes and departure times, changing vehicles, and using our knowledge of the geography to lose watchers or pursuers when we were on the move.

Then the terrorist activities became even more overt. Specifically, they began to actively plan and practice assassination attacks on US personnel, including CT unit members like myself. It was an escalation that we were not prepared for. Armed with only 9mm pistols and driving unarmored vehicles, it was abundantly clear that any altercation would be squarely one-sided in the terrorists' favor. That was illustrated during one of our escort runs to the housing compound. I was working with Rob (call sign RODEO) and Billy (call sign AMIGO). My radio call sign was SNAKE. I was in the lead vehicle in front of two SUVs fully loaded with embassy personnel. We were shorthanded so Rob was going to ride with Billy in the follow vehicle. We conducted a radio check prior to our departure from the office.

"RODEO, RODEO, are you and AMIGO ready to move?" I asked before setting out on the run.

"Roger that, SNAKE," Rob said.

I smiled and gave Rob the thumbs-up. It was funny to hear him trying to sound cool. I headed toward my car. Billy and Rob were waiting in the car behind mine with Billy in the driver's seat and Rob riding shotgun. It was similar to some formations we had run in Somalia, comfortable in its familiarity.

I pulled away from the office, heading toward the housing compound with my vehicle in front of the other US vehicles. Several minutes into the drive an International Scout sport utility vehicle shot out from a side street and slid up next to the left side of my vehicle, paralleling us as we moved down the street. As soon as I saw the vehicle pull out, I radioed to my colleagues.

"Possible contact left! Looks like we've got company."

As the Scout kept pace with my car, I could clearly see that the driver was the only one in the front section of the vehicle. In the very back of the vehicle, though, where the cargo area was located, the side window had been removed and two Arab-looking individuals were squared up, facing me through the open space.

I instantly assessed the situation and started to plan some evasive action while I began taking deep breaths to slow my breathing and pulse. There was no time to think about anything but the situation at hand. I was hyperaware of what was going on around me. I began to specifically focus on the actions of the two individuals in the back of the Scout. Were they armed? I could not see any weapons, but they could have had AK-47 rifles below the window in possible preparation for an attack. The aggressors could easily lift up rifles to fire directly into my vehicle or any of the other vehicles in our motorcade and we wouldn't have fared well since none of our vehicles were armored.

My possible immediate actions were severely limited. The convoy vehicles following directly behind kept me from immediately braking, and the lack of side streets on the other side of the road left me with only a quick acceleration or a quick aggressive smash into the Scout to try to spoil the aim of its potentially deadly passengers. I was watching them closely with my peripheral vision when Billy's voice cut through the static in response.

"SNAKE, we see 'em. What's the plan?"

"AMIGO, hold straight but prepare to slam on the brakes to ruin their aim."

"Roger that, SNAKE. Standing by."

The Scout stayed next to me for the next minute, at which point the driver gave me the universal symbol for slitting a throat before swerving off down a side street.

I wasn't sure if it was a dry run for them or just harassment. Either way, I was quite happy that no weapons had edged out through the Scout's windows.

"Lucky break, kid," I heard Billy say over the radio. "They had us dead to rights!"

The result of that event was an edict issued by the US Embassy to the Sudanese government formally declaring that the increased hostility by terrorist elements within Khartoum was not acceptable in any way, shape, or form. This was the equivalent of the United States issuing a verbal warning with a far more aggressive action looming on the horizon. The Sudanese reacted quickly and strongly, and the aggressive actions ceased. The terrorists still conducted surveillance, but in a more discreet manner, and they stopped any overt actions that could be considered borderline lethal.

One of the biggest things I learned in Khartoum was not about terrorism; it was about leadership. Specifically, I was "schooled" on the importance of taking care of your people and that if you do that, they will take care of the mission. Former Command Sergeant Major Billy Waugh brought that to my attention when he singled out the behavior of our station chief, Cofer Black. Cofer was the type of leader whose concern for the well-being of his team almost surpassed his mission focus. Over the years I'd bear witness to this behavior by Cofer on many occasions, not only in the field but also when he was the head of the Counterterrorism Center a bit later in both our careers.

As for me, well, I'd survived one of the most dangerous places in the world, a hotbed for the terrorists gathering to rest up before deploying again to put their diabolical plans into effect across much of the world. I often think about how much of the groundwork for what would become 9/11 had been laid in places like that, and what more we could have done. For the time being, though, we'd done the job we'd been brought in to do, and I left Sudan with the knowledge I'd dodged yet more bullets in the figurative sense, which was a hell of a lot better than the literal one.

I was, understandably, not sad to be leaving that place, maybe because the nature of the job was so different. In the POC you worked as a team, while much of the counterterrorism work more often involved solo labors that forced you to deal with the threats on your own, which made for a lonely and dangerous world.

12

Washington, DC ▪ January 1995

My assignment with the CTU was a continuous blur of travel to countries with a variety of threat elements and often very different terrain. From the Middle East to Asia, I bounced between countries suffering from insurgency problems, terrorism, or both. I felt like I was spinning through a revolving door, never sure of what I would find on the other side.

The missions varied to a great degree. In one country, I'd be doing countersurveillance to protect CIA personnel and in the next I would be surveilling "bad actors" from some of the most infamous terrorist groups in the world. In almost every case, when I arrived in country I had to immediately get up to speed on the geography and threat conditions before going operational. The assignments lasted anywhere from six to eight weeks before I would be replaced. I'd then head back to DC for two to three weeks to regroup physically and mentally. During that time, I tried my best to have a regular life and as normal a relationship as possible with Luna. And I have to give her credit because she did her absolute best to make it work, but it was hard for both of us.

Relationships don't function in a vacuum. There are expectations on both sides, a normal give-and-take. That, though, was impossible in our case, because I wasn't just a businessman or executive jetting around the world to close this deal or that; I was an operator who couldn't reveal where I was going or what I'd done when I got back. That's not a recipe for a successful relationship. Lots of people are busy. Lots of people have incredible demands placed on their time and pressures confronting them. But working in the kind of hostile environments required by my job was something entirely different. And when I came home, I had to leave that all behind me, like it never even happened, which was growing increasingly difficult for both of us.

When I was out of the war zone, all I wanted to do was relax. Being in a high-tempo op environment working against threats that had lethal capabilities while serving your country meant you were on Uncle Sam's time 24/7, until the very moment you got on the plane to go home. I wanted my freedom when I got back. Freedom to sleep, eat, or do nothing on my own schedule. I knew those were selfish impulses that wore Luna down. However, my time back in the US was extremely limited, each brief respite coming with the knowledge I was going to be sent away again soon enough.

And the next stop in my counterterrorism journey was Africa.

An African Country ▪ October 1995

As the leaves were starting to turn their vibrant autumn colors in the US, I was deploying to the capital of a country in Africa boasting mixed relations with Washington. The crowded city had been built along a ridgeline above a beautiful bay and was covered in a blanket of dust and sand from the nearby deserts. Due to the horrific terrorist/insurgency threat in the country, Western diplomats were not able to safely use commercial aircraft to get into the city. Instead, they would board a small aircraft in Madrid and fly into the capital,

Arab Souk in a Northern African Country.

landing in a special section of the airport away from the main terminal where protective details from the various countries sat waiting on
their passengers.

Even as our plane circled to land I knew that this, like Somalia
and Sudan, was its own special kind of hell on earth. Before I left
Washington, I'd received in-depth briefings from some of the regional

analysts to learn about the country; that, for instance, the main threat was an insurgent terrorist group that practiced tried-and-true, old-school terrorism methods, with no pretensions of trying to win over the hearts and minds of the people. This group was only interested in creating chaos and viciously attacking their enemies, regardless of any innocents who got in the way.

Vladimir Lenin allegedly wrote that "the purpose of terror is to terrorize," and no group I'd come into contact with before fit that bill more than these guys. Upon entering a village, they would rape, pillage, and plunder until nothing was left but corpses and flies. They would kill farmers and goat herders at random. They put no value whatsoever on human life, including women and the youngest and most helpless of children. And they'd been staging almost daily attacks in the capital for years, often several per day, trying to maximize the damage they could do and pain they could inflict. One of their most bloodthirsty methods was to set off a secondary explosive charge ten to fifteen minutes after the first explosion went off in an effort to kill police and medical personnel, thereby terrifying first responders charged with helping those injured in the first explosion.

The strategic importance of this particular country made American support, and thus my mission, all the more vital. To put it in perspective, Islamic militancy had surfaced in a big way in the 1990s, especially in countries like Saudi Arabia, Egypt, Algeria, Israel, Jordan, and Lebanon. Some of the more notorious terrorist groups operating in these countries included the Islamic Movement for Change, the Tigers of the Gulf, and the Combatant Partisans of God in Saudi Arabia; the al-Gama'a al-Islamiyya (the Islamic Group, or IG) in Egypt; and the Armed Islamic Group (GIA) in Algeria. Groups operating in Israel, Jordan, and Lebanon included Hezbollah, the Islamic Resistance Movement (better known as Hamas), the Palestinian Islamic Jihad (PIJ)-Shaqaqi Faction, the Democratic Front for the Liberation of Palestine (DFLP), the Popular Front for the Liberation of Palestine (PFLP), the Popular Front for the

Liberation of Palestine General Command (PFLP-GC), and the Abu Nidal Organization (ANO).

From Morocco in Northwest Africa to Malaysia in Southeast Asia, militant Islam continued to thrive and grow. Adherents of militant Islam accounted for some 15 to 20 percent of the Muslim world, according to Daniel Pipes, an expert on the subject. This meant that more than 150 million people were part of the problem we were facing. To make matters worse, they were experts at hiding among nonthreatening civilians. They didn't wear uniforms and rarely identified themselves, much less announce their true intentions.

Talk about getting dropped into a hornet's nest!

To their credit, the host government had city maintenance personnel ready to respond immediately to the scene of an attack, where they'd be positioned to carry out at least patchwork repairs and cover up the effects of the explosions. If nothing else, the goal was to try and minimize the public's exposure to the damage being done. The problem was these work crews could do nothing to repair the damaged psyches of the local people.

Due to the significant threat level in the city, once we landed in this African capital my plane was met by a multivehicle motorcade bristling with armed protective personnel. This reception wasn't just for CIA members—*all* US citizens arriving in country were met at the airport by six or seven vehicles filled with heavily armed security consisting of the State Department RSOs, some vetted local security personnel, and a POC team. Additionally, all movements off the US Embassy compound required an armed protective detail.

As the passengers were hustled out of the plane and across the tarmac into the waiting vehicles, I was met by my CTU teammate, "Chris J." A blonde-haired, buff, steely-eyed former Marine Corps sniper, he hardly blended with the Arab or European-Arab mixed population, but could he drive! He immediately handed me my pistol, holster, extra magazines, and radio. I strapped on my weaponry, stowed my gear in the back of the lightly armored white sedan, and climbed in. We rocketed out of the airport area and onto the road that the US Embassy motorcade would use to return to the embassy grounds. Our job was to scout the route and warn the motorcade of any dangers from the airport to the embassy compound. No rest for the wicked or the weary; hey, I was working less than ten minutes after touching down in country!

Due to the threat level, the State Department prohibited most US Embassy personnel from leaving the embassy compound unless they were heading to the airport on their way out of the country for R&R or the end of their tour. Meanwhile, CTU and the POC units would travel to parts of the city that few in the embassy could even find. That included the city's main market area, where, if our vehicle broke down or was trapped, it would be nearly impossible for the POC team or embassy security staff to reach us in time. The terrorists had eyes and ears everywhere and were likely to attack as soon as they ascertained that we were foreigners.

Chris and I would do deep recon trips into the city. Just the two of us in the sedan with four music CDs, one of which featured country music from Dwight Yoakam. Even now when I hear Dwight on the radio, I have flashbacks of flying down those streets with Chris at the wheel singing along to honky-tonk country tunes cranked on the stereo!

The United States Embassy was located in a section of the city shared by a number of other foreign embassies. The host government's security services were very careful to provide a measure of armed men in the area, especially near the gates. The embassy compound had several housing units within it and also boasted a second compound with additional logistical, administrative, and general housing. The second compound contained the motor pool, a bar maintained by the US Marine security detachment, and the embassy storage warehouse.

There were several walled areas adjacent to the embassy compound, but only two had been deemed secure enough to be inhabited. One compound had a large villa and two smaller buildings, and the villa housed both the POC element and the chief of our office.

On this, my first deployment to that particular country, the CTU team stayed in a small compound adjacent to the back section of the main compound. It had a high wall and reinforced gate, but it still wasn't nearly as secure or fortified as the other residences. As the new guy I got the second-choice bedroom, the one without air-conditioning, while my teammate Chris had the preferred bedroom complete with air-conditioning. Of course, my room featured an "unobstructed" view of the rear of the compound—unobstructed meaning there were no insect screens, so every night I had to spray myself head to toe with insect repellent or risk waking up drained of blood from the swarms of mosquitos. I kept my bedroom door slightly open to try and get some cross ventilation. Being a light sleeper, I could hear a pin drop in the house, along with the buzzing of those pesky mosquitos that managed to gain entry.

Less than a week into the tour, having come almost directly from my harrowing experiences in Sudan, I was pretty high strung. One night just after I had drifted off to sleep to the sound of mosquitos "buzzing the tower," I heard a sharp crack in the hallway. I shot out of bed, grabbed my pistol off the side table, and swung it toward my door as I slid up against the wall. From that position, I had decent cover and could see a slice of the hallway as I brought my pistol sights up to engage whatever threat was moving in my direction.

While this was happening, part of my brain was still processing the noise, recognizing it as familiar. The other part of my mind was tactically preparing for action when my sleepy teammate Chris walked into view. He looked up and stiffened when he spotted the bore of my pistol tracking him. At that point I fully realized what had happened. The door to the other bedroom, the one equipped with air-conditioning, had warped over time so it would occasionally stick and have to be forcefully opened, causing the wood to make a sharp cracking noise. Chris, who was on his way to the bathroom to take a piss, found me training a gun on him. To say he was a bit unnerved would be a serious understatement.

The host government security services consisted of local police, military, and special counterterrorism units. During my tour, I learned to recognize the different elements by their uniforms, weaponry, and tactics. The police were the least dangerous, as they were just trying to maintain order, keep traffic flowing, and deal with ordinary crime, something that was a factor in a country with an estimated 40 percent unemployment rate. The military units were more dangerous and prone to setting up unexpected checkpoints. They would often have machine guns set up that covered the center of the checkpoint, as well as the approaches to and from it, making it a death trap for anyone crazy enough to try to run them.

The problem was as we neared these checkpoints we weren't always sure who was manning them, because they weren't always "real" soldiers. Terrorist elements were known to ambush military elements moving around the city and out in the countryside and strip the bodies to acquire their uniforms and guns, which enabled them to impersonate actual soldiers. This made us extremely careful of fake military checkpoints that would often spring up on the outskirts of town, resulting in the execution of unwary individuals who fell into the trap.

The most dangerous element of the country's government by far was its counterterrorism unit, who were the most hard-core terrorist hunters I'd ever encountered. They wore hockey masks to both disguise their identities and incite fear in the populace. They never took action absent being certain that they could overpower their targets. The unit moved about the city covertly, usually traveling in unmarked vehicles, and when they arrived on the scene, someone usually died. They would strike suddenly and were known to spray indiscriminate fire with their AK-47s. The sight of them suddenly swarming into an area with their hockey masks was terror itself, making it difficult to determine who was actually worse, the hunted or the hunters.

About halfway through my tour, the insurgents stole an ambulance from one of the local hospitals. They zipped through town, nearly running down bystanders en route to the French Embassy. When they arrived at the gate, they tried to trick their way past the French military police guards by saying that someone was hurt on the compound and they needed to get in. The guards weren't fooled by the ploy and the terrorists, their plot forfeit, tried to ram the gate instead. A vicious shoot-out ensued and after the dust settled, fourteen terrorists were killed and several French police were injured. The reports of the especially brazen attack served as a warning that we needed to be ready for some unorthodox attacks, so we heightened the security at the gates of our embassy as well.

Those actions made the embassy safer, but had no effect on the dangers we faced when we were out on the roads. During a recon of the main market area, Chris and I parked our sedan on a semi-deserted side street with a good view of a number of local shops and vendors. Citizens were moving through the area, meandering among the market stalls and bartering over the price of figs, fennel, grain, spices, and other wares. There was a good mix of older men, women, and young children but a conspicuous lack of what Americans would call "millennials" these days—military-aged males, between the ages of fifteen to thirty-five, who matched the profile of the terrorists we were conditioned to look for.

Several minutes into our stop we felt a "disturbance in the Force," a distinct change in the atmosphere and activities among the people. The locals began to react to the movement of three vans slowly moving down the street toward the market. Though totally unremarkable on the surface, there was something ominous about the way the vans were creeping through the area. The real giveaway was probably the fact that the vans were similar to vehicles reportedly used by the dreaded hockey mask–wearing counterterrorism units. As if choreographed, the majority of shoppers in the market began to warily move, exiting the area with purpose, but without the kind of haste that might be interpreted by security personnel as guilt or panic.

In possible reaction to the dissipating crowd, the vans suddenly accelerated to the center area of the market and then locked up their brakes, the side doors opening before the vehicles had even fully stopped. A swarm of the hockey-masked hunters, all wearing black uniforms and carrying their deadly AK-47 assault rifles, fanned out and moved purposefully through the stalls. Knowing that violence was only a heartbeat or trigger pull away, we backed our sedan down the street and around the corner in an effort to exit the area. Our timing was good, as a blocking force of uniformed police took up our previous position near the corner in an effort to prevent anyone from fleeing the area or to engage anyone crazy enough to try and support any terrorists trapped somewhere in the market.

Suddenly the sound of gunfire split the air and a cacophony of echoes reverberated off of the old buildings that made up that part of the city. The hunters had found their prey and a battle ensued, a losing one for the terrorists yet again who'd been confronted by an overwhelmingly superior force that treated them with the same level of mercy with which they treated their victims. As all eyes turned to the market, we seized the moment to slowly swing around and exit the area, aware that we'd barely escaped being trapped in a lethal operation characteristic of the deadly campaign that the host government was waging against a committed enemy. They were fighting fire with fire, and as much as I hate to say this, sometimes that's exactly what it takes. The only way to defeat those types of terrorist groups was to become as ruthless as they were. That's a hard lesson to learn for most Americans, and even harder to accept, but to paraphrase Dorothy's famous line in *The Wizard of Oz*, we weren't in Kansas anymore!

More than any other of my CTU deployments, my time in that particular African country remains crystal clear in memory, though not for the right reasons. Maybe the constant bombings in the city or the reports of small towns being massacred by radical Islamic terrorists was taking its toll. Or maybe the fact that the host government had to resort to an "Old West" approach to its antiterrorism efforts left me discouraged and disillusioned. Other deployments had placed me in countries facing occasional violence, but it was constant there.

Reflecting on that now, it's almost like I was getting a glimpse of the world the US would soon be facing. It wasn't just my imagination; the world had been evolving right before my eyes over the years I'd spent at the Agency. Terrorist groups around the world were growing in power, numbers, and capability, as the United States would tragically witness just a few years later on September 11.

I left that country feeling torn. I knew that our people were handling the mission, but I felt troubled by the level of violence being inflicted by the terrorists. Innocent citizens were being butchered: women, children, and simple farmers who just wanted to live their lives in peace. To make matters worse, I knew there was nothing anyone could do to help them, so long as they were caught between a ruthless, cutthroat terrorist group and a necessarily ruthless government response. Only when the host government got the upper hand would the violence begin to wane. No easy task.

Washington, DC ▪ November 1995

I needed a rest after my tour in Africa. It was bound to happen with the serious ops tempo I'd experienced there that left me on edge 24/7. The timing was good, as it was getting close to the holidays, and I decided to take some well-earned leave. Luna was thrilled, rejoicing in the semblance of a normal life we could enjoy, however briefly. We were able to do things and be a normal couple for a change, and Luna had no problem making it very clear to me that was what she wanted. Part of me did as well, but not then, not yet. I'd taken an oath to protect and serve my country, and I knew I'd have to get back to that world before long.

Actually, I wanted to, *needed* to. Every deployment had been successful from an ops mission standpoint as well as from the perspective that we kept our people safe; indeed, no Agency life was lost while I was doing my job. In the big picture I might not have been turning the tide on terrorism, but I was doing my part in the battle.

Luna's family lived in Virginia and, while being separated for Christmas was painful, I needed to get back to Milwaukee to spend some quality time with family and friends. Looking back now I can see that I wasn't ready to make a serious commitment to Luna, given that I never even considered taking her to Milwaukee to meet my family. My trip back home turned out to be a great time. Seeing my father and stepmother, my stepfather, and my brothers. Hanging out with my cousins and helping out at wrestling practice at my old high school.

It was just days after Christmas that I got a call from the Agency.

My stepfather passed the phone to me, saying, "It's work."

He had a serious look on his face, knowing it didn't bode well. It was my boss from the CTU. He said I needed to come back to Washington as there was a priority assignment. What could I say? The fact that they called me at home over a holiday spoke volumes about the urgency of the situation.

"When do you need me?" I asked.

There was a pause on the line, followed by, "Can you get here by tomorrow?"

Of course I said yes, and then the hard part began. I had to tell my family the big lie: a training assignment had opened up in Europe and I had to fill the slot. The look on their faces told me that they clearly didn't believe me. They knew that the US military was engaged in operations in Bosnia and that was where I was probably headed. Nonetheless, I had to keep up the lie, if for no other reason than to help them cope with my being absent for the holidays.

I reported to work early the next day and was immediately briefed on our mission, along with the other members of the CTU team. While I did not speak any of the local languages of the area, my teammates Sasha Dzeltov and Robert Chankoff spoke Serbo-Croatian and Russian respectively. We were told that General William Nash, the commander of US military forces in Bosnia, had asked the president for help with some possible terrorist threats to his troops.

Our primary mission was to look for signs of any terrorist activities among nongovernment agencies (NGOs) and provide force protection for the troops based out of Eagle Base, near Tuzla Airport. The Agency provided each of us with some money to purchase cold weather gear, since winter in Bosnia was extremely harsh. We hit the local REI store to buy Gore-Tex jackets and other essentials we'd need to deal with the snow and icy conditions in Tuzla. We literally had only two days to prepare before we were to catch a commercial flight to Croatia, where we'd be meeting up with our handling officer.

I had originally scheduled my return from Milwaukee for just after New Year's, and I knew Luna was looking forward to spending some quality time with me before my next assignment. Luna would be happy to see me early, but that would change as soon as she found out that I was deploying again almost immediately and would most likely be gone for another month or more. Yet another disappointment coming her way...I knew I was going to pay for that. I wasn't even sure Luna was ever going to speak to me once I told her I was leaving for "training" in Europe instead of being back in Washington. I was getting the feeling she thought the travel had worn me out, and she probably expected that I'd be opting for a desk job in the near future, although I gave her no such inclination.

I thought it was best to tell her in public and made a reservation at a new restaurant in DC. I hoped that a romantic dinner would help to ease the blow.

"This is so nice," Luna said as the maître d' showed us to our table.

The low lights, dark wood, and oversized booths were going to set the perfect mood for the conversation.

"I'm glad you like it," I said.

I slid into the booth and Luna eased in next to me and snuggled close. I could see on her face how happy she was. She looked beautiful. Her long, dark hair hung down past her slight shoulders. Her dark eyes danced as they locked onto mine.

"To what do I owe this?" Luna asked.

"No reason," I said. "Can't I just take you out for a romantic dinner? But…"

"But what?"

"I do have something I need to tell you."

"Okay," she said expectantly, her eyes widening.

"Luna, you know how much you mean to me and I want to make you happy…"

Luna interrupted, pounced on me, and began kissing me. "Yes! Yes! Yes!" she started screaming.

I sat there and said nothing. Didn't move a muscle. I think I might've held my breath.

Did she think I was proposing? She thought I was proposing! What am I going to do now?

When I didn't respond, Luna began to realize that we weren't on the same page. She slowly slid away from me in the booth, lapsing into silence too. It was so uncomfortable, each of us waiting for the other to speak first.

"You're not proposing, are you?" Luna finally asked me.

I knew I had to respond gently and thought for a moment. "Not today."

Luna crossed her arms. The sparkle left her eyes and it was replaced with a glare. "So what were you going to tell me?" Without giving me a chance to respond, she crossed her arms even tighter and continued. "What aren't you saying, Tom Pecora?"

"Well…"

Her arms got even tighter. "There you go again!"

"Okay, I just wanted to take you out for a great dinner to try to make up for the fact that something has come up and I have to go on another trip for work," I said, trying to sound like it really was nothing, just routine.

"I thought you were done with all that."

"I never said that."

"Your eyes did, when you got back. Your eyes said you were never going to leave me again because every time you come back, there's a little less of you there. I thought you knew that. I thought you'd finally figured it out."

"Er," I started, not able to complete the thought.

"You aren't *really* going on a work trip, are you?" she asked.

"That doesn't really sound like a question," I responded.

"Are you?" she asked, her hand on her hips and her teeth clenched.

"I am," I said, "but that doesn't mean I won't miss you."

Needless to say, Luna was angry and she let me know it the entire time. She proceeded to give me every reason in the world why I shouldn't go, going so far as to suggest other types of jobs I could take instead, even though she had no idea what I really did for work. I tried to appease her, but nothing worked. The only solution that would satisfy her would be to not take the mission, and that wasn't going to happen.

"I can't take this, Tom. If you go, you need to know that I won't be here when you come back."

"Are you seriously doing this right now? It's work, Luna; it's what I do. You're not being fair."

"Maybe I'm not, but if you leave, I leave. Take your pick."

She waited for an answer.

"What are you going to do?" she asked.

"You don't have to go," I said, lamely.

"Neither do you," she replied, her voice shaky.

"I do."

"Then I do too," she said.

There was nothing more to say. Luna slept with her back to me the entire night. She was still asleep when I left the apartment and caught a cab to Dulles Airport. I had no idea where Luna was going, but once I closed the door of the cab, I was on my way to my next mission and it was time to push her out of mind.

13

Tuzla, Bosnia ▪ December 1995

Robert, Sasha, and I flew commercially to Split, Croatia, to prepare for our insertion into Tuzla, Bosnia. We stayed in a small hotel on the outskirts of the city along a beautiful river. Split had remained remarkably untouched by the war. The city lay along the Mediterranean and featured a beautifully scenic coastline, very resort-like. We walked the quaint city and talked to the people, who seemed friendly, warm, and welcoming.

We learned that Tuzla, where we were headed, had been cut off commercially from the world for more than two years. The people had to adjust to living without boots, sunglasses, backpacks, and gloves, because the city had been under blockade by enemy forces that precluded even those staples of winter life getting in. We arranged a trip to the Croatian markets to adjust our clothing so we could better blend into the indigenous population in Bosnia. We took a small cab into the city of Split, where the markets were located, packed with junk and used clothing. I had been to markets all over the world and found that one to be comparable: food and other staples in one section, new and used clothes in another, intermixed amid the usual clutter of useless knickknacks. Robert, Sasha, and I were laughing as we tried on tattered hats and gloves with missing fingers.

"Are we really turning in our two-hunded-dollar gloves for these cheap mittens?" Robert asked, his pinky finger poking through the top of the finger hole.

"We want to blend in, don't we?" I replied.

Robert handed the mittens to the merchant. "I'll take these."

Sasha and I laughed.

"How about this hat?" I asked, my puffy black hair sticking out of the top of the black wool.

"Hard to tell where the fraying wool ends and your 'fro' begins," Robert replied. "You realize we don't have to worry about being shot because we're going to freeze to death."

"Well, at least we'll blend into the frozen wasteland," Sasha quipped.

"Lucky us," Robert said.

"Stop whining," I told them. "I see a cafe."

We spent the evening enjoying ourselves prior to heading on to Tuzla, where we rang in 1996 together while staring at the Croatian mountains. Snowcapped and glistened in the moonlight, the mountains weren't very tall, but the range was vast. We listened to the rattle of the AK-47s echoing off the mountains as the locals fired into the air in celebration of the New Year. I couldn't help but hope that would be the only gunfire I'd hear over the next couple of months, but I strongly suspected it wouldn't be.

After all, we were preparing to help safeguard US troops surrounded by hostile forces. Once General Nash heard the Agency had a unit that was uniquely qualified in tracking potential terrorist attacks, he asked for our assistance. The general was concerned terrorists had infiltrated the NGOs in the area and that they'd target his forces and his base. He wanted an undercover element that could look for the terrorist signature and report directly back to him on any possible threats. And for good reason, given the fragile state of the nation's psyche and all the pieces the peacekeeping force, led by the United

CTU Deployment to Bosnia. Bosnian boy among the rubble in Tuzla, Bosnia.

States military, was trying to help put back together in the wake of a war riddled by ethnic cleansing and unspeakable violence.

"Civil war in Bosnia-Herzegovina erupted in April 1992," writes John S. Brown, retired brigadier general and former chief of military history at the United States Army Center of Military History. "Over the next three and a half years between 140,000 and 250,000 people had been killed. At least four out of every five deaths were noncombatants. While an unknown number had been wounded or maimed—many from the thousands of land mines that saturated the country—the horror did not stop there. Perhaps as many as 12,000 women were raped, and 520,000 Bosnians found themselves homeless. Ethnic cleansing created over 1.3 million refugees, many of whom had fled to other countries or were trying desperately to escape the fighting and poverty that engulfed the region. Dozens of diplomatic initiatives and temporary truces failed before a U.S.-brokered agreement in late 1995, the Dayton Peace Accords, finally ended the fighting and permitted U.S. military forces to enter the country as part of the North Atlantic

Treaty Organization (NATO) international force charged with the responsibility of enforcing the peace."

When the signing of the Dayton Accords (officially the General Framework Agreement for Peace in Bosnia and Herzegovina) in Paris on December 14, 1995, brought the Bosnian War to an end, Bosnia and Herzegovina declared independence and looked forward to rebuilding from the atrocities both countries had experienced. Prior to the US military taking over operations on Christmas Eve, the city of Tuzla had been attacked by Serbian militants.

Back in Croatia, our CTU team was celebrating the first day of January 1996 by heading to a small airstrip at the edge of town, where we boarded a turboprop aircraft along with a number of other passengers and some cargo. I drew the short straw and ended up without a seat for the hour-long flight to the Tuzla Airport compound. Because the plane was full I stood in the aisle in the rear, holding onto the cargo straps in lieu of a seat belt. The flight was bumpy and I was tossed from left to right and back again.

"How ya hanging in there, Tommy boy?" Robert asked, his face green from the turbulence.

"Better than you are," I replied.

Just then the aircraft did a steep dive into its landing approach, forcing me to wrap my arms around the cargo straps to stop from falling forward. We were told that this was an evasive maneuver the plane performed on every flight, in response to the threat posed by surface-to-air missiles (SAMs). Our military hosts met us on the tarmac, grabbed our rucksack luggage, and piled us into an old Lada Niva, a Russian-made SUV.

We were taken off the base and driven down a winding road through the countryside to the main city of Tuzla. A Muslim city of about two hundred thousand, Tuzla was located in the northeast corner of Bosnia. After Sarajevo and Banja Luka, it was the third largest city in Bosnia and Herzegovina. The city would have been quaint with its brick and cobblestone roads and lots of pastel-colored buildings, but the fact that some of the buildings were heavily pockmarked with bullet and shrapnel marks destroyed that illusion. Beyond that, Tuzla was relatively untouched by the war, except for a major artillery attack launched by Serb forces. An artillery shell had struck the Old Town "Korzo" square area during the evening, killing seventy-one people. It was the worst disaster to hit this city during the four-year war. A large memorial with photographs of the victims took up a section of the square. Photos, poems, flowers, and verses from the Muslim holy book—the Koran—had also been placed on the numerous graves of other victims of the war, of which there were plenty. During the height of the fighting, prior to my arrival, 405 soldiers and civilians were killed and 537 injured.

Tuzla's most striking feature, other than the local architecture, was the number of refugees and wounded Bosnian soldiers hobbling around. Some soldiers, many of whom were amputees, sat in wheelchairs on street corners or blocked traffic on main roads to gain attention. Others went door-to-door begging for food and money. Refugees who hoped to return to their homes were stranded there. Most of them were women and children who no longer had husbands, fathers, or homes. And many had been beaten or raped. It was difficult—all but impossible, in fact—to assess the physical and psychological damage caused by nearly four years of war, so much of which was utterly devastating.

The other less visible casualties in the city were its many citizens riddled by mental illness, given that an estimated half of the population suffered from some form of post-traumatic stress disorder according to doctors and international aid groups. For the forty thousand Bosnian Muslim refugees in Tuzla who fled from the city of Srebrenica when Serb soldiers overran it, the trauma rate was nearly *80 percent*, doctors said. All three sides in the war—Serb, Croat, and Bosnian—had been accused of atrocities, including the widespread use of rape. But the Red Cross estimates that of the estimated ten thousand women who were raped during the war, most were Muslims targeted by Serb men.

Some speculated that the relatively small damage and low number of fatalities in Tuzla might have been attributed to the strong defensive actions of the Bosnian Army's 2nd Corps. The military unit had managed to hold the Serbs at bay far enough away in the hills outside of town to keep their artillery from shelling the city, with the exception of that single shell that struck the town square.

When we arrived in Tuzla, we were dropped off near the only so-called high-end hotel in town. To try to apply a star-type rating system to that hotel would be impossible. It was an old place before the war and, with the blockade, its services and infrastructure had deteriorated even further. It turned out that it was the hotel where most of the Western journalists and other foreigners stayed. By the time we checked in, it was early evening. We decided to meet in the lobby and then planned on doing a short walk around the town prior to grabbing some dinner. We had been told there were a few restaurants down the street, so we decided to brave the cold and walk.

It was dark outside, more like pitch black since the street and signal lights weren't functioning, which lent the city an ominous look, especially with the light fog and falling snow. It was like something out of a scene from the Cold War, pulled right from the pages of a John le Carré novel. The people were grim, heads hung low, feet shuffling, never laughing or cracking a smile. In short, it was one of the most depressing places I had ever been. We had been told that the local hospitals' psychiatric wards were full due to all the nervous disorders afflicting those battered by so much war raging around them nonstop. Children were among the most affected, given that so many had lost parents. Put simply, it was a humanitarian disaster on an epic scale.

With no desire to brave the darkness any longer than necessary, Robert, Sasha, and I stopped at the first restaurant we found. It was filthy, in dire need of new furniture, paint, and flooring. But we were hungry and they had food. Sasha was able to translate the menu and served as our interpreter with the waiter. I ordered what appeared to be sausage and rice in a pita but tasted like ants and a chew toy. It took everything I had to not spit it out in my napkin.

"Oh man, this is awful!"

"I've had worse," Sasha said, continuing to eat.

"Better get used to it," Robert said. "You don't have many options for the next couple of months."

He was right. I picked up whatever it was in front of me and continued to eat. Then I gagged.

The guys laughed.

"Won't be so funny when I puke all over you."

"Actually, that may be even funnier," Robert said.

I held up my middle finger and kept forcing myself to chew.

"If it makes you feel better, I think the hotel will be serving hot dogs for breakfast," Sasha said.

"You know what, screw you guys," I said. "I hope you get bitten by bed bugs."

"Asshole, we are all in the same room. I don't think the bed bugs stick to just our beds," Robert laughed.

"Let's see who's laughing after we spend the next week scouting the city. My Wisconsin blood is going to be just fine. Let's see how your Florida-living ass does in the cold."

"You've got me there," Robert conceded, nodding.

We spent the next week walking the city in order to become intimately familiar with our surroundings. It was freezing. Although I had bragged that my Wisconsin upbringing would help me deal with the cold, the truth was I hated the cold and was struggling to stay warm in my used Croatian overcoat. The only trick to not losing complete feeling in limbs was continuous movement and stopping in coffee shops to warm up. I gave up trying to drink the awful local coffee and settled on drinking fruit tea, which tasted like warm Kool-Aid. The only people who seemed to have any energy were the foreign news correspondents who had descended on the city like locusts, taking advantage of the fact that it had finally broken free from the blockade.

Our official point of contact, Steve Banks, worked out of the CIA office that was located just outside the downtown area. Surprisingly, the office had been able to rent two upper floors in a very old facility. We often joked with Banks, telling him we would rather take our chances with gunfire than risk getting tuberculosis in the office! After conducting a surveillance detection route to ensure we were not followed, we would meet with Banks to discuss our assignments, receive intelligence briefings, and pass him our reports so he could send them up the food chain to the CIA liaison officer, who in turn provided our reports to General Nash's military intelligence officer. The US military had some serious concerns about the local militants, both Bosnians and Serbs, as they were competent and violent fighters. In addition, there were the terrorist groups that had reportedly infiltrated some of the NGOs. Both groups would consider the US military personnel at the base to be very tempting potential targets.

With all the threats in the area, we were very careful to keep a low profile. Add in the significant press presence and you had a recipe for an extremely dangerous environment that could erupt at any moment. In public, walking around or driving in the city, the team avoided speaking English; instead my teammates would converse in either Serbo-Croatian or Russian with the local population. The local citizens were totally demoralized, and many feared the United States was going to leave, meaning the war along with all the atrocities that came with it would return.

The locals had suffered a great deal not only from the war itself, but from the massacres that had become part and parcel of it. It was always civilians, those who wanted nothing more than to raise their families in peace, who ended up paying the greatest price. That's the thing many people back in the US lose sight of. The natives living in such areas are the ones blown up in terrorist attacks, uprooted by incursions into their towns, villages, or cities, or, in the case of Tuzla, subjected to mindless massacres that splinter families and destroy the morale of an entire nation. It was those people I felt the worst for. My mission wasn't to help them, at least not directly, but all the hopelessness, defeat, and futility took an emotional toll that was almost as wearing on me as having my guard up 24/7.

A few weeks into our time in Tuzla, we acquired our own Russian *Lada Niva* sedan. That gave us the ability to move outside the city and run the routes between Tuzla and Eagle Base, where the majority of the US military forces were assembled. Eagle Base was on the outskirts of the airport. We were able to get familiar with the geography and find the possible surveillance points and ambush sites that our enemies might use to attack American troops when they left their base. We also saw more of the devastation that the Bosnian War had left behind. Some of the farmhouses and fields were unaffected by the fighting, but most were deserted. Many of the smaller villages were decimated—their mosques shot up, the houses abandoned, walls pockmarked with bullet holes, and windows covered with small tree trunks in a pitiful effort to try and keep more rounds from getting in.

As we began traveling through those small towns and villages outside of Tuzla, we realized that we would be able to operate more securely and with greater secrecy if we resided in a suburb rather than in the city center. It would be a better method to "disappear into the background," hiding among the people. We moved out of the hotel and into a series of rented safe houses located near the neighborhoods where we needed to operate. That significantly lowered our profile. We ended up switching safe houses several times to make it difficult for a terrorist group to track and surveil us.

With our new wheels we began planning and executing surveillance on the actual Eagle Base entrance. We also provided countersurveillance for US military foot and vehicle patrols, all our work aimed at determining if any local insurgent or terrorist group was surveilling our troops in an effort to plan an attack. Several times we spotted suspicious behaviors by some of the locals, and these incidents were documented and reported to General Nash's staff for follow-up investigation that included, on at least two occasions, helicopter overflights and surveillance of the vehicles we'd tagged. During the next several weeks, we conducted day and nighttime static surveillance of different sectors of the city, looking for any surveillance and operational signatures that spelled trouble.

The few roads that went over the mountain between Eagle Base and the city of Tuzla were the key operating areas, since that was where the terrorists would concentrate their activities. They'd look for critical observation points and ideal ambush sites, where they could watch the US military elements and plan attacks. Several times we observed vehicles and people in those locations and would alert Eagle Base to the activity so appropriate action could be taken. Given that our mission was infiltration and reconnaissance, offensive action was left to operationally-based units that likely included the Special Forces.

Besides the ever-present human threats, we also had to deal with Mother Nature. The narrow country roads we traveled were slick with slush and ice, dangerous at any speed, so we had to move with caution. That meant watching for large UN military convoys, some of which included armored vehicles. The largest were the tanks and armored personnel carriers. It was hard to pass by each other on the roads, especially after a storm. Occasionally, we'd come across a vehicle that had slid into the drainage ditches that lined many of the roads. If a vehicle were to come in contact with insurgents in that scenario, they'd be sitting ducks. And the insurgents knew the intricacies and oddities of the roads, land, and climate far better than any US soldiers.

Our job was not just watching for terrorist surveillance; we also provided some guidance to the US military on how to more safely operate in an environment where insurgents and terrorists were always looking for vulnerabilities. The US troops were not schooled in force protection; it wasn't something they were trained to do, at least not at that time. After Bosnia, "force protection" became an established military activity, referring to the preventive measures taken to mitigate hostile actions against Department of Defense personnel, resources, facilities, and critical information.

In Bosnia, the US military's lack of awareness of the threat was extremely evident, especially near Eagle Base's main entrance. We observed that the base had configured the entrance to accommodate parking. They allowed local vehicles to park directly along the road that led into the front gate, creating a "fatal funnel" effect for troops moving in and out of the base, whether they were on foot or mounted in vehicles. The local vehicles parked in this area were in an ideal location to be used as car bombs, or in the current vernacular, vehicle-borne improvised explosive devices, or VBIEDs. We advised General Nash to change the configuration of the front gate area to prevent any local vehicles from parking in the area to minimize any risk of a VBIED attack.

Fifty days into our tour, a glorious thing happened. The town lit up, literally. With the return of security to the area, some of the streetlights and traffic signals became operational. More goods were arriving into town, so stores began to have something to put on their shelves. Very much needed public services became available, including more power and water. Many homes began receiving running water again, something they had not had since the beginning of the conflict. That had an immediate effect on morale, including ours, as we had gone over a month without running water. We had been able to take sponge baths but hadn't had a proper shower in weeks. That first shower was simply wonderful. The water was chilly, but I stood under the thin, wobbly spray for longer than normal just to make sure I was getting all the accumulated dirt off of me.

Nothing really dramatic happened during the tour. That was the goal! We were in the prevention and protection business, after all, the dramatic to be avoided at all costs, especially when American lives were at stake. Many of our soldiers were just kids really and, in many cases, far away from home for the first time. They needed someone to watch their back.

That's literally what we did. And my posting in Bosnia ended without a single American life being lost to insurgents or terrorist attacks in the Tuzla area.

Now that's what I call a successful mission.

14

Washington, DC ▪ March 1996

I returned home to an empty apartment. As heartless as it may sound, I had forgotten that Luna had threatened to leave while I was gone. I guess I was still expecting her to be there when I returned home. As I said, the best way to survive deployments in war zones was not to allow any distractions to interfere with the mission. Anything but the environment and the immediate task before you had to be filed away in your brain to deal with later. Part of that has to do with emotional compartmentalizing, but a greater part is focus. You simply can't afford to concentrate on anything other than keeping yourself, and those in your charge, alive. Everything else pales by comparison. If it isn't part of the mission, you leave it behind. If you can't do that, you can't do the job.

Beyond that, there wasn't anything I could do about Luna's leaving. The real world may have stood still for me, but it certainly kept moving for everyone else stateside. I understood that, I understood the reality of my world, and I accepted it. I tossed my suitcase down, threw off my shoes, took a hot shower, and went to sleep in a real bed in the modern comforts of the Western world.

During the two years I worked in the CTU, I completed ten assignments in the Middle East, Africa, Europe, Latin America, and

East Asia. The opportunity to do clandestine work had been the reason I'd joined the CIA in the first place. However, there was a rotation involved, and my time with the unit was up.

I returned to the Office of Security to wait while I looked for another assignment. I was temporarily assigned back in the POC, but this time it was in a training and administrative capacity only. I helped create a training course that specifically addressed protective operations techniques in support of clandestine operators. I was putting my two years of real-world ops experience to good use by helping teach the POC members what the operations personnel did, the kind of tradecraft they used, and how we, the POC, could best support them. Knowing how your protectee operates and how to conduct low-profile protection were two especially important traits, instrumental to whatever success the POC would enjoy in the future. When they entered the hostile environments of Iraq and Afghanistan, for example, the POC used low-profile operating methodology that allowed our case operators to successfully operate in those dangerous environments and kept them safe while they were doing it.

By June I'd found another rotation at the CTC, this time providing protective operations training with the Counterterrorism Training Group (CTG). I had no reason to stay in town; in fact, without Luna the emptiness of my apartment gave me more reason to travel, and the position promised me travel to more hospitable locations. It would be a welcome break from the violence and chaos associated with typical counterterrorism work.

The new position required me to design specialized protective operations courses for foreign government protective services. Over the course of the next three years, I provided training in the US as well as nine locations in Central and South America, Southeast Asia, the Middle East, and Europe. I trained personnel in a variety of security organizations whose task was to provide the same type of protective services as the US Secret Service did for our presidents.

Like most positions in the CIA, my new job required more training before I began to deploy. Most notably, I attended the United States Secret Service Firearms Instructor Training Course at their training headquarters in Beltsville, Maryland. I also received firearms instructor training from a firearms company. Those courses prepared me to provide extremely intensive firearms training for our foreign students. The safe handling of firearms was deemed a high priority, since many foreign students lacked that critical skill, which led to unnecessary injuries and deaths due to negligent discharges. The extremely sad aspect of those incidents was the fact that most victims were from within their own units, an issue I would hammer again and again in my new role.

From that position, I'd get a chance to work alongside some outstanding firearms instructors, some of whom had previously been in military and law enforcement units that included the regular US Army, Army Special Forces, Navy SEALs, Marine Force Reconnaissance (Force Recon), US Secret Service Counter-Assault Team (CAT), and the Los Angeles Police Department's Special Weapons and Tactics (SWAT) unit.

Over the next three years, I ran courses that consisted of two weeks of protective operations training followed by a week of firearms training. Most of the instruction was conducted in the host country, in their facilities with their equipment, to include their assigned weapons. To prevent a language barrier from affecting our instruction, we often brought along interpreters.

But bullets have a language all onto their own.

January 1998

My three years at CTG flew by. I traveled regularly, but at the same time my schedule felt much more leisurely in comparison to my past deployments, to the point I was even able to enjoy some of the tourist attractions at each location. It was the first time in quite a while where

CTG Training for South American Presidential Security Personnel.

I was able to work in countries that weren't so war-torn or fraught with danger and risk, all except one country in South America and a couple in the Middle East. It was just what I needed after those dangerous earlier assignments. You can only keep your guard up for so long before you need a breather.

I returned home from my fifth deployment to a country in South America in January of 1998, but I was only going to be in the US long enough to do my laundry, pay my bills, and repack. Snow was falling lightly outside, my favorite time to visit the Korean War Veterans Memorial in DC. It was magical when the snow lightly dusted the soldiers, one of the true highlights of living in the capital for me. I didn't really think I had the time but decided to make the time. Figured I could make it there and back before it was time to switch over the laundry from the washer to the dryer.

I was about to walk out the door when the phone rang. Strange. No one should've been calling me. After all, I hadn't been home in three weeks and nobody knew I was back.

"Hello?" I answered, wondering who might be on the other end of the line.

"Hello, Tom."

"Hi, Richard. Everything okay?" I asked my stepfather, fearing the worst. "*Everyone* okay?"

"Why wouldn't everything be okay?" he asked.

"Because you're calling me."

"Can't I call and say hi?" he asked.

"Sure, but I know you, and you hate talking on the phone. If you're calling me, it's because something's going on. What is it?"

I heard him sigh. "You got a phone call here, while you were gone. A young lady named Allison." My stepfather paused, waiting for me to say something. "I seem to recall that was the girl you dated while you lived in London, right?"

"It was," I said, reframing Allison in my mind and recalling our time together. "What did she want?"

"I have no clue. She didn't say. Any ideas why she'd just call you out of the blue?"

"No, not really."

It had been more than a decade since I'd last seen Allison and I couldn't remember our final parting or how exactly we'd drifted apart. Maybe she was traveling in the US and called me on a whim. What else could it be?

Either way, I was traveling soon so any chance for a visit was out of the question. I decided not to let the mystery distract me from my visit to the Korean War Memorial. The light snow crunched under my boots as I made my way from the parking area to the memorial. Despite my best efforts, I couldn't keep my mind off that call from Allison, my memories crystallizing. We'd had a great time together in England, but it was a summer fling, after which she went her way and

174

I went mine. I couldn't imagine what she could possibly want, and there was no time to fixate on it further. I was leaving in the morning, and whatever Allison wanted to talk to me about would have to wait until I got back from my next assignment.

* * *

I spent the next three weeks in the capital of a small Baltic country training the minister's protection detail. Though it wasn't a war zone, it was close. There was some kind of political conflict brewing that had led to a series of bombings in the capital. The city had a rough feel that made you not want to linger too long in one spot. The locals were on edge and the security services were busy patrolling the main streets. Besides the political issues, there was a significant crime element, from street urchins trying to pick your pockets all the way up to a more sophisticated mafia element that controlled much of the city.

The security issues were good reasons to not venture outside our hotel when the sun went down. In terms of grand theft auto, I was told that the thieves were partial to Mercedes-Benz vehicles and that there were probably more stolen Benzes in country per person than anywhere else in the world.

It was hard to judge the good guys from the bad in that country. And the locals that I ended up training came across as the biggest group of bona fide thugs I'd ever worked with. My students were straight out of central casting, looking more like low-life mafia enforcers than a protection detail for the government. But they were my students, and I had a job to do.

At one point I was teaching some of the important aspects of "walking formations," specifically the need for the rear protective agent to be vigilant and watch the rear section of the formation by constantly scanning the area. The group refused to pay attention to that issue, so when one of the students who was playing the role of the rear agent wasn't following instructions, I snuck up behind him and startled him. He did not take kindly to that and proceeded to berate me in his language, his insults so profane the local interpreter we were using refused to translate for me. It was the most hostile student I had encountered, but I couldn't let his attitude affect me. I was going to give those trainees my best, thugs or not, and if they failed in their jobs it wouldn't be a reflection on the training I'd given them.

A day before we were to start the firearms section of the course, our class coordinator took us to look at a shooting range near a riverbed area outside of the capital. Unfortunately, the "firing range" had a backstop consisting of a rock wall, making every shot a potential ricochet almost certain to turn the day into a disaster. We convinced him that we needed a safer location to conduct the training and settled on a wide field with miles of open range between a mountain and us.

The weapon of choice for the minister's protective unit was a Chinese Tokarev 7.62x25mm pistol. Upon interviewing the students and reviewing their training records, it was decided their firearms skills were so lacking that training would be conducted only on a one-to-one basis and that the students would not be allowed to carry any firearms while at the range. Our precautions proved not just wise but also prescient, as a member of the unit who wasn't part of our training course shot himself in the head while fooling around with his pistol in the anteroom of the minister's office. The local newspaper covering the story called it an "accidental suicide."

During the CTG tour I had gotten used to the creature comforts of home, as I was able to spend more time in my own place between trips, seeing family and friends. It was work that I could actually talk about with non-Agency people, and I was living as close to a normal life as I had since I'd worked in the Security Duty Office back in 1992. Although I enjoyed conducting protective operations training, teaching the principles and methods that our own Secret Service had successfully applied, I began to miss actually doing the work. I missed being "operational" as I'd been with the CTU, and before that the POC, conducting a mission or protecting our personnel. That was one of the problems associated with the type of work where you feel the rush that only comes when there is danger involved and you are pitting your skill and experience against an adversary. As Ernest Hemingway so aptly described it for soldiers, "There is no hunting like the hunting of man, and those who have hunted armed men long enough and liked it never cared for anything else thereafter."

Such a predilection can be just as applicable for those who have worked in the protective fields. Civilians use terms like "adrenaline junkie" or "action addict," both carrying a negative connotation that doesn't at all reflect the actual job. The feelings instilled by that type of hazardous work are primal, touching the ancient memories buried in our DNA going back to the caveman who had to struggle against life-threatening conditions on a daily basis to protect his family and provide food and shelter for them. Thus, it was a condition that was normal for thousands of years, and only in the past several hundred have we become so "domesticated" that we have lost our understanding and appreciation for this "risk-taking" gene. The world will always need people willing to run toward the sound of gunfire! So, while embroiled in more mundane work, all I could think of was getting back to making a difference in the kind of war zones pretty much everyone else avoided at all costs.

Little did I know I was about to get my wish, though not at all in the manner I was expecting.

15

After I arrived home from the Baltics and got settled in, I started thinking about that phone call from Allison. Somehow, I still had her telephone number. I dug it out of my stored stuff and sat at my kitchen counter contemplating giving her a call. But what would I say?

Hi Allison, it's been a long time!...

Heard you called after thirteen years, so what's up?...

Hey Allison, thanks for the call. It was so nice to hear from you....

Ugh! It was so awkward! I felt like a teenager again. I had to just pick up the phone and call. Whatever came out of my mouth would come out.

I took a couple of deep breaths and dialed the number.

Oh, shit! It's ringing! Breathe! Breathe!

A woman with a heavy British accent answered. "Hello?...Hello?"

"Hello," I finally managed. "Is Allison there, please?"

"This is Allison."

"Hi," I said lamely, in a shaky voice. I wanted to hang up then and there, but I didn't.

"Who is this?" Allison asked.

"It's Tom, Allison. Tom Pecora."

"Tom! How have you been? I'd given up hope you were ever going to call me back."

"Sorry it took me so long. I was out of the country on business when my stepfather told me you'd called…"

I could hear myself continuing to ramble, but for some reason I couldn't stop myself. Yup, a teenager all over again.

"Tom, Tom," Allison finally interrupted, "it's okay. You can relax. I'm sure you're wondering why I called you."

"Well, yes."

"I'll get right to the point." Then it was apparently Allison's turn to take a deep breath and settle herself, the roles oddly reversed. "This is going to be as hard for me to say as it is for you to hear. Remember that great summer we had together?" She didn't let me answer. "And at the end of the summer, how you were ready to go start your life back in America? You made that clear and I didn't want to stand in your way. It wouldn't have been fair."

I tried to jump in but she wouldn't let me.

"So when I found out I was pregnant, I made the…"

"What?" I interrupted. "What did you just say?"

"Please let me just say what I have to say," she said, and then picked up where she'd left off. "When I found out I was pregnant, I didn't say anything. But now my daughter, *our* daughter, is asking questions about her father…about you. Look, I'm not calling to ask you for anything. You can hang up right now and forget this call ever happened and you'll never hear from me again. And I'm not asking you to be a part of her life now, because I didn't invite you into her life then, and that was so very wrong, and I see that now. But there's an amazing twelve-year-old girl here who wants to know her dad, to know you." She stopped talking for a second and picked up again. "If you are willing."

I was speechless.

I had a child, a daughter!

*My daughter Kirsty
visiting me in
Washington, DC.*

She was twelve and I never even knew she existed—casting my life that had passed in the interim in an entirely different light. All the missions. All the postings. All the deployments. All the danger. Nothing to ground me, until Luna came along, and I'd pretty much chosen my job over her.

What was my daughter's name?

I didn't know what to feel, a number of emotions slamming through me and leaving me as stressed as that ambush in Mogadishu. Allison had hid this from me for all these years. I had missed all those years while my daughter was growing up. I had the chance to be in her life now.

But did I want to?

As all of those thoughts bounced through my brain, I realized I had to get a grip. Allison was still on the line. She was right; at the time we met I wanted no part of settling down or anything resembling a long-distance relationship after our summer together in London. I wanted to get back to America and start grad school and then a career. Allison had been doing what she thought was right, and at the time it probably was.

"What's her name?" I asked finally.

"Kirsty."

"Kirsty," I repeated.

"Kirsty, like the American actress, Kirstie Alley. And she's fabulous!"

"How could she not be, with you as her mother?" I said lightly, recalling how well the two of us had gotten along.

"It takes two, love."

"Not in this case, Allison, not really. When can I meet her?"

"When would you like to?"

"Twelve years ago, but I'll settle for tomorrow," I said.

* * *

I bought Allison and Kirsty plane tickets to Washington, DC, for June, when Kirsty had her summer break from school. I had never felt that type of excitement before.

I met them at the airport. I had flowers for Allison and a teddy bear for Kirsty. I had no idea what to expect. All Allison had told me was that she was like a typical twelve-year-old girl. But, growing up in a house of all boys, I had no idea what that meant.

I recognized them both the minute they walked out from customs. Allison hadn't aged at all. She was as beautiful then as she'd been when I left London a dozen years before. Kirsty looked like her mom, but she had my deep-set brown eyes. My heart was racing at the sight of her. I didn't know what to think—more accurately, I *couldn't* think. My brain had frozen up solid.

Allison smiled and waved at me. Kirsty had almost no expression on her face. For someone supposedly excited to meet me she looked like I felt: in shock. I saw Allison give her an elbow and whisper something into her ear.

I was so afraid to speak, I'd coughed out some words before I even realized I was talking.

"Hi, Kirsty. I'm so excited to meet you. I brought you something," I said, handing her the bear. "And for you," I said, handing Allison the flowers, hoping she didn't notice my hand was shaking.

All the danger zones I'd been in, all the death and violence I'd witnessed, and I'd never felt anything like the trepidation I did in that moment.

"Thank you, Tom," Allison said with a smile. "They're beautiful."

Kirsty just stood there staring at me. I felt like I was struggling to breathe.

"What do you say, Kirsty?" Allison asked our daughter, gaze tilted toward the teddy bear.

"It's okay," I told Kirsty.

I could tell she was uncomfortable, unsure of how to react, so I added, "Hey, don't sweat it."

Don't sweat it.... Had I really just said that to...

Ughhh!

...my twelve-year-old daughter.

Double ughhh!

"Young lady," Allison urged.

"Thank you," Kirsty said.

"Kirsty, he's your dad!" Allison said, embarrassed.

"That's fine," I interjected. "Give her some time. We haven't even known each other for five minutes yet. She can call me anything she wants," I said, looking at Kirsty and trying to sound reassuring.

Kirsty flashed me a smile, and I practically melted. A smile from my own kid? I knew right then that I wanted to *keep* making her smile, twelve years of smiles crammed into the next few days.

I spent the next five days showing Kirsty and Allison around DC. Unfortunately, Allison came down with some kind of stomach bug (we later found out it was vertigo), so for several days she was out of commission. That ended up being an advantage, as I got to spend some one-on-one time with my daughter. I took her putt-putt golfing and out to lunch at restaurants she'd never eaten at before, like Subway and Taco Bell. We wandered around the mall and made small talk, breaking the considerable ice and slowly getting used to each other.

When Allison felt better we started to hit the tourist sights: the Mall area in Washington, several of the Smithsonian museums, and a couple of famous places a short drive away such as Thomas Jefferson's home at Monticello and Great Falls Park looking over the waterfalls. I was able to get some very good photographs with Kirsty, some of which revealed a real smile starting to show on her face, especially when she succeeded in splashing me with some cold water from the pool of my apartment building.

The second half of the trip was a visit to Milwaukee to see the family. That would be an interesting moment for Kirsty, as it would be expanding her family members tenfold since the family on the English side was relatively small. Kirsty met my father and stepmother, my brothers, my stepfather and my uncle, and several of my cousins. We went to a small water park where she witnessed me thrash around in the shallows in a dunking match with one of my best friends with whom I'd wrestled in high school. As she became more comfortable with me, and more familiar with my family, Kirsty became more talkative and her personality started to shine through. It could not have been an easy experience for a twelve-year-old, but she handled it exceptionally well. I was not used to being around young children, so it was a challenge for me too, but we found some common ground and began to build a relationship.

At the end of the week I saw Allison and Kirsty to the airport for their flight back to London, already missing my daughter the moment she disappeared down the jetway. As I watched the plane take off, I realized how unique of an experience it had been. I was a father, with all of the new responsibilities that went with the role. It was the first time I felt as if I had a special reason to stay alive when I was out on a mission, coupled with a real reason to come home, because now I had someone to come home to, figuratively if not literally—at least, not yet.

I decided that day, after I dropped Kirsty and Allison at the airport, that I was going back to the POC. I knew that I would be able to work my schedule to have more breaks between assignments where I could route my travel through London to be with my daughter.

Everything had changed.

PART FOUR

THE NEW NORMAL

16

Washington, DC ▪ May 1999

Two months after meeting my daughter for the first time, I started my new position as a Senior Team Leader in the Protective Operations Cadre (POC). Our work was covert—no one outside of the Agency was really supposed to know we even existed, so the name was not made known to the public.

I was just glad I was back in the "game." I was looking forward to the work and my ability to use my travel schedule to arrange return trips through London. The POC mission had increased over the past several years and so had the number of full-time staff officers assigned to the unit. We then had permanent team leaders managing the uniformed and staff security officers on rotation from their day jobs. The POC application process had gotten tougher, with the highest marksmanship standards in the Agency, and physical fitness requirements that surpassed any other group except for the Agency's paramilitary officers. The standards were necessary in large part because the locations where the POC was deploying were some of the most difficult operating environments in the world. The CIA was sending us to protect our personnel while they conducted clandestine operations in places even the military wasn't operating.

For me, the beginning actually started at the end. My first trip out as a new team leader was back to Africa, the same area I had worked with the CTU.

Africa ▪ July 1999

Africa is hot in the summer, and not like a hot day in the States. It's the kind of hot that makes you feel like your skin may actually catch fire. And it's dry, so dry that the flies swarm your skin to drink the sweat as it pours down your brow. It was a good thing that most of the men on my team were used to the desert and roughing it.

In the early 1990s, it was widely feared that several countries in Africa were on the verge of an Islamic revolution. In the region where I was, extremist Islamist insurgent groups had fought against the host government and its army in a civil war. In nondemocratic societies where autocratic rulers and tyrannical oligarchies frequently flourish, massive violence is normally the only course of action available for altering the status quo.

Having studied terrorist groups and their methodology, and having been previously deployed there as a CTU officer, I was no stranger to the tactics of the extremist Islamic terrorists in the region. On almost a daily basis, the groups would set off bombs inside the city with little regard for innocent civilians. While their main objective was to hit local security services and government offices in order to strike maximum terror in the population, they'd often settle for markets and other places where large numbers of people gathered. Random attacks on bystanders walking in the city were common, with a preference being to slit the throats of women who were walking without a head covering (*niqab* or *burka*). At night, insurgents would snipe the security service personnel and police as they stood watch outside government buildings or were on patrol.

Outside of the city, they terrorized the population by sneaking into villages at night and slitting the throats of every man, woman, and child. They would also randomly kill shepherds and farmers who were tending their flocks or out in their fields, leaving their family members to find them. The groups truly took terrorism at face value. Our teams came across hundreds of dead during our time in country from a combination of knives, bullets, and bombings.

During daylight hours, when the terrorists launched one of their typically violent attacks in the city, the POC team would deploy to the incident location to assess the damage, determine if there were any changes in their methodology, and report back to the chief so we could provide headquarters with the latest assessment of conditions. From a tactical point of view, we needed to keep a sharp eye on what our enemies were doing so that we could adjust our TTPs (tactics, techniques, and procedures). Since the terror groups liked to place secondary explosive devices to take out responding medical and security services (police and military units), we had to be especially careful when approaching the area. Additionally, the local security services would be very jumpy, so precautions were taken to remain as low profile as possible on those recon missions. We tried to avoid checkpoints as much as possible, since insurgents were known to set up fake checkpoints or even gun down the security forces to take over a checkpoint.

Typically, though, when we arrived at the scene of an attack the perpetrators were long gone, leaving only bodies and debris behind. The local government would immediately begin repairing the damage and cleaning up the debris. We speculated that they wanted to hide the extent of the problem and lessen the impact of the bloodletting on the local population, both of which were somewhat futile pursuits in the face of the almost daily attacks.

The POC had been deploying to the region since 1995, around the time of my last deployment there as a CTU. The POC typically operated in daylight hours, moving in and around the city with our protectees, making airport pickups, and conducting atmospheric patrols. We moved in multiple-person teams in fully armored vehicles.

POC Team Leader on rooftop in Northern Africa.

We were armed with 5.56mm automatic rifles and Glock 9mm pistols. We had citywide radio communications, and we used local maps to navigate our way around—at that point in time there was still no Global Positioning System (GPS) technology available for us. We usually conducted multiple-car movements, but occasionally we would do lower-profile movements in close proximity to the embassy. Our POC team sometimes supported US personnel when they made airport runs or had dignitaries they had to take out into the city. The RSOs used local nationals that they had trained to be security personnel, relying on them for their language capabilities and area knowledge to get them from point A to B. The POC, though, operated on its own, learning the city, annotating maps to make them more accurate, and passing on our collective knowledge to every succeeding team.

We became very adept at recognizing real security service checkpoints as opposed to fake checkpoints set up by the terrorists. Even with the real checkpoints, there was significant danger because the host security services were suffering appalling losses and were correspondingly nervous. If even one soldier or police officer fired a shot when we were traveling through those checkpoints, all hell would break loose and the only thing between us and death by gunfire would be the armor of our vehicles.

We normally limited our travels to short distances. It was generally far too dangerous to travel at night, especially outside the city, due to intense terrorist activities, security force patrols, and the inability to assess and negotiate through potentially hostile checkpoints. But at times we would conduct nighttime operations, with special planning to account for the increased risk from not only the marauding terrorists but also the local security services out hunting for the terrorists. Precision planning, multiple contingencies, and good tactics were applied to reduce the risk to manageable levels.

At one point, the CIA chief decided that we needed more outside information about the country, so he suggested taking a reconnaissance trip to cover the area between the capital and the second largest city. It would be the longest road trip ever conducted by the POC in country. According to the chief, it was going to be both an atmospherics and reconnaissance mission to gather information for analysts who were trying to determine the progress the host government was making in combating the terrorist groups riddling the country.

The POC team's job was to make it happen, starting by doing everything we could to prepare. Nothing could be overlooked, yet there was so much that we couldn't foresee, given the unprecedented distance we'd be traveling over roads we hadn't previously performed reconnaissance on.

It was too dangerous to overnight at our objective—the sister city of the capital—or to travel at night due to terrorist ambushes. That meant we needed to travel several hundred miles in one day. I advised the chief that, based on the distance and the amount of daylight, we needed to get a very early start, no later than sunrise.

I woke up the team before dawn to conduct a pre-trip inspection and gear assembly.

"Good morning, boys. Are we ready for an adventure?" I asked.

The other three team members were experienced operators, to include my old teammate from Mogadishu, Bill. Each team member had an assigned area such as communications, weapons, or vehicles. Bill was in charge of our vehicles, and he gave us all a briefing on the requirements.

"This is the most dangerous run that the POC has made since we landed in this shithole. Each vehicle needs to have a full gas tank, and we will put an extra jerry can of fuel in the rear cargo areas. There ain't no gas stations or rest stops along the way. Got it?"

"Got it," Dylan Ruck said.

"Yep," echoed Nate Aaron.

We decided to take the two fully armored SUVs. Bill and I would be in the lead SUV with the chief, while Nate and Dylan would be in the follow vehicle.

We loaded up and exited our compound just before the sun was coming up. As we moved toward the edge of town we could see people beginning to move about, starting their day. The traffic was still light and we went through several of the security checkpoints protecting the city, the soldiers tired from their long night-shift duties. The countryside outside the city changed from desert to farmland as we moved along the highway. There were sections that appeared like some of the Midwest states, especially where there were large fields growing vegetables. But we never forgot how hostile the countryside could be, keeping a sharp eye out for potential ambush sites or checkpoints.

The fertile areas gave way to winding roads moving through low mountains. At one point we entered a tunnel that seemed to go on for hours, but it was the confined space that made the movement through it seem so long. We finally made it to the sister city without incident or even a distance sighting of potential insurgents. I could sense the relief in my guys. Halfway done and so far, so good.

We escorted the chief on a short walk through the downtown area as he observed the city and gathered the atmospheric intelligence we'd come to collect. We managed to leave slightly ahead of schedule, and I couldn't help but be pleased with how well we were doing. The mission could not have gone more smoothly, and we were on track to make it back to the capital before sunset.

Unfortunately, on the road back through the mountains we encountered more traffic slowing us down. Some of the local trucks were not able to keep up their speed moving through the mountain passes. I couldn't believe it. Being slowed by or stuck in traffic made us more vulnerable to attack from any terrorists lurking about.

"You'd think we were in Los Angeles? What the fuck!" Dylan spat, anxiety lacing his voice.

"Once we get through this section we'll get back up to speed," I said, trying to keep everyone calm.

"It's worse in LA; there's more road rage!" Nate joked, trying to reduce the tension.

"Guys, keep alert and your eyes on your sectors," I said, not wanting to show I was feeling the same anxiety they were. "It's traffic. We are just another couple of vehicles in the middle of the crowd."

"Shit!" Dylan said again.

To further complicate our situation, we were falling behind schedule. The sun was starting to set and, although the orange and pink hues were beautiful, there was nothing hopeful or promising about nightfall. We were still an hour out from the capital, which left a whole lot of time to be ambushed. Our alert levels were at maximum, and every mile seemed to just crawl by. Not that I was superstitious, but sometimes when you start feeling like things are going your way, something happens.

"Just twenty more minutes," Nate said. "Almost there."

Just as the words left his mouth, two large armored vehicles with their lights off, full of personnel and brandishing a big mounted machine gun, pulled up alongside our caravan.

Here we go, I thought.

"Fuck! Fuck! Fuck!" Dylan ranted.

"Just be cool. Don't make any sudden moves," I cautioned.

The trucks continued to ride next to our convoy along the highway.

"What the fuck are they doing?" Nate asked.

I tried to get a better look, but it was hard to see since we were then in almost total darkness due to the lack of lights along the highway.

"Slow down a little and let them pull ahead so I can get a better look," I said.

Finally I was able to see, and I breathed a slight sigh of relief. They were local army armored personnel carriers, and they were running without lights in an effort to surprise any terrorist forces moving on the highway or trying to set up ambushes. Maybe they thought that's who we might have been, or maybe they were just shadowing us protectively.

The last twenty minutes passed without any further potential threats, to the point we even abandoned the countdown. The team and I were beyond relieved when we returned to our compound alive and well. That night we celebrated our survival by heading straight to bed.

In the five years the POC was operational in Africa, not a single member of the cadre was killed or even injured. The POC provided protective operations support to intelligence operations in the war-torn region that would otherwise have been too dangerous to do, and lost not a single person while doing it.

As for me, it was another successful mission and another chance to route my travel home through England to see my daughter.

17

Washington, DC ▪ October 2000

Although I enjoyed the POC mission, the travel and lack of any home life was taking its toll. When I wasn't deployed, I was either visiting family in Milwaukee, England, or on vacation in Asia. I didn't want to admit it, but I was getting a little long in the tooth for that kind of activity.

Not that I couldn't keep up—the youngsters found that out during a Counter-Assault Team training course that only vetted personnel were allowed to take. The qualification test was grueling and was only a preview of what the course would be like. It turned out that I was the oldest POC member to qualify for the course, and I led a four-man team that won almost every competitive tasking.

That included shooting on the move while wearing full body armor (steel plates front and rear) and full ammunition loads for both our 5.56mm rifles and Glock pistols, along with a gas mask. We also had to run, climb, and maneuver around obstacles while conducting vehicle bailouts, close-quarter battle (CQB) drills in the shoot house, and counter ambushes against our motorcades. It was a hell of a course and the toughest physical challenge I ever faced at the Agency.

As for instructors, we had the best, culled from veterans of the special operations community that included Marine Force Recon,

United States Government

COUNTERTERRORISM TRAINING GROUP

Recognizes that

Thomas Pecora

Has attended the

Counter Assault Team Course

Issued this _16th_ day of _December 1999_

Program Coordinator

CAT Course Completion Certification—December 16, 1999.

Army Special Forces, and Navy SEALs. We also had instructors from the most elite law enforcement communities that included a former Los Angeles Police Department SWAT commander and even a former US Secret Service sniper. And, while I loved the training and the challenges of the POC mission, I could see that there were other positions where someone with my experience would be valued and where I could contribute in an even bigger way.

I decided to begin looking for new opportunities, and no sooner had I considered that road when along came a beauty. A Chief of Security position in Southeast Asia opened up, and after reading the job description I knew it presented a rare opportunity to put all of my security skills to use, not just those on the protective operations side. Other than one former POC member, I had no real competition and, after the interview, I was tentatively selected to the position with a start date of summer 2001. I was intimately familiar with that area of the world, having worked there as a CTU member and from several personal vacation trips with my brothers and cousin for scuba diving.

I completed my final tour with the POC as a Senior Team Leader working a protection detail in the Middle East. The city we were based in had some level of danger to it, mostly when you found yourself in the wrong place at the wrong time, but that pretty much described all the areas in which we worked. The danger turned out not only to be from terrorist and insurgent groups, but also from the bevy of government border guards who never hesitated to point their guns at us when we entered their checkpoints, even when they knew we were US citizens. It's truly a nerve-racking experience to look into the eyes of an eighteen-year-old soldier, with no life experience, who's pointing a gun at you and clearly hating both his job and everyone who isn't stuck sitting there with him!

I was on my way back from that assignment when I got the final confirmation that I would indeed be heading to Asia for my next position. While I'd miss the excitement of traveling to new locations and the opportunity to route my flights home through London to see Kirsty, I was ready to embrace it as the next chapter in my Agency adventures.

December 2000

Since I had some vacation time owed to me, I decided to take another dive trip to the Philippines before I started my "official residency" in Asia. My brothers, cousins, and I figured what better time to visit some dive spots south of Manila, not knowing how extremely memorable the trip would become or how much of a precursor it would be for some of the things that loomed in the future when I was posted to Asia.

Our arrival in Manila was uneventful and the resort we visited in Puerto Galera, on the island of Oriental Mindoro, was a diver's haven. Puerto Galera was a short ride on a *banca* boat (a large canoe-like boat with outrigger for stability) from the southern tip of the island of Luzon. On December 30, we caught the boat back to Luzon, where we piled into a van for the several-hour drive back to Manila to pick up a late-arriving friend. We were in high spirits, as the diving had been great, and we were looking forward to spending some time relaxing in a beach resort. Then, about an hour outside of Manila, the driver of our van got a cell phone call. Laying his phone back down, he told us there had been a major terrorist bombing attack in Manila.

During the next two hours, as we drove toward the capital, four additional bombings ensued, including one near the US Embassy. A total of twenty-two people died while close to a hundred were injured when the five, almost simultaneous, bombings rocked five areas in metro Manila: at a light rail transit station, in Plaza Ferguson (directly across the street from the US Embassy), at a bus station in a suburb of Manila near the Ninoy Aquino International Airport in Pasay City, and adjacent to a gas station in Makati City, the business district of Manila. We decided it was too dangerous to drive into Manila, so we diverted around the capital and headed north to Subic Bay, where the old US naval base was located.

There wasn't a lot of information available because the city was in a panic, but once we arrived at a beach resort near Subic Bay I called a friend who was working at the US Embassy to find out more about the situation. Little did I know I would become intimately acquainted with the person responsible for all five of the bombing incidents. The event was later called the *Rizal Day bombings*, as the thirtieth of December was the national holiday celebrating the nineteenth-century nationalist Dr. José Rizal, a Filipino rebel who had fought against Spain and was executed in 1896. After several days with no further incidents, we felt it was safe enough to return to Manila to catch our flights back to the US.

A portent of things to come? To say the least.

Southeast Asia ▪ June 2001

I took over as the Chief of Security in a country in Southeast Asia in mid-June 2001. It was a chance to go PCS (permanent change of station) as compared to all the TDY (temporary duty) trips I normally did to foreign countries. As anyone who has done both TDY trips and a PCS posting will tell you, there is a big difference between the two. When you're PCS, you're able to really get to know the area. Both the work staff and the local people treat you differently as a resident as opposed to a transient, and rightfully so. Instead of working hard to learn your way around, you have more time to explore, and you can be "normal," enabling you to enjoy the little conversations that happen when you visit a restaurant or bar over time. With that posting I got one of the primary things that I was looking for, in the form of less travel. Though I was going to be much farther away from my family in the States and my daughter in London, I was going to be in one place for a while; or at least in one region. It was going to be my "home" for the next three years. I was hoping to have Kirsty come and visit me, since she had never been to Asia.

Knowing how terrible the traffic could be in big Asian megacities, I asked for housing close to the office. I was lucky and was slotted to live in an apartment building within walking distance (five to six blocks) of the office. Most of the time I drove, but when the traffic situation became too snarled I could opt to walk to or from work. The walk allowed me to unwind from the stress of the job, and I got a chance to watch the normal activities of the local people who lived and worked in that section of town.

As I approached my building one morning, I took a moment to contemplate why I loved the country so much. To start with, I was living in a beautiful historical apartment building built in 1923. The small neighborhood where my apartment and its walled compound were located was one of the few areas of the city that had survived the horrendous bombings by US forces during World War II. My two-bedroom apartment had beautiful old wood floors, antiques, and a huge walled-in porch. The apartment compound was a square lot, and tall trees were planted along the inside of all four of the walls to provide shade and keep the city noise out.

But nothing could shield us from the myriad of threats we'd be facing.

Many of the countries in Asia consist of a large number of islands. Malaysia has more than 878, the Philippines has 7,107, and Indonesia has a whopping 17,508 in its territory and is the world's largest island country. The larger countries in Southeast Asia include Vietnam, Cambodia, Laos, Thailand, Myanmar, Malaysia, Singapore, the Philippines, and East Timor.

The Philippines is an archipelago of 7,107 islands covering a total land area of about 115,831 square miles bounded by the Philippine Sea to the east, the Celebes Sea to the south, and the South China Sea to the north and west. In the north, across from the Luzon Strait, is Taiwan; to the west, across the Celebes Sea, lies Vietnam. The Sulu Sea, which is in the southwest, sits across from Borneo.

Indonesia is the world's most populous Muslim majority country at 87 percent, most of whom are Sunni Muslims. Christians make up almost 10 percent of the population. It has an estimated population of more than 257 million people.

Malaysia describes itself as a secular state with Islam as the state religion. More than 61 percent of the population practice Islam, while 20 percent are Buddhist and approximately 9 percent are Christian. Population estimates in 2017 were 31 million people.

While countries like Thailand, Malaysia, and Singapore had their terrorist threats, in 2001—when I began my tour in Southeast Asia—my attention and my counterterrorism work were focused mainly on two countries: the Republic of the Philippines and Indonesia. That was due to the terrorist and criminal activities at play.

With a population of more than 96 million, the Philippines is the only major Christian region in Southeast Asia. Its capital of Manila is located on the northernmost major island of Luzon. The other two major island areas are Mindanao and the six islands comprising the Visayas. The Philippines is beautiful if you like tropical beaches, lush vegetation, and year-round warm weather, which was something I especially liked having grown up in the frozen north of Wisconsin.

The two major languages spoken in the Philippines are Tagalog (Filipino) and English. I have found the Filipino people to be among the friendliest in the world. They respect their elders, the older children help take care of the younger, and they have an incredible sense of hospitality. Unfortunately, the Philippines struggle with some of the highest levels of poverty in the region, with more than one quarter of their population falling below the poverty line (earning less than $234 per year). Even under such desperate conditions, you will hear Filipinos laughing, singing, and joking around. They have a strong spirit.

Two of the largest foreign-located US military bases—Clark Air Base and the naval base at Subic Bay—had been closed in 1991 and 1992 respectively, but the Filipinos were still very much influenced by the United States and continued to follow American sports (especially basketball) and music. As an American, I had some serious status and, having worked in so many countries that did not necessarily like the US, it was a wonderful change of pace to visit a place where we were respected and admired. There were a lot of US expatriates in the Philippines. Many were service personnel who stayed behind after the military bases closed as well as service personnel who, when they retired, chose to return to the Philippines with their wives or to take advantage of the low cost of living. It was also a great place to vacation for those who liked to scuba dive or visit clear-water beaches not overrun with tourists.

There are many famous American buildings in Manila, one of which is the US Embassy consulate, a historical site that's remained relatively unchanged since World War II. The flagpole and base still have bullet marks from when US and Filipino forces took back Manila from the Japanese in February and March of 1945. The consulate sits directly along Manila's harbor with its back facing the bay. Sunsets are spectacular looking out on the water, and the annual Fourth of July party was an "A" list event that everyone tried to get into.

The Philippines enjoy a rich history, and without a basic understanding of that, it would be difficult to understand the complicated threat environment I would face in my three-year tour in the region. For example, most people have no idea the level to which terrorist elements in the Philippines were interwoven into the events of 9/11. My next tour would bring just those elements to the forefront.

18

Southeast Asia ▪ Summer 2001

When I arrived for my tour in Asia, much of the US focus was on terrorism in the Middle East, but there was also plenty happening in Southeast Asia. Many Asian terrorist groups threatened the status quo of the region by seeking to create independent Islamic states in majority-Muslim areas, overthrow existing secular governments, and/or establish a new supranational Islamic state encompassing Indonesia, Malaysia, Singapore, the southern Philippines, and southern Thailand. In pursuit of these objectives, they planned and carried out violent attacks against American and other Western targets as well as against Southeast Asian targets. Additionally, Al-Qaeda used its Southeast Asia cells to help organize and finance its global activities.

In the spring of 2001, the US Embassy in Manila was dealing with a terrorist situation involving the kidnapping of several US citizens by the Abu Sayyaf Group (ASG). The ASG was an Islamic separatist organization that had carried out several high-profile assassinations and bombings, rightfully earning a reputation as the most violent Islamic separatist group in the Philippines. While most of the ASG's activities were centered on Mindanao and the Sulu Archipelago in the south, where the Sunni Muslim Moros were concentrated, the ASG also engaged in terrorist acts in the capital of Manila.

The ASG was founded in 1991 by Abdurajak Abubakar Janjalani, who had studied in the Middle East and became radicalized after traveling in Saudi Arabia, Libya, and other Muslim countries. While studying the Iranian Revolution in 1988, Janjalani reportedly met with Osama bin Laden in Pakistan and may even have fought alongside him against the Soviets during their occupation of Afghanistan, after which Janjalani developed his mission to transform the southern Philippines into an Islamic state.

Janjalani, formerly a member of the Moro National Liberation Front (MNLF), left that organization and began to recruit other disappointed MNLF members into what would become the ASG. Throughout the 1990s, the ASG turned to violence to gain recognition, engaging in bombings, kidnapping, assassinations, and attacks with a special focus on Christians and foreigners. The ASG also targeted the Philippine military, consistent with the organization's professed goal of resisting the Philippine government and establishing an independent Moro state.

ASG's loose relationship with Al-Qaeda, stemming from Janjalani's connection to bin Laden, continued, with Al-Qaeda supporting the ASG with funding and training. In 1991 and 1992, Al-Qaeda member Ramzi Yousef, a major participant in the 1993 World Trade Center bombing, traveled to the Philippines several times and, in 1994, allegedly provided training for ASG operatives. During that time, Yousef and other Al-Qaeda members, including Khalid Sheikh Mohammed, collaborated with the ASG in the Bojinka plot, in which eleven airplanes were to be bombed over the Pacific Ocean. Thankfully, the botched manufacturing of explosives in Yousef's Manila apartment led to a fire and the discovery of the plot in January of 1995, preventing it from ever becoming operational. Yousef's arrest in Pakistan later that year, as well as Khalid's inability to enter the Philippines after the discovery of his connection to the plot, weakened the Al-Qaeda–ASG relationship.

After Philippine police forces killed Janjalani in a 1998 shoot-out, the ASG fractured into two factions. Fragmentation and deterioration

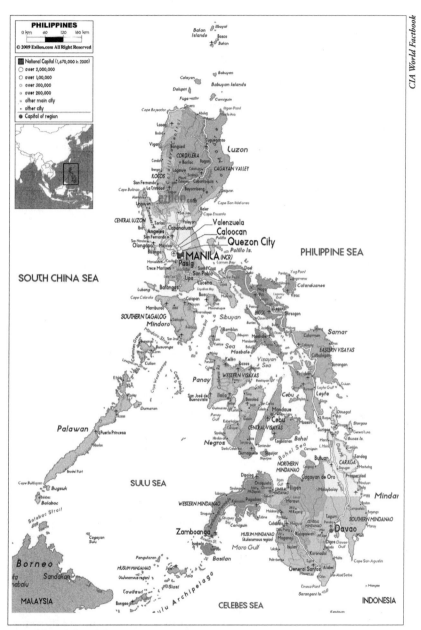

Republic of the Philippines, September 5, 1989.

of discipline within the ASG, combined with the loss of Al-Qaeda's assistance, pushed the organization to substitute its terrorist activities for kidnappings conducted specifically to obtain ransom money necessary for the group's financial survival. And on May 27, 2001, the ASG conducted its first international attack, kidnapping twenty people from the Malaysian resort of Dos Palmas in Palawan Province, an island chain about 375 miles southwest of Manila. The sixteen tourists and four staff members were grabbed from their thatched bungalows at gunpoint while they ate breakfast beneath the sun over the sea. The hostages were then put onto a boat and taken south toward the Mindanao area, a stronghold for Abu Sayyaf.

Three Americans were among the captured, including two missionaries, Martin and Gracia Burnham from Kansas, who were there to celebrate their eighteenth wedding anniversary. The other American in the group, Guillermo Sobero of Corona, California, was executed by the guerrillas several weeks later. Because American citizens were in danger, the United States government was very involved in assisting the Filipinos with the international incident. During my tour in the region, I would be part of a collective US government team to whom a lot of that task's heavy lifting would fall.

Needless to say, I walked into a shit storm when I flew into the Philippines on the first day of June. The US Embassy and Philippine government were doing everything they could to hunt down the ASG terrorist group that had taken the hostages. Kidnapping of US citizens falls under US Embassy and FBI jurisdiction, so they had the lead on the Burnham case, but because of the terrorist connection all US government agencies with deep local experience worked closely with the Philippine military and police. The combination of the kidnapping and other activities by several terrorist and secessionist Muslim groups led the US government to send additional military elements to the country to assist the Philippine military with added training and support.

The operation to rescue the American hostages was a major priority, and as soon as I arrived I began spending long days working nonstop to support the team's efforts. It was a grind but my spirits were high, and I welcomed the opportunity to be involved in something so vital right out of the box that fell within my particular area of expertise.

As the CIA security officer assigned to the region, I wore a lot of hats. During my tour in Asia, besides all my security duties I also served as the Deputy Chief of Support, managing one of the largest fleets of Agency armored cars outside of the US, supervising several drivers, and coordinating all visitor support to include airport pickups/drop-offs, lodging arrangements, communications, and security briefings. I was heavily involved in the procurement of office and operational supplies, and I assisted my boss Tony with the logistical/administrative activities necessary to keep our Agency personnel active and safe in the various environments in the region.

With my extensive training and experience with terrorism, I was often called upon to provide tailored security briefings for US State Department and select military and law enforcement personnel. Being able to provide that type of current threat information was critical to keeping personnel safe and helping them understand the variety of threats they would face while operating in that part of Asia.

I also provided personal protective guidance for my management and coworkers, helping develop tactics and techniques unique to the Asian environment to keep our people safe. On occasion, I similarly lent hands-on security support to our case officers when they were operational. This included POC-type armed protective security during their high-threat meetings, as well as in and around their residences when they were possibly under direct threat. I used my Counter-Terrorism Unit skills by conducting countersurveillance for their meetings and some countersurveillance coverage around our officers' residences and other US government facilities. I directly supported US military force protection efforts by providing security guidance to personnel on the threat environment in the Philippines, especially in and around Zamboanga City. Later in my tour, I provided security and logistical support to a number of counterterrorism operations.

Beyond that, I was directly responsible for the physical security of our offices, our residences, and our information. This included being the firearms custodian, lending guidance on all firearms issues and regulations governing the issuance and accountability of weapons, as well as providing instruction and training on a regular basis to ensure our personnel kept their marksmanship skills honed.

While US government operatives hunted for the hostages and assisted in the training of Philippine police and military units, the ASG and other terrorist groups remained violently active. On June 2, 2001, forty gunmen invaded the Dr. Jose Torres Memorial Hospital and St. Peters Church compound in the southern part of the Philippines. The attack ended in the capture of two hundred people. On August 2, 2001, ASG stormed a small village in Lamitan, Basilan, where they captured thirty-two residents. They also attacked and took captive fifteen people from Golden Harvest, a coconut planation, and ended up hacking off the heads of two of the captured men in a despicable act—meant to strike terror in the hearts of an entire country—that eerily foreshadowed the tactics of ISIS.

It was turning out to be a rough summer, with no end in sight. Things were different than when I had first started with the Agency. Technology had advanced and enabled the US government to provide better and more accurate intelligence to the Philippine military and police units. As the *New York Times* reported on June 8, 2002, "The Americans flew sophisticated spy planes to help pinpoint the hostages in the dense jungle. American eavesdropping equipment intercepted satellite-phone calls made by the guerrillas and, Filipino officials said, even heard them ordering provisions for the Burnhams, including peanut butter."

Unfortunately, Mother Nature was not without her sense of humor, as no matter how powerful thermal imagery and advanced satellite surveillance capabilities might have been, a triple-canopy jungle proved just too thick to penetrate. The US government had to rely on human sources, something difficult to do in the clannish tribal jungle environment of the southern Philippines. Eventually, between intelligence activities and the collaborative efforts of the Philippine military and police, US and Philippine forces began to take down a number of the bad guys.

As the summer ended, the Burnhams were still being held captive and the US had employed lots of resources trying to find them and put an end to ASG's reign of terror once and for all. But, despite receiving really good intel, the US had yet to come up with a firm location on the hostages, keeping any thoughts of a rescue off the table. And before the United States could ratchet up efforts further, our world was shaken and changed forever.

19

Southeast Asia ▪ September 11, 2001

Pretty much every American knows where they were when they first heard about the attack on the World Trade Center on September 11, 2001. Since most countries in Asia are close to a twelve-hour time difference from New York, it was just after 8:30 p.m. and I was returning from dinner when my cell phone rang. It was the deputy, and he breathlessly told me to immediately get to a television because there was a possible terrorist incident occurring in New York. I told him I was just about to enter my apartment and would have my TV on in two minutes. I ran up the three flights of stairs, unlocked my door, and hit the remote.

I normally watched US news channels, so when I turned on my TV the first thing I saw was live coverage of one of the Twin Towers. From the apparent damage in the side of the building, it appeared something had struck it at a high floor. The news anchor was talking about the fact that an aircraft had slammed into the tower, and that it was on fire. I stood there, stunned, trying to soak in all the initial details while simultaneously dialing my cell phone and landline telephones to get in touch with two other station officers who were recent arrivals and who I knew did not have access to a television.

I reached Alan Denton, a former US Army Special Forces NCO and Explosive Ordnance Disposal (EOD) technician.

"Al, looks like we may have a terrorist event happening in New York," I said. "I'm watching the live coverage on TV."

"What kind of terrorist event, Tom?" he asked me.

"Looks like a large plane struck one of the Twin Towers. Hold on, I have to call Ed Horton, the new communications officer. He just arrived too and doesn't have a TV either. Stand by."

As Al waited on the landline, I called Ed on my cell.

"Ed, this is Tom Pecora. It looks like an airplane just flew into one of the Twin Towers in New York. I have Al Denton on my landline and I will narrate what's being broadcast live on TV."

Silence filled the line while the shock set in.

"Thanks, Tom," Ed said, his voice scratchy and drawn. "I'll stand by here at my apartment. If management needs me, I'm available."

I began to narrate what was happening in New York to provide Al and Ed situational awareness. Suddenly, another plane flew into view across the television screen and struck the other tower. One aircraft potentially straying off course and striking a tower was one thing, but two? Clearly, it wasn't a coincidence. It had to be a coordinated terrorist attack, of a magnitude the US homeland had never experienced before.

I continued to relay information about the events as they unfolded, including the attack on the Pentagon and a possible fourth aircraft, which we later found out had been commandeered by brave passengers who stormed the cockpit and caused the plane to crash in Pennsylvania well short of its likely target of the Capitol Building. Alan explained that those large aircraft almost always had significant amounts of fuel on board, and that once they hit the towers the igniting of all that fuel would turn the situation truly horrific. His words turned out to be prophetic, as later investigations revealed all the immeasurably intense heat from that burning fuel melted the steel girders that provided the buildings their structural integrity.

*Supporting US Military
operations in the
Southern Philippines.*

When the first tower fell, it hit me like no other world event ever had before. As an Agency employee, a security officer, and someone who had spent so much time working counterterrorism, I knew our world had been changed irrevocably. And, as the rest of 9/11 unfolded, I knew that we were in a new world and a new fight.

The next day I reported for work earlier than usual, and found a somber and strained environment with the other American employees just going through the motions of their jobs, obviously consumed by the events of the previous night that had been as sleepless for them as it had for me. The locals working in our building were uncharacteristically quiet too as they watched us trying to do business as usual. In my office, things were in a frenzy as we tried to gather as much data as possible about who had hit us and the implication for Asia.

Later that day, when I went to a local shopping mall to pick up some much-needed supplies, I could not believe how normal the local people acted, as if they were oblivious to the major event that had just occurred in the United States. I couldn't get my mind off the fact that we had suffered such a vicious attack on American soil. To say we took to our work with a new sense of mission and urgency would be an understatement. Somehow, the bad guys had gotten past our defenses and struck on our shores. Now it was time to shake off the rage-infused shock and redouble our efforts to protect the American homeland. Every action took on a new significance, as we began the essential job of responding to the attack.

As a security officer, I immediately consulted with several embassy Regional Security Officers (RSOs), the people who were specifically responsible for the security of our embassies in the Asian region along with every United States citizen in their respective countries. I also contacted my security colleagues back home and across the world. I began to compare notes with them to see what they were doing in response to the unprecedented attack, and to collaborate on additional ideas on how we could protect our own employees and assist with the larger mission of protecting the homeland. As a first step, most of the US embassies were increasing security staffing and local guards, as well as adding physical security elements such as portable vehicle barriers to strengthen their perimeter and prevent unauthorized vehicle entry.

To my shock, I found out that the senior RSO who ran the State Department Diplomatic Security Service office in the Manila embassy had not made any arrangements for additional security measures to be put in place in and around the compound in response to the 9/11 attacks. A major cause for concern, in my mind. The fact that the Philippines was currently struggling with both domestic and foreign terrorist groups made it even more imperative that American and Filipino authorities increase their security posture and find out what was going on in their AO (area of operations) to prevent, preempt, and disrupt terrorist plots.

I informed my management about the discrepancy between what the Manila embassy security elements were doing and what the vast majority of other US embassies were doing throughout Asia, Europe, and the Middle East. The issue was then brought to the attention of the Deputy Chief of Mission, who was the acting ambassador at the time. He called a meeting with senior members of the embassy staff and the senior RSO. The result of the meeting was a decision to immediately implement additional security measures, to include the posting of a Philippine National Police Special Action Force (SAF) squad around the Manila embassy as well as increasing police units and local guards at the main embassy housing areas.

We knew that Manila was vulnerable, since less than a year earlier there had been a major terrorist attack there. Specifically, twenty-two people were killed in that series of daring and deadly bombings in five locations on December 30, 2000. There was also a continuing stream of threat-assessment reporting about plans by the various secessionist/terrorist groups to attack targets in Manila and other major cities in the Philippines.

Like every other American, I was having a hard time digesting what happened in New York. It still didn't seem real. Although I had been surrounded by terrorists my entire career, I'd never seen them carry out something that outlandish and organized. All US government elements—military, intelligence, and diplomatic—were put on high alert to keep their eyes and ears open for chatter of any plans for future attacks anywhere in the world. The entire Agency went into high gear across the globe.

To get a better handle on what was happening in other parts of the world, I contacted a friend of mine, Dave Burkstrom, who was working counterterrorism back in Washington.

"Hey Dave. How are things in the House of Flying Daggers?" (That was how we affectionately referred to CIA Headquarters.)

"Hey Tom, long time! Same bureaucratic nightmare with a scoop of frenzied activity on top these days."

"Dave, any idea who's taking responsibility for the Twin Towers?" I asked him.

"No one yet. But the consensus opinion is Al-Qaeda."

"These guys are getting crazier and crazier," I said.

"That's why it's a good thing that we're here," Dave replied.

I agreed with Dave wholeheartedly on that point, except our battle had just gotten exponentially harder. We were now up against not just a bunch of rebels with machine guns fighting for a tiny bit more land or a new government. We were up against devious, kill-crazy fanatics who wanted to take over the world. And they had successfully pulled off an immensely sophisticated operation in which they were able to steal commercial aircraft and kill thousands of people at one time.

And just as the authorities back stateside were nowhere near catching the masterminds behind 9/11, there in the Philippines the US was no closer to getting back the Burnhams.

November 2001

I finally got to take a bit of a break from work when my father, brothers, and cousins came out to Asia for a visit, a trip that had been a year in the making. Since they liked to dive and enjoyed the beaches in the Philippines, we decided to meet up in Manila. When I met them at the airport, they told me the planes were almost empty on their flights on the way over, making for a very nice opportunity to lay across several seats and catch some good sleep en route. It was the first trip back to Asia for my father since he'd served in the US Army in World War II on one of the Pacific islands.

I drove them all around the city, tourist spots like Chinatown and the famous Manila American Cemetery, which contains the largest number of graves of our military fallen from World War II—a total of 17,191—most of whom lost their lives in operations in the Philippines and New Guinea. The achievements of the American armed forces in the Pacific, China, India, and Burma are immortalized in twenty-five mosaic maps, and the seals of the American states and territories are carved into the floors. The cemetery was a monument to the honored fallen from both the United States and the Philippines who died fighting in the Philippine campaign. We took the boat trip to the island of Corregidor, an island fortress that had withstood months of bombardment by the Japanese before finally surrendering. We ended up at a resort in Subic Bay enjoying the tropical weather and the beach before returning to Manila.

After my family left for home, it was back to the grind, but we were making some progress. By then we knew Al-Qaeda and Osama bin Laden were behind the 9/11 attacks, and we had already begun to disrupt their operations. The Burnhams were still missing somewhere in the jungles of Mindanao or, more likely, on one of the smaller islands used by the ASG to avoid Philippine police and military units. If we could get them back, it would be a victory against the mentality and mindset that had murdered more than three thousand Americans, the lives of two more taking on even more weight in the face of that.

December 2001

We were just beginning to scratch the surface of our new reality, the new normal, the new world we were facing. In December 2001, the Singapore government discovered a plot by Jemaah Islamiyah (JI) elements to attack US entities and buildings. According to open-source reporting, the plan was to attack six different targets simultaneously in Singapore using six truck bombs, each rigged with three tons of ammonium nitrate. The potential targets included the US and Israeli embassies, the Australian and British high commissions, the Sembawang Wharves and Changi Naval Base (both used by the US military), as well as commercial buildings housing American companies. The plan was to be initiated by two foreign terrorists code-named "Sammy" and "Mike."

The Singapore authorities successfully arrested thirteen suspected JI members, eight of whom apparently received training in Afghanistan from elements of Al-Qaeda. In fact, some of the primary evidence about the plot was said to have been discovered in Afghanistan, after Al-Qaeda operatives fled their homes and offices in fear of the coming American retaliatory strikes.

One piece of evidence seized in Afghanistan was a blurry videotape showing apparent terror targets in Singapore accompanied by narration from one of the men in custody. Two of the cell members, Sammy and Mike, had ordered the terrorist cell to get twenty tons of ammonium nitrate to make truck bombs, according to the Singapore government. The cell already had four tons of the explosive compound in Malaysia and had made plans to purchase the remainder.

Sammy was believed to be linked to Al-Qaeda, while Mike was described as a trainer and bomb maker with the Philippine Muslim separatist group Moro Islamic Liberation Front (MILF). According to the reporting, both Mike and Sammy instructed numerous cell members to conduct surveillance of the various targets, procure the bomb-making materials, and arrange the transport and hiding places. Sammy would bring in foreign suicide bombers a day before the planned attack, while the local JI members would leave the country.

In response to the disrupted plot in Singapore, I flew in along with several CIA security officers from the region to work with the RSOs to conduct a security assessment. The US Embassy in Singapore is situated in an "Inman building," a structure built following the specific security recommendations made by the *Inman Report*, formally known as the *Report of the Secretary of State's Advisory Panel on Overseas Security*. The report was released in 1985 in response to the US Embassy and Marine barracks bombings in Lebanon in 1983. The report was normally referred to by the name of its chairman, Admiral Bobby Ray Inman, and it recommended a range of security improvements including increased setback between embassies and public streets.

The US Embassy in Singapore was the product of a major building program to improve security in existing embassies and build new structures to replace those that could not meet security standards. During the review, we found some deficiencies and the RSO immediately implemented changes to address those issues. It was a successful collaboration of security expertise.

After I left Singapore, the US intelligence community identified Sammy as Mohammed Mansour Jabarah, a Canadian-Arab linked to Al-Qaeda. Mike was identified as Fathur Rahman al-Ghozi, an Indonesian Jemaah Islamiyah bomb maker who had been working with the Philippine MILF. In a joint operation by US and Philippine government elements, both Sammy and Mike were arrested in the Philippines in December 2001.

Meanwhile, the planner and financier of almost all the major terrorist events spanning the 2000–2003 period was certainty the most dangerous terrorist in Southeast Asia. JI's Riduan Isamuddin, also known as Hambali, facilitated the carnage by organizing the money. Hambali, an Indonesian, was regarded at the time to be among the worst of the worst of the Al-Qaeda–affiliated elements. His involvement provided the starkest case that Al-Qaeda directly financed Jemaah Islamiyah to unleash terror throughout Southeast Asia. After he was captured, his US interrogators reported that he harbored the "most extreme Islamic ideology" they had ever encountered.

Hambali was acquainted with Osama bin Laden's inner circle. In the 1980s, Hambali had trained to fight the Soviets in Afghanistan alongside Al-Qaeda's Khalid Sheikh Mohammed, known as KSM, currently the highest-value detainee in the prison facility at Guantanamo Bay, Cuba. We also learned that there was significant reason to believe Hambali was involved in the 1995 Bojinka plot to bomb eleven US commercial airliners.

* * *

To put the attacks in perspective, let's look at the timeline of the events in Southeast Asia from 2000 through 2002:

In December 2000, JI leaders Hambali and Faiz bin Abu Bakar Bafana, a Malaysian, arrived at the Manila International Airport and were met by al-Ghozi. Hambali and Faiz were visiting the Philippines to personally monitor the MILF's *jihad*. Al-Ghozi later admitted that, during the visit, he and Hambali had cased the US Embassy in Manila as an alternate target to the Singapore attack.

It was only later discovered that the architect of the famous Rizal Day bombings on December 30, 2000, was JI bomb maker extraordinaire Fathur Rahman al-Ghozi—a.k.a. Mike. Twenty-two people died while close to a hundred were injured when those five simultaneous bombings rocked five targets in metro Manila. Al-Ghozi and company left Manila that night for Iligan City, then Marawi City.

In November 2001, al-Ghozi went to Singapore to surveil the intended targets. In December 2001, Faiz was arrested in Singapore and the plot began to unravel. In a cooperative operation between US and Philippine elements, al-Ghozi was located and arrested on January 15, 2002, in Quiapo, a small suburb of Manila, by a task force of agents from the Bureau of Immigration and the National Police, allegedly while he was preparing to leave for Bangkok.

On January 17, 2002, acting on al-Ghozi's tip, police seized fifty boxes of commercial-grade explosives weighing almost a ton, four rolls of detonating cord, three boxes of blasting caps, seventeen M16 rifles, and two rifle grenade launchers in General Santos City, Mindanao, in the southern Philippines.

On October 12, 2002, a bombing attack on two pubs in Bali, Indonesia, killed 202 people, including 88 Australians. According to US intelligence records, Hambali had passed $86,000 of Al-Qaeda funds to Bali bomber Huda bin Abdul Haq, a.k.a. Mukhlas, to carry out the attack. Hambali also personally organized the simultaneous multicity church bombings in Indonesia on Christmas Eve, 2000, as well as the bombing of the Philippine ambassador's residence to Indonesia. And, he took part in an Al-Qaeda summit in Kuala Lumpur where the attack on the USS *Cole* was planned. Hambali was arrested on August 11, 2003, in Thailand, and after a short stay there ended up in the Guantanamo prison.

January 2002

The shit hit the fan on January 15, 2002, when US special operations elements landed on the island of Mindanao in the southernmost part of the Philippines as part of the Asian segment of Operation Enduring Freedom. Specifically, Special Operations Command–Pacific (SOCPAC) troops were the core elements of Operation Enduring Freedom–Philippines, an operation in support of the government of the Republic of the Philippines' counterterrorism efforts.

Our military began to work with and train Philippine soldiers and police units to help them fight not only Abu Sayyaf but also the Indonesian-based terrorist group Jemaah Islamyia (JI) that was infiltrating the Philippines via the porous islands to the south of Mindanao Island. Both Abu Sayyaf and JI were growing in numbers and in strength. They threatened not only the people in the Philippines but also all US interests in the Philippines and throughout Southeast Asia. The Filipinos trusted us and knew we could work with them to address the serious threat.

The first deployment of troops in the effort arrived in January 2002 and involved more than 1,200 members of SOCPAC. They were part of the Joint Special Operations Task Force–Philippines (JSOTF-P). An average of 500 to 600 US Army, Navy, Air Force, and Marine Corps special operations personnel were employed continuously. They provided training, advice, and assistance during combat operations to both Philippine special operations units and select conventional air, ground, and naval units. They also conducted civil-military and information operations on Basilan, the Sulu archipelago, and elsewhere in Mindanao; provided intelligence, surveillance, reconnaissance, medical evacuation, and emergency care; and aided planning and intelligence fusion at joint operational commands and force development at institutional headquarters. And they did all this in close coordination with a variety of US government entities, to include the CIA. I was assigned to assist the effort.

The mission of the JSOTF-P was to provide civil assistance programs and military training programs in the jungles of several islands near Zamboanga City, the provincial capital city of the island of Mindanao. It was on those islands that a variety of secessionist/terrorist elements were hiding and where it was suspected the Abu Sayyaf Group was holding their hostages, including the American Burnhams. Unfortunately, the Philippine government was very strict about enforcing an advisory-only edict when it came to activity by US troops, so no combat activity was allowed. Additionally, before our troops could be involved in any lethal action they were required to get specific approval from the White House and the Philippine government. US and Philippine forces also worked together to complete humanitarian and civil assistance projects and improve living conditions in the southern Philippines. As a result of those combined efforts, support for terrorists waned markedly. We were winning the hearts and minds.

In the end, Operation Enduring Freedom–Philippines contributed to the successful degradation of transnational terrorist threats in the Philippines and the improvement of its security forces, particularly special operations units. All this while the US was still mired in the middle of a major mission to rescue those hostages from the Abu Sayyaf criminal/terrorist group. Our government just had to do more and learn more. Between the 9/11 attacks and the infiltration and attacks by local terrorist groups in the region, we had our hands full. Luckily, the US military arrived in full force.

It was not like Somalia or Bosnia, where the US ended up going in blind. This time, American special operations forces were supported by a large contingent of logistics staff stationed in Zamboanga and in the central city of Cebu. The terrorist activities in and around the city of Zamboanga became the focus of both the Philippine and United

States governments. In preparation for the massive influx of US military personnel, as someone who had worked in a variety of war zones I was asked to assist with the planning and security oversight and support for the US military, law enforcement, and intelligence operations to recover the hostages and fight the various terrorist elements that posed a threat to the citizens of both countries.

I looked for the basic physical security elements necessary to accomplish the US government mission. This included finding a site with sufficient perimeter security as well as the necessary logistical capability (power, water, space). Wearing my support hat, I had to factor in transportation, living conditions, communications, and medical elements. I began spending a lot of my time in support of the personnel working in the high-threat environments. It was a well-laid plan, fought not against another country but, instead, against terrorists.

In April 2002, the kidnappers demanded a $1 million ransom for the release of the Burnhams. The mother of Martin Burnham helped to raise $330,000 to be paid to Abu Sayyaf. The Bush administration eased its opposition to such payments and acquiesced to the plan in the hope that it would free the couple and avoid the necessity of a military rescue, administration officials said at the time.

The FBI, in what would later be described as a botched operation, ended up losing the money when it was handed over to the terrorists who promptly disappeared with the cash and still didn't release either of the Burnhams. This put the US government in a peculiar position, since the strict policy of our nation was that we did not negotiate with terrorists and did not pay ransom, under any circumstances. It also put all the US citizens in the Philippines at risk because the previous adherence to the "no negotiation/no ransom policy" discouraged kidnappers from going after them. Only the more radical Muslim terrorist groups were willing to take the risks.

In October of 2002, the Burnhams were finally located. It had been seventeen months since they'd been kidnapped, but the efforts of a huge number of American agencies and elements working with the host Philippine government had finally paid off. The Philippine Scout Rangers encountered the ASG encampment where Martin and Gracia Burnham along with Ediborah Yap, a Filipino nurse, were being held. A gun battle ensued between the ASG captors and the Scout Rangers. According to Philippine military reports, during the firefight Gracia Burnham, forty-three at the time, managed to run away and fell into the hands of Scout Rangers. She and her husband, as well as Ms. Yap, had been shot during the firefight. Unfortunately, Martin Burnham was found dead, while Ms. Yap died shortly after the battle. Gracia suffered a gunshot wound to the right thigh. Emaciated and wearing camouflage shorts and shirt, she was evacuated first to a Philippine military hospital in Zamboanga City, then to Manila for treatment of the wound and of tropical diseases contracted during her rugged jungle experience at the hands of her captors.

The US military reported that American troops had not been directly involved in the incident, which took place in the jungles of Zamboanga del Norte in Mindanao Province, five hundred miles south of Manila. A Pentagon official said that in the firefight, four Abu Sayyaf guerrillas were killed and the rest, about fifty, fled. During the protracted search for the Burnhams, American military officials had questioned the Philippine forces' ability to mount a successful rescue operation, given the deep jungle, the troops' lack of experience, and, the Americans added, an apparently symbiotic relationship between some soldiers and the guerrilla group. The US was only providing general training to various units within the Philippine military, but no training that specifically emphasized hostage rescue had been given to the Philippine Scout Rangers. A Pentagon spokesman later commented that the gun battle was a "chance encounter during a larger operation" as opposed to a planned rescue effort.

When I heard the news that the Burnhams, or at least one of them, had been rescued, I chose to walk to my hotel rather than make the short drive. I wanted a chance to slowly contemplate what had happened over those long months and to try and unwind a bit from the stress and fatigue that came with an extended mission like that. I was able to head back feeling some degree of satisfaction that at least Gracia Burnham was free, although it was far from the result I'd been hoping for. Still, a mother was returned home, something that may not have happened without the sacrifices made, the efforts expended, and the resolve exhibited by so many. The calling I had chosen, the world I lived in, was definitely one built on teamwork. Nobody wins alone, but plenty lose that way.

And I was about to learn more hard lessons along that same line.

20

Southeast Asia • March 2002

As my tour progressed, I began to really enjoy getting to know some of the indigenous locals who provide the backbone for all US government efforts in foreign countries. Americans visited these countries on short trips (TDYs) or were posted for three to four years at most, while the local employees worked for decades at the various US government offices (embassies, consulates, joint military bases, and so on) within these countries and knew their jobs inside and out. They had to put up with training the "new people" every couple of years and the numerous changes that relative transients like us wanted to make to the system, most of the time not even understanding the system well enough to really make efficient changes.

Watching how the Asian employees, especially the Filipinos, dealt with that constantly changing management staff really helped me later in my career when I dealt with similar circumstances in the war zones of Iraq and Afghanistan and pseudo war zones (low-intensity conflicts) in Southeast Asia. But that's for later.

I had a great supervisor during my tour in Asia, Tony, who really understood how important it was to get to know the local staff. After I had been in the job only a couple of weeks, Tony told me, "Tom, we are going to ask if we can join the local Employee Association Bowling League!"

Being from Milwaukee, the capital of the world for bowling (or so I thought), I was so excited!

"Tony, that's a great idea! I like bowling and I've always wanted to join a league just for fun, since I'm not very good."

"Don't worry about your skill level," Tony quipped. "It's a great way to break the ice with the local people who really run this place, and we can make some friends and balance the work-to-fun ratio."

Since no one had ever asked to join their league, the local employees were surprised and, as we later found out, a bit nervous about it. Being the very friendly and accommodating people that they were, they allowed us to join. We had our own team shirts made and bought some bowling balls, bags, and shoes. The first night of bowling arrived and we all met at the bowling alley in the local mall. The owner of the alley turned out to be a five-time World Bowling Champion. (So much for Wisconsin being the bowling capital of the world.) As we warmed up for the game I walked over to Tony.

"I have to say I've never seen such a quiet group of bowlers in my life!"

Tony answered, "Tom, you're right. They normally are smiling, laughing, and chatting. Not sure what to make of this."

After we bowled our first game, which was against the Telephone Operator team, things started to loosen up and we began to see some smiles and hear chuckling among the locals. By the third and final game, they were back to their lively selves, hooting and hollering for each other, laughing and smiling. It was then that it hit me.

"Tony, I think I know what was going on before. They were nervous when we started bowling, thinking we were going to be great bowlers, but as soon as they found out how really bad we were, things lightened up."

Tony began to laugh as he realized how crazy that sounded but how accurate my assessment was. The league allowed us to meet local workers from all parts of the US government offices and entities and gave us something to talk about other than work. We ended up placing dead last in the league, but they gave us a trophy for being the "All American Team." We made so many friends and got a lot of favors done for us that made our jobs easier, which really helped us with our mission. I have never forgotten the lesson that it's always easier to work with friends, especially during a crisis, than with strangers.

February 2003

As things began to really heat up between the US and Iraq, we began to prepare for trouble from Iraqi elements in Thailand, Indonesia, and the Philippines. There was a history of bad behavior by Iraqis in the Philippines against US targets, dating as far back as 1991. Specifically, on January 19, 1991, when two Iraqis unsuccessfully attempted to plant a bomb near the US government's Thomas Jefferson Cultural Center in the capital's Makati financial district. One Iraqi was killed and another wounded in the attempt. A Philippine investigation also implicated two Iraqi students and two Iraqi diplomats, one of who held the high-ranking post of consul general.

Investigators said the diplomats had been identified as agents of Iraq's intelligence service. Philippine and Western intelligence agencies then began to scramble to unravel what they suspected was a vast Iraqi-sponsored terrorist network in Asia. The bombing was the first terrorist attack solidly linked to the Iraqi government since the Gulf War began, suggesting that Iraq was trying to make use of the broad intelligence network that it had set up in the 1980s to procure advanced technology and weapons systems and otherwise promote its interests abroad during its war with Iran, according to intelligence sources. Western intelligence agencies suspected Iraq of using its embassies in Manila and Bangkok to smuggle in arms and explosives in diplomatic bags for use in terrorist attacks.

In a similar incident, on February 12, 2003, the Philippine government ordered an Iraqi diplomat to leave the country over his alleged contacts with a Muslim rebel group. Iraqi diplomat Husham Hussein was accused of having links with Abu Sayyaf, which the United States classified as a terrorist organization. The case against him centered on a bomb attack in October 2002 in the southern city of Zamboanga. The police blamed Abu Sayyaf for the bombing, which had killed an American serviceman. The day after the attack, Philippine spies monitored a telephone call to Hussein by a suspected member of Abu Sayyaf. Both Washington and Manila had linked the group to Osama bin Laden's Al-Qaeda network, although it was best known for ransom kidnappings. The Philippine government stated that it considered Husham Hussein undesirable and gave him forty-eight hours to leave the country. It was the second time an Iraqi diplomat had been expelled from Manila, the first being back in 1991.

Hussein's expulsion put us on red alert for other nefarious activities by Iraqi embassy personnel and their contacts. Surveillance activities and investigations were initiated, and I was called back to the Philippines to use my countersurveillance experience working with our officers who were busy tracking every lead. I provided security overwatch on high-threat meetings by covering the venue, observing possible hostile forces, and being prepared to intervene if the meeting went south. I also provided some residential surveillance for one officer who was very involved in counterterrorism.

July 2003

Rumors of another possible coup had been circulating for months, but as is the case with rumors, it was hard to find the source. During my various trips to the Philippines I had made substantial contacts within elements of the Philippine police, army, and navy as well as the National Intelligence Coordinating Agency (NICA)—the Philippine's version of the CIA—and none of them could provide any substantial details. United States government personnel were out hitting all their sources. Resources were spread thin and they were doing the best they could to cover the country so, as the rumors grew, efforts were made to dive deeper into the community to find out what was happening; but nothing concrete was surfacing.

The Filipino people culturally enjoy gossip, which often made separating fact from fiction a challenge in its own right. The last actual coup had taken place in 1989, but there had been several bursts of coup madness over the past year that turned out to be false. That left the US government struggling to determine what to do, and that similarly left them unable to fully prepare for the actual coup attempt when it finally came.

Early in the morning on July 17, 2003, about three hundred Philippine soldiers took over the Oakwood Premier serviced apartments in Ayala Center, Makati City, to demand the resignation of certain officials and air their grievances against the military establishment. Calling themselves the Magdalo Group, these soldiers railed against alleged anomalies in the armed forces pension program, the military procurement system (including the purchase of substandard equipment for soldiers), and the construction and repair of various facilities at Marine Base, Cavite, as well as the alleged transfer of arms and ammunition to unauthorized parties. They also called for the resignation of then President Gloria Macapagal-Arroyo, then Defense Secretary Angelo Reyes, then Philippine National Police Director General Hermogenes Ebdane, and Victor Corpus, then Chief of the Intelligence Service, Armed Forces of the Philippines (AFP).

I just happened to be on a short trip to the Philippines to conduct a security survey when, very early in the morning, I got my first inkling that something was happening, as I began to receive text messages from my contacts saying that Philippine military elements were on the move and that at least one element was unaccounted for. As I was getting ready for work, my cell phone rang. It was one of the bosses.

"Tom, you need to get into work as soon as possible. Looks like the coup rumors are true. Philippine soldiers have taken over the Oakwood hotel in the Glorietta shopping center."

"Wow! I'm on the way."

"Be prepared to begin working with all of the US government elements, as they will be setting up a command center to work the situation."

"Roger that."

The US Embassy in Manila had a room that could easily be converted into a command center, and the administrative staff was prepared to bring in the numerous laptops, landlines, and other electronics that would be used to gather, analyze, and disseminate information back to Washington. By the time I got there they were already pretty far along in the process, and major planning meetings were being held. The "war room" was complete with a sea of laptops that were going to be manned twenty-four hours a day monitoring every facet of the potential coup.

The local CIA chief saw me enter the conference room and walked over. "Thanks for coming in early, Tom. I know you have your security protocol, but we're spread thin and we need you on top of this right now. Shit has hit the fan!"

For me, the first task was personnel accountability, especially for visiting personnel. Once I was able to make positive contact with US personnel, I assisted with moving any family members living near the Oakwood to safer accommodations. I then began to work my contacts via my cell while I simultaneously assisted with the strategic deployment of US government personnel to specific locations within the city to gather information. I needed to keep track of where we deployed people and what was happening in those areas.

Because the Oakwood was one of the hotels that US Embassy personnel used for long-stay lodging, there were several of our people trapped in the building when the incident occurred. It just so happened that a senior manager was staying in the Oakwood, and when he received an early-morning text message that something was amiss he went down to the lobby area in his robe. To his surprise, the elevator opened to a scene of uniformed Philippine soldiers carrying weapons moving about. Being of Japanese American descent, he immediately spoke to the first soldier he encountered in English with a heavy Japanese accent stating that he was a Japanese tourist and asked what was happening. The soldier told him that the building was being taken over and that if he wanted to leave he should immediately pack his stuff and get out.

I made contact with people I knew within the Philippine police, military, and private security to find out the apparent intentions of the rogue military elements holed up in the Oakwood. I added my data to that of the embassy work group that included the legal attaché's office (FBI), DEA, Immigration and Naturalization, and the various State Department offices (political, economic, diplomatic security, and so on). All this information was provided to the embassy staff personnel manning the war room who organized it, documented it, and then transmitted it back to Washington via situation reports. This went on for eighteen hours. At 10:00 p.m., President Gloria Arroyo announced that the occupation of Oakwood was over. The rebels agreed to return to their barracks and were out of the Oakwood premises by 11:00 p.m.

The bloodless mutiny ended unsuccessfully for the soldiers because they failed to rally enough support from the public or other members of the armed forces. All the military members involved surrendered and were charged in a general court martial and, later, with attempting a coup d'état.

* * *

I'd thought I would have Kirsty come visit me, since she had never been to Asia. We'd planned to do it early in my tour, but it turned out that I couldn't spare the time until my last year due to the continuous crisis situations that occurred from my arrival all the way through

2003. Because there were raised threat levels in Malaysia and Indonesia, and since I had more extensive knowledge of the Philippines, we decided that my daughter and her mother would meet me there.

I was really looking forward to showing Kirsty all the great things in the Philippines, the full red-carpet tour. I arranged for Allison and Kirsty to fly as close to nonstop as possible to avoid any chance of a missed connection. They arrived in Manila a bit jet lagged but no worse for wear after flying more than twelve hours from London. On the drive in from the airport, I filled them in on some of the planned activities and introduced them to the wonders of Manila traffic: five cars traveling along in a two-lane section of road, left turns from the right lane, and cars so close on your sides that you could touch them if you opened a window. They also got to see some of the poverty that plagued Manila when we drove through a major slum area on the way to our lodging.

Kirsty got pretty quiet as we moved past the shanty buildings where little children played in the trash. She had never witnessed third world poverty, and I could see it was leaving a stark impression. I knew that once we got deeper into the trip, she'd see the indomitable spirit of the Filipino people, who keep a smile on their face, a song on their lips, and a laugh ever ready to burst—a spirit of positivity I'd come to know and respect.

When we drove into the small walled compound where I was staying, the loud sounds of the city were instantly muted by the closed gate and tall trees that lived along the outer walls. Their thick foliage successfully battled the eternal street sounds in the area, one of the things I liked most about the little oasis. I took Allison and Kirsty upstairs and settled them into the spare bedroom. It was getting late, so I told them to get their rest and that we would start with a short tour of some of the historic US buildings in Manila.

The next morning we drove to the embassy, parked, and got our breakfast. It was such a treat for me to show them the historic landmark with the flagpole still wearing bullet holes from World

War II. I incorporated the US Embassy consulate building into the tour, an easy task since the building itself was such a museum-like gem. A historical monument, it had photos on the walls showing the carnage of World War II. And the view from one of the seaward-facing balconies was just as interesting, as large cargo ships could be seen moving through the Manila harbor toward the massive shipyard less than a mile north of the embassy.

After two days exploring various sights in Manila, we began the long road trip to Baguio, a mountainous region of Luzon known for cooler weather and pine trees. Being my first trip there, I had to work the maps. The signage was not ideal, and since commercial GPS wasn't yet available I had to make some educated guesses that, in the end, got us up the mountain without incident. We stayed in what used to be one of the spare bungalows on the US ambassador's residential compound, in what was formerly the US military's Camp John Hay. After we brought our luggage in, I opened one of the windows facing the downward slope of the mountains just in time for a small cloud to drift in through the window. The view of pine trees dotting the mountain landscape was beautiful.

Our next stop was the beach community of San Fernando, La Union, famous for surfing. The beach might not have been impressive from a standard sunbathing standpoint, but for catching gnarly waves I was told it was near perfect. We settled for the hotel pool.

The next day, we headed south to the Subic Bay area, former home of the massive US naval base. I found a hotel in the beach city of Barrio Barretto thanks to a friend who owned a nice bar/restaurant, an American Navy service member who had met his Filipino wife while working on the naval base and had decided to stay on when the base closed in 1992. He had a great cook and a nice view of Subic Bay from the back of his restaurant. The main reason we were there was to visit Ocean Adventure, an aquatic theme park where you could arrange to swim with a whale. It was something Kirsty was very keen to do and, of course, nothing made me happier than making her happy.

The day we went to Ocean Adventure, the weather didn't cooperate, but a light rain wasn't about to waylay our plans. It turned out the rain hardly bothered the wildlife at the park, and Kirsty got her wish when she and her mother swam with a cute little whale that was trained to do tricks with the customers. He allowed them to hold on to his dorsal fin and pulled them across the water and even pushed them with his snout. They got lots of photos, and I got to see the biggest smile on Kirsty's face when she posed with the whale in the shallows.

It wasn't all smiles on the trip, though. Kirsty was a teenager and going through the vacillating mood swings common to that age. It did not help, either, that her dad was a bit of a control freak. I think the term "square" originated in a conversation about me.

The trip back to Manila was uneventful and, in what felt like no time at all, I was driving them to the airport for their flight back to England. It was a great experience for me to have family visit and to spend so much time with Kirsty.

Of course, neither she nor her mother had any idea that I was in the CIA. They thought I was just a security officer working for the United States government in Asia. A good time was had by all, but it was also time for me to get back to work. Things never really slowed down in Asia, and we were about to receive a very distinguished visitor.

October 2003

We received official notification that President George W. Bush would be making a visit to Manila on his way to Thailand, where he was to attend the Asia-Pacific Economic Cooperation summit. I was called into the boss's office in early September to discuss the upcoming visit.

"Chief, you wanted to talk to me?"

"Yes, Tom, take a seat. As you know, the president is coming to Manila in October, and we have the lead on threat intelligence and are working closely with the Secret Service and the rest of the

Supporting President Bush's Visit to the Philippines, October 1993.

embassy elements to make this a seamless visit. Since you have a lot of experience working with the Secret Service and in protective operations when you were with the POC, I'm going to ask you to be heavily involved with all the prep for this visit."

"Sounds good. I can do this, as long as I get all the comms traffic and I can sit in on the planning meetings."

"I can make that happen," the chief replied. "The Secret Service will be sending in an advance team at least a week before the event, and we will have to really support them with their activities."

"No problem. These guys will be the advance agents in charge of protective intelligence, and I'm very familiar with their requirements."

"Great. I'll brief you as more details come in. Be prepared to fly into Manila early enough to get up to speed. Stay on your toes; you know how quickly things can go to shit there."

"I do indeed," I chuckled. "I'll make this my top priority."

The first step for any senior-level protective operations visit is to prepare the threat assessment. It is a complicated and in-depth process of evaluating any and all *possible* threats and distilling the long list into a shorter, more critical *probable* list of threats. In the protective world, we call this "protective intelligence" (PI). I was lucky to have direct access to our own analysts and, with my guidance, we would be able to craft a near perfect PI report for the Secret Service.

An invisible layer of protection, PI is the outermost ring of security and it is a critical element. The MNLF was largely defunct, a political element trying to be relevant, but the MILF was still very active, and their on-again/off-again collaboration with the Abu Sayyaf Group made both groups a serious threat. Of course, we still had the coalition of the Communist Party of the Philippines and the New People's Army—the CPP-NPA—skulking around and, while they kept a low profile, they were still players; especially on the island of Luzon where Manila was located.

I also looked at the logistical pieces of the visit. I arranged to acquire the use of several armored vehicles that we'd loan out to the Secret Service, and had the vehicles taken in for servicing and cleaning to make sure they were fully prepped and up to snuff. Since I knew some people with excellent connections with all the Philippine security and police elements at Manila's Ninoy Aquino International Airport, I knew we would be helping to coordinate the diplomatic clearance process for bringing in all the aircraft that would be involved in the visit. Besides Air Force One, there would be support aircraft needing secure areas to park and from which most of the US presidential support elements would operate.

I then began the arduous task of working with the various US government and embassy offices as they all tried to create their own "plan" for the visit. The "protocol" elements of the personnel detachment are somewhat the enemy in any protective operations visit. They were so politically-centric in their thought processes that they couldn't seem to understand they would have to adapt to the required security protocols and not the other way around. A presidential visit was probably the highest-profile diplomatic event an embassy could host, and the embassy was desperate to put on a good show amid the hotbed the region had become.

This required a doubling up on the workload across the board, because normal business had to be maintained at the same time all the labors associated with visit preparation were factored in. Of course, different offices were jockeying to get as much face time as possible with the president and his staff. This ego involvement was another issue that made my job difficult, but I was used to working with these "staff" types and used all my diplomatic experience and skills to herd those cats. If I couldn't get them to bend on a particular issue, I knew that in the end the Secret Service would.

The Philippines' progress against the terrorist threats had not come without setbacks. The infamous bomber Fathur Rahman al-Ghozi, architect of the Rizal Day bombings and a member of the JI terrorist group who'd planned the attacks in Singapore, escaped from a high-security detention cell in the middle of Camp Crame, the headquarters of the Philippine National Police, located in Quezon City. We were already hard at work putting together a threat package for the Secret Service, and the fact that the notorious terrorist had slipped from custody and was loose somewhere in the Philippines did not help us.

A week before President Bush's visit, the Secret Service advance team flew in and the frenzy began. One of my bosses worked with the senior advance agent, while I was joined at the hip with the number-two advance agent whose main job was protective intelligence. This couldn't have worked out better, enabling me to brief the advance team on our threat assessments as well as accompany them when they traveled to all the possible venues to be visited. Since none of the Secret Service agents knew the city, I did most of the driving, which also helped educate me on the possible routes the motorcade would take and allowed me to add my two cents about the driving patterns, traffic issues, and local environmental issues that are critical for route and contingency planning.

Besides the possible meeting venues, we also made trips to all the potential high-interest sites as well as to several hospitals. As you may recall, when President Ronald Reagan was shot in 1981 there were no Secret Service agents on standby at the local hospital, something that almost cost him his life because the hospital was unprepared for his arrival. This was not going to happen in Manila. There would be a Secret Service agent stationed at all the closest hospitals whenever the president was nearby.

The local press was on top of things, reporting that the Communist Party of the Philippines–New People's Army (CPP-NPA) had issued a statement insisting they had dispatched hit squads with a mandate to assassinate the president. Other militant groups reiterated their plans to push through their widespread mass actions to protest President Bush's visit. And against that backdrop, the Philippine government insisted that their military and security agencies had the situation in hand.

Then, on October 13, 2002, the US ambassador was contacted by the general in charge of the Philippine National Police (PNP). The general told him that Fathur al-Ghozi had been killed. Like a classic line out of the old movie *Casablanca*, the rumor was that he had either "committed suicide" or "died trying to escape." While this was a big relief for us, taking a bad player and major threat off the board, the implications that it may have been a case of "extrajudicial killing"—a.k.a. the killing of a person by governmental authorities without the sanction of any judicial proceeding or legal process—put the US in a difficult position. The US normally tries not to associate with any element of a foreign government that engages in extrajudicial killing, but with an imminent presidential visit, it appeared that the issue was resolved.

On October 18, 2003, the day of the visit, as part of the advance team I would be visiting each venue prior to President Bush's arrival. I was on the tarmac as Air Force One arrived and, as soon as it parked, my Secret Service partner and I drove off to the next venue. So went the next several hours, arriving at venues, checking motorcade approaches, parking areas, and the venue security before moving on to the next stop. A textbook operation, until President Bush stopped at the Philippine Congress building to give a speech. While he was speaking, local groups protesting the US military presence in the Philippines gathered in sufficient number to make the primary and secondary motorcade routes untenable. While we looked for alternative options, President Bush remained in the building.

Finally, the crowd dissipated enough for the motorcade to make its way to the next venue where the president was scheduled to meet some local people along a rope line. This was a very typical protective operations procedure where the protectee moves along a rope/fence line that provides a physical barrier between him and the public. Protective security moves on either side of the protectee, observing every movement by the largely unscreened crowd. Additional security elements move through the crowd, directly behind the public and in line with the protectee. Their job is to spot any movement or activities by people in the crowd facing, in this case, the president himself.

When we arrived at the rope line venue, the advance agent asked me to augment the Secret Service agents in the crowd, so I positioned myself approximately seven feet in front of the president while he moved along the rope line shaking hands and talking with the local Filipinos. I was on hyperalert status watching hands and movement by people directly in front of the president as well as to his left and right. Being asked to cover this position while I was armed was a serious compliment, as the Secret Service obviously trusted me to be that close to the president and to cover him when he was in such a potentially precarious position. Quite frankly, there is probably no greater protective operations job than being part of the US Secret Service's Presidential Protection Detail, and for a few precious moments I was in the inner circle protecting President Bush himself.

My posting to Asia flew by. The three years that I lived in the region would turn out to be longest stretch of time I spent in one place during my entire twenty-four-year career. The world had changed during my time there, and a new kind of war had broken out that continued to rage on. It was a war within the borders of Iraq that had really become more of a war against terror itself.

A war that needed soldiers with the kind of expertise that I could lend.

21

Baghdad, Iraq ▪ September 2004

By May 2004, US armed forces and their coalition allies had liberated Iraq. At first the people were friendly and appreciative. As our military began to pull out and turn control of the government back over to the Iraqi military, though, things slowly began to change. The threat level rose drastically. Terrorist attacks struck on almost a daily basis.

The insurgency had proved to be alarmingly dynamic, with shifting tactics that had earned American commanders' respect as well as contempt for the rebels' seeming indifference to the fate of the civilians who'd become their most numerous victims.

And with that as the backdrop, I walked right into one of the biggest chapters in the history of *Route Irish*, generally considered the world's most dangerous road. Route Irish, also known as the Baghdad Airport Road, was a twelve-kilometer (7.5 mile) stretch of highway linking the International Zone (a.k.a., the *Green Zone*) and Baghdad International Airport (BIAP). Between BIAP and the safety of the Green Zone was a terrifying void that had to be traversed by all who went to the Iraqi capital.

But one constant had been the vulnerability of the airport road—a journey so loathed, particularly by foreigners, that it had become a

241

kind of personal bellwether for the state of the war. Because Route Irish was basically the only way in and out of Baghdad, it was an insurgent's dream, a hunting ground populated by prey of all sorts and sizes—senior military convoys, government security details, busloads of Western coalition personnel, businessmen, journalists, supply convoys, and of course the US coalition and Iraqi military patrols, just to name a few. The list goes on and on.

Insurgent attacks throughout the Iraqi theater of operations fell into one of several categories, all of which were taking place regularly along Route Irish. These included improvised explosive devices (IEDs), unexploded IEDs or unexploded ordinance (UXO), hand grenades, indirect fire (mortars, rockets, and unidentified indirect fire), rocket-propelled grenades (RPGs), small arms fire, vehicle-born improvised explosive devices (VBIEDs), and more complex forms of attacks.

The skeletal remains of charred and wrecked vehicles, as well as the holes blasted in the road surface from the IEDs and VBIEDs, were there for all to see, a portrait of the death and suffering that occurred in the area on a daily basis. "There is at least one attack a day on Route Irish," an article in the *Sydney Morning Herald* reported in June 2005. "Invariably, the aftermath reveals a collision of fate and randomness that makes it seemingly impossible to fend off these strikes, which have the unsettling effect of making the firepower of the coalition, Iraqi forces and private security contractors as grave a risk for those who travel Route Irish as the insurgency bombs."

The danger was everywhere. It could be a suicide bomber, vehicle-borne or on foot; a roadside bomb with the explosives hidden in a discarded sack, animal carcass, or feigned damage to the roadway; or a barrage of mortars or rocket-propelled grenades. Suicide bombers in cars packed with explosives lurked at on-ramps, waiting for American convoys or other targets. Insurgents in cars with darkened windows mingled in traffic, then lowered their windows for bursts of machine gun fire. Insurgents disguised as members of a road crew would try to bury daisy-chained artillery shells beneath the roadway, rigging them with wires so they could be command-detonated or, if they were really sophisticated, remotely detonated using garage-door openers or cell phones.

So feared had the route become that an American security company ran an armored-car taxi service to the airport from the Sheraton Hotel on the east bank of the Tigris River. The cost, one way per person, was $2,390, almost certainly the world's most expensive airport cab ride. But it didn't matter if you traveled the road in a US military convoy of armored Humvees, a supply truck, or a taxi—arriving safely was an occasion for celebration and a sense that luck, or benign providence, had prevailed.

Besides connecting Baghdad and BIAP, Route Irish also linked a number of well-known neighborhood areas to each other. Although it was commonly referred to by the military as a Main Supply Route (MSR) designation "Route Irish," the route from the International Zone to the airport stretched over two MSRs: Route Aeros, the section leading into and out of the International Zone, and Route Irish, which stretched east from the airport and then turned south (past the junction with Route Aeros) to a junction with Highway 1 (MSR Tampa).

Initially, the insurgents used small arms fire in their attacks. When the US responded with armored vehicles, though, they progressed to placing IEDs, usually artillery shells rigged to explode by wire. US military and security forces adjusted by adding more heavily armored vehicles and removing all the guardrails and other potential hiding spots for IEDs. The insurgents would then try to place the explosives in potholes or dig them into the dirt along the side of the road. All this effectively resulted in a continuous game of cat-and-mouse, as the insurgents would try to anticipate and adapt their tactics to beat ours. The constant patrols, both day and night, put a lot of US military personnel at risk, but there was no other way to keep the road open.

It was going to be my first major management assignment, as I was not going to Iraq to do POC-type work. Instead, as the new

Chief of Security for all CIA operations in Iraq, it was my job to plan, implement, and maintain a countrywide integrated security program supporting hundreds of CIA personnel spread across the country. I was to oversee the hundred-plus security team members, including several POC teams and US Army personnel detailed to support our Baghdad site. Within my team I had specialists such as physical security technicians and bomb dog handlers, and there were POC teams strategically placed in different parts of the country to support operations. Each team generally consisted of staff POC team leaders and POC contractors. I needed to protect the people who were in harm's way collecting intelligence to keep our leaders informed and to assist the US military with their efforts in the war-torn country.

By the time I arrived, the insurgents had learned how to use remote detonator switches using cell phone technology. Efficient killing was nothing that I hadn't seen before, but there was no real predictability to their attacks, as there were multiple factions fighting with little coordination. We faced everything from small arms fire and crude IEDs to more sophisticated car bombs and missiles launched via remote control.

The CIA was on the ground in a big way there, and in fact was dual hatted. Besides looking for weapons of mass destruction (WMDs) and collecting intelligence on Al-Qaeda elements and Iraqi insurgents, we also were collecting tactical intelligence in support of the US military mission. That explained our growing presence and the need for a large headquarters-type compound in Baghdad. And we ended up with a compound fit for a prince—literally, in the form of a palace previously owned by one of Saddam Hussein's sons, Uday. Not to say we took the complex over in all its palatial splendor, since the US military had hit it with a JDAM—a bunker buster–type bomb that left the structure in ruin. The Agency commandeered the parts of the compound that had survived, moving into several of the smaller buildings within the site. One of the minor palaces on the compound was converted into the station's command center, and we moved in housing trailers for our personnel.

The palace was strategically located near Saddam Hussein's main palace that initially housed the Coalitional Provisional Authority (CPA) but would later become the US Embassy. We augmented the existing compound walls with concrete barriers and built an armored entry gate fitted with a "Delta" barrier, a hydraulic vehicle roadblock rated to stop a small truck. We stationed a bomb-sniffing dog and a handler at the gate to ensure nothing hostile could pass through.

While my flight over was uneventful, my arrival in Baghdad was memorable. The aircraft that flew me into BIAP had to fly in a very tight corkscrew fashion to reduce altitude and land due to the threat of surface-to-air missiles (SAMs). Upon landing, I was greeted by one of the senior officers in charge of security for our operations in the BIAP facility. As everyone in country communicated via push-to-talk (PTT) radios, we were all assigned radio call signs. The BIAP security officer went by call sign TAYLOR, as in Sheriff Taylor, the sheriff from the old Andy Griffith show. TAYLOR gave me an initial security briefing on the threat level and emergency procedures in case we were to receive indirect fire from mortars or rockets or small arms fire, along with the location of the nearest bunkers in which to take refuge. We then went to the chow hall for lunch.

I was later issued my weapons and body armor and prepared for the ride from BIAP to Baghdad. I loaded into the back seat of a dusty newer model sedan, while other personnel got into several other fully armored vehicles that would be making the shuttle run to the "Villa," as we called the CIA compound in Baghdad. Each vehicle in the convoy had POC personnel in the front seats. As the new incoming Chief of Security, I rode in the front vehicle with a staff POC team leader named Ralph Charles in the right front seat and a contract POC officer in the driver's seat. Ralph, call sign GRUMBLES, was an older POC officer who had a lot of experience in war zones. The other officers were relatively new to the POC, all former military guys on their first or second forty-five to sixty-day rotation.

The Agency had hired POC contractors from a variety of private companies that were able to supply experienced operators who had previously served in the US military or, in some cases, SWAT-type law enforcement units. The military guys came from a variety of the armed forces but were typically the best of the best. We had former Special Forces, Rangers, SEALs, and Force Recon Marines working with us. They were chosen because they had excellent soldiering skills, as well as their assumed ability to adapt to the unique mission of the Agency; something not all of them did well, as it turned out. Since we operated differently than the military, keeping a low profile and being strictly defensive versus offensive was a mental challenge representing a totally different mindset than what those warriors were accustomed to. But once they got the hang of things, they were great.

"Hello, sir. Welcome to Iraq," GRUMBLES greeted.

"Thank you. How has it been in these parts the past few weeks?" I asked.

"Insurgents have been quiet over the past couple days."

"Does that mean something is cooking?" I questioned, wondering if it was going to turn into an exciting ride to my new home.

"Ain't any pattern that we have found to their madness, sir. It just seems to happen in spurts."

My luck held as our ride down the dreaded Route Irish went smoothly with no major obstacles, except for dodging potholes and slowing down for US military convoys. As we pulled up to the Agency compound, I couldn't help but be impressed. It was by far the most secure CIA compound I had been to outside of the headquarters in Langley, Virginia. The walls were made of prefabricated concrete barriers, called *T-barriers* because from the side they looked like an upside-down "T" with a wide base and a tall, vertical, reinforced blast-proof slab. They were designed to protect us from shrapnel and all but the largest rockets. They were also almost twelve feet high, so they gave us the privacy we needed.

The arid conditions in Iraq were reminiscent of Death Valley, California, as temperatures could soar to as high as 130 degrees, while in the winter there would be snow in the mountains and downright chilly conditions in the plains. In the south of Iraq, there was a more tropical area complete with swamps. I arrived in Baghdad during the hot summer months, and I could feel my perspiration instantly dry in the blast furnace heat. The dress code varied according to the type of tactical personnel. Security, POC, and ops people who were preparing to go out of the compound wore more action-oriented attire. Hiking boots, long pants, and sweat-wicking shirts were the norm. Some wore nonmilitary cargo-style khaki pants and a variety of shirt types to include photographer's vests, while the administrative and analytical types wore jeans, shorts, polos, or T-shirts. A very casual attire environment, overall.

I was dropped off near the housing office, where I was given the key to my "pod" (what we called the small trailers we lived in), linens, and other incidentals. I stumbled around through the labyrinth of the housing area. There were rows and rows of pods, like a huge trailer park in the desert. It was the first time I had seen a setup like that. I found myself gawking at the variety of weird decorations people had put up in front of their pods. Pink flamingos were a common theme. I dumped my gear and then worked my way back in the direction of the main office building, where I hoped to meet up with the Security Chief I was replacing, get issued my radio, and begin what I knew would be a rough orientation process.

After getting lost, I finally asked for some help and was shown to the Personnel Accountability Section (PAS), one of the security elements that fell under my responsibility. PAS had a radio call sign, OPERATOR, and was led by an interesting chap who went by the call sign of DIRTY BIRD. DIRTY gave me a brief overview of the PAS operation and then had me photographed for the first of the many badges I would acquire during the tour. I also was given a chance to choose my radio call sign. As both of my previous call signs, RATTLER and SNAKE, had been taken, I chose SLINGER, a personal inside joke given that it was short for GUNSLINGER, something I had been called once by someone who had no respect for the POC. For much of my tour in Iraq, the call sign succeeded in confusing people as many had no idea what it meant.

I found out that the old Security Chief was busy with some administrative work in preparation for his flight back to the US that weekend. I busied myself talking with one of the security officers who'd done several forty-five-day tours in Baghdad. A former US Marine, call sign MULE, he was a wealth of knowledge about how things operated in Baghdad and on the Villa compound. Since my Deputy Chief of Security was on home leave and would not be back for at least two weeks, I knew I needed someone with this type of experience close at hand.

"MULE, you have just been temporarily promoted to Acting Deputy Chief of Security, and you will be no farther than five feet from my side until the Deputy returns from his home leave. Is that understood?"

With a small smile on his face, MULE said, "Totally understand, Chief, and I will not let you down!"

"Excellent, so let's start with an orientation tour of the Villa compound, including some narrative about each of the security positions we're maintaining."

MULE proceeded to give me a full tour of the station building and all the satellite offices (POC, cafeteria, gym, logistics and admin offices, and so on). We toured the main gate to our compound and the remainder of the compound grounds. He showed me the outside of the bomb-damaged palace as well as the swimming pool that had been part of the palace's immediate area.

"…And over there is where Uday would swim with his girlfriends," MULE said, interrupting my train of thought.

"Swim, huh?"

"Yes, and it's said that he'd have many lady friends over and, when he finished with them, if they hadn't suited his needs, he'd drown them and feed them to the lions."

My face must have reflected the horror I was feeling. I couldn't even think of a suitable response.

"The lions were moved to the Iraqi National Zoo," MULE told me.

"Glad the lions were taken care of," was the only thing I could think of saying.

After hearing the grisly truth about the pool, I made a vow to never set foot in it and to look at keeping the damaged parts of the palace off limits. A great deal of Uday's palace had been destroyed during the war but, from the remnants, I could still see that the décor must have been very grand. Large pieces of marble had been pushed into piles. Massive pillars still stood, reaching high into the sky. Several smaller buildings on the compound hadn't been destroyed and were being put to use.

"And this is the Babylon Bar," MULE said when we reached the next structure.

I wasn't surprised to see a bar, because the Agency is always "wet." The Babylon Bar had been set up in an extension off the chow hall. It was one of the very few places where libations were available within the Green Zone. The other bars in the Green Zone were downright dingy in comparison. For those who were after something altogether classier, the only place to be seen was our bar. The Babylon, staffed by volunteer bartenders, was open most nights, but the big night was Thursdays. Open to outsiders by invitation only, people had to be sponsored by someone living and working in the Villa to get in. It was a great icebreaker for meeting people and a bargaining chip to get things done. Personnel, both US and foreign, working in the Green Zone or in the Coalition Provisional Authority (CPA) were keen on attending the Thursday night party.

The CPA was a mixed bag of Iraqi officials, UN foreign officials, UN military command elements, contractors, and both US military and State Department personnel, all working to stabilize Iraq. Later, a large part of the CPA building would be converted into the US Embassy staffed by American diplomatic personnel.

Outside the bar there was a patio with lots of tables and chairs. In an effort to fight the stifling heat, there were also "swamp coolers" installed on the very edge of the patio roof. These swamp coolers were small tubes perforated to allow water mist to drift down into the patio and, as this water evaporated, they succeeded in cooling the area by ten or more degrees. The actual bar was inside the facility on the left as you entered and was complete with neon signs and other decorations that smacked of home. On the right, against the wall, were tables and sofas. In the back on the right was the TV room with a large-screen TV on the wall. To the back left was the dance floor, complete with a revolving mirrored disco ball.

Through a doorway to the left of the dance floor area stood a room with a pool table and bathrooms. The back of the bar butted up against the chow hall that had a self-service cold cuts sandwich station as well as snacks and drinks available 24/7.

On Thursday nights, the place would begin to fill up at about 7:00 p.m. and would stay that way until the bar closed at 1:00 a.m., with security personnel ensuring all patrons were out of the bar and all visitors off the Villa compound. The attendees were a mix of men and women from the Villa population as well as visitors from the CPA/US Embassy, with a few foreign military mixed in. US military personnel were not allowed to drink while in Iraq, but a few in civilian attire slipped into the bar on occasion.

* * *

During the drive into the city along Route Irish, I had seen only a small portion of the Green Zone, the heavily guarded diplomatic/

government area of closed-off streets in central Baghdad where US and other coalition forces lived and worked. The Green Zone, officially called the *International Zone*, occupied a three-square-mile cluster of national monuments, palaces, and parkland where the CPA made its headquarters before it went out of existence on June 28, 2004. The zone, along the Tigris River, was a city unto itself, with broad, tree-lined avenues that wound among apartment buildings, garish palaces, and government ministries, many of them caved-in more than a year before by US bombs. Within the Green Zone there were houses for the civilian ruling authority run by the Americans and British, and offices of major US consulting companies. The precise boundaries of the Green Zone would shift depending upon construction efforts and the expanding requirements for safe housing by the personnel living and working within the zone.

The Green Zone was commonly referred to as the "ultimate gated community" due to the numerous armed checkpoints, coils of razor wire, and chain-link fences and the fact it was surrounded by T-barriers. Part of the Green Zone was referred to as "Uday's Play-ground," as it was comprised of the presidential palace (the CPA, then the US Embassy annex); numerous villas for Saddam's family, friends, and former Baath party loyalists; an underground bunker (Believer's Palace); the Tomb of the Unknown Soldier and Military History Museum; the new Baath Party headquarters (unfinished); the Al Rasheed Hotel; the Convention Center; and a large park.

Due to the numerous Iraqi interim government entities occupying space within the Green Zone, traffic and population had increased. There was even a taxi service working within the zone supported by the Iraqis. Also, several independent local shops, including an Iraqi flea market (a *souk*), provided an array of international and local goods. The US government had clearly done a solid job of making that part of the city into a decent place for their people to live. They had cleared much of the rubble and ruin, but it was impossible to mask that it was still an active war zone.

The Villa compound was inside the Green Zone, and the station was located within one of the minor palaces on Uday's compound and consisted of a multistory building with a large central hall and arching cathedral-type ceiling, with offices along the outer walls. My workstation was a movable desk and chair situated in the basement stairwell area. I worked just steps away from the Deputy Chief of Support and near the Chief of Support's office. It was a critical arrangement, as there was really nothing you could do in a war zone without security needing to know about it and weighing in to mitigate risk.

My deputy, call sign DUKE, had been in country for more than six months, and he had a good handle on the administrative tasks of our job. One of my most important responsibilities was emergency management planning and crisis response. Working with my PAS office, I conducted countrywide personnel accountability, provided crisis management support, and ensured the safety and security for all Agency personnel within Iraq.

My supervisory responsibilities included leading all the security elements that managed a multitude of security officers via my deputy and the security officers at BIAP. I also worked directly with the POC country team leader and the POC operational team leader in Baghdad. The security technicians who supported all the major physical security projects across Iraq also kept me informed of their projects and schedules.

In terms of field support, I was tasked with providing very specific security assessments and assistance to operating bases spread throughout the Iraqi theater. My duties required me to travel to establish relationships with base chiefs as well as continuously monitor security programs to ensure requirements were being met and to anticipate any potential changes. This included assisting with security support and planning for construction projects, which at times meant I had to go out with a team of support officers to survey a potential site to determine its suitability.

Upon my arrival in Baghdad, I'd immediately realized that it was too big a job to rely solely on my expertise, so I decided to capitalize on the enormously talented and experienced personnel on my security staff. Since I had a continuous rotation of TDY personnel with huge variances in skill sets, I began to hold weekly staff meetings with most of my Villa-based security personnel. In the first meeting, I explained how vital it was for the security team to have situational awareness, to be up to speed with all the current threats.

I started the meetings by reviewing current threat trends and then moved on to scheduled projects and activities. But I always ended by going around the room asking for specific input from each individual officer in the form of critical observations, areas for improvements, and general comments relevant to our security operations. I let them know how important each of them was to our overall effectiveness and how valuable I considered their input.

The first few meetings, only one or two people would make a comment. I immediately implemented their suggestions and ensured the security team was made aware of the changes. Soon the team realized how serious I was about their suggestions. This helped me build up a sense of teamwork among my staff, providing a feeling of ownership for the individual team members and vesting them in our day-to-day operations. The great progress we made early on led to a high confidence level among my team and a desire by the TDY personnel to come back and serve in Iraq. I was convinced in the effectiveness of that leadership method and used it successfully for the rest of my career. But in that first month, I was seriously focused on how I was going to survive my tour in Iraq. Hardly a given, as circumstances grew increasingly complicated and dangerous.

22

Baghdad, Iraq ▪ October 2004

The days were long, usually twelve to fourteen hours, but they passed quickly. There was never a dull minute. And the nights were just as busy. I tried to get some sleep, but I had to keep one ear open so that I could listen for the occasional chatter from my security elements. I had my radio set to scan all ten channels during the night. Being a light sleeper meant I was very good at picking up on any urgency in the voices of my security personnel. In most cases I was awake and on the radio before they had even decided to contact me. I knew this was only a temporary thing, as I was sure that once I trained them to know the "wake up the chief!" threshold, I could reduce my channel surfing to the two critical channels, PAS/Security operations and an administrative channel.

The second week I was in country, I was sleeping when I was suddenly bounced out of my bed by an ear-splitting explosion that rocked my trailer. It was 6:00 a.m. From the floor I reached up for my radio and flipped the channel selector to "All" channels. Sitting on the floor in my skivvies, radio in hand, I took a deep breath and said:

"All Villa personnel, take cover! Take cover! All Villa personnel, take cover now!"

As I calmly sent that alarming message, part of my mind wondered what the hell I was doing in a trailer in Baghdad in the middle of a rocket attack. I had to be crazy. But there was no time to linger on that thought.

I immediately switched radio channels so I could talk directly to OPERATOR, my PAS and 24/7 security operations center in the station building. I requested a situation report and told them to prepare to issue orders to my static security elements to begin a sweep of our compound for any effects of the blast and to determine if we had any casualties (wounded, killed, or missing).

I jumped into my cargo pants and boots that I had placed at the foot of my bed for just that type of immediate reaction. I waited in my trailer for a few minutes listening to the radio chatter from my static security officers as they called in from their posts at the main, secondary, and tertiary gates. They reported seeing smoke coming from the other side of the wall closest to the CPA compound. I left my trailer and began to work my way to the station to hook up with my PAS office.

The smoke was billowing out and over our wall into one of our housing areas. I had to pull my shirt up over my face so I wouldn't choke. It was amazing that the explosion hadn't done more damage; it had hit just on the other side of the security wall near my row of pods.

Many of the residents were peeking their heads out to see what was going on.

"Stay in your pod or go into a bunker!" I yelled. "Wait for instructions from OPERATOR. Your immediate supervisor will be around to account for everyone's whereabouts soon," I announced.

As I walked toward the station, I sent out an announcement over the radio advising my static security elements to begin to search the compound to assess the damage. Entering the PAS office, I was immediately given a situation report. It appeared that a 122mm rocket had detonated in the roadway area between our compound and the main CPA compound. The rocket had struck a portable generator on a trailer that was attached to a Humvee. Both the generator and the Humvee had been destroyed but, luckily, no one had been injured and no other material damage sustained.

I had my PAS office begin a full accountability drill for our personnel using what we call a "warden tree" organizational chart. Supervisors from all units would account for their personnel and then report in to PAS, who would check the information against our daily personnel reports and our warden tree organizational chart. Within twenty minutes we had full accountability and I verbally briefed my boss on the incident. I then completed a preliminary report for transmission to HQS.

It was only the first of many indirect fire attacks from rockets and mortars during my one-year tour in Iraq. Most of the days were spent counteracting some sort of threats on our vehicles or dealing with the increasingly creative means our enemies were employing to hide and detonate explosives. SVBIEDS (suicide vehicle-borne IEDs) were all the rage among terrorists, as they were the most effective weapons in their arsenal against our armor. The insurgents would even go so far as to wait along Route Irish for convoys so they could jump out from behind cover and blow themselves up when they were in range.

Both the US military and the private security convoys got wise to the tactic and added rear gunners (using rear doors that had ports to shoot through or could open to allow a gunner to fire on any vehicles moving up to the rear of a convoy). Unfortunately for us, to keep a low profile we couldn't utilize that type of defense as we moved around Iraq.

Surprisingly, most attacks on our personnel consisted of "blue-on-blue" encounters—friendly fire incidents involving US military elements misidentifying our vehicles and firing on them. It was an unfortunate side effect of working in a military environment where US and coalition soldiers were afraid of any vehicle that was not easily identifiable as nonthreatening (read military vs. civilian). The US Department of State motorcades, with their big SUVs and high-profile activities, were more easily identifiable by both friendlies and hostiles. It made each day without a casualty worthy of a celebratory drink at night.

And there was no respite, because the insurgents continued to change their strategies and tactics. Rather than approach from the rear, they began to hit convoys from the front by either letting the line of vehicles catch up with them or waiting on the on-ramp areas until just before the convoy reached their position. Route Irish had become a SVBIED hunting ground, and the number of attacks increased to the point that heavily armored vehicles would not be enough to prevent a significant number of deaths.

October of 2004 proved to be an especially active period for insurgent attacks on Route Irish. Most of the attacks involved small arms fire, RPGs, IEDs and VBIEDs, and they prompted a reassessment of the coalition's responses during operations along the route.

As part of my duties, I worked closely with a variety of other US government elements, but I worked closest with the Department of State's Diplomatic Security Service (DSS). The senior DSS officer in country is called the Regional Security Officer (RSO). The other DSS officers that support the RSO are called Assistant Regional Security Officers (ARSO) . The RSO works directly for the ambassador, the most senior US government official in country. The president gives the ambassador Chief of Mission (COM) authority over every executive branch employee in the host country, except those under the command of a US area military commander or those on the staff of an international organization.

The ambassador, using COM authority, has full responsibility for the direction, coordination, and supervision of all US government executive branch employees within the host country or in the relevant mission to an international organization. Additionally, all executive branch agencies with employees in the host country must keep the COM fully informed at all times of their current and planned activities.

As the president's most senior government authority in country, the ambassador sets the rules for how the rest of the US government entities operate, with some exceptions. While the ambassador's authority does not cover the US military, his or her wishes must be taken very seriously by the senior US military commander in country, and they normally coordinate their activities very closely. This is important background to understand how all those in the US government have some regulatory obligations to work together under the COM authority.

The RSO, as the head of the Regional Security Office, is responsible for the security of every US citizen in country. The Regional Security Office provides guidance and threat assessment information to the US population in country. In Iraq, they established a tactical operation center (TOC), a fusion clearinghouse that collected threat data from the US military and other coalition forces, as well as information reported to them from private security elements. The RSO TOC in Iraq had an all-source analyst who was cleared to see up to Top Secret (TS) data from various other sources. This allowed the TOC to keep track of the threat environment and provide predictive guidance to all the government entities that fell under the ambassador/COM authority.

One evening, my chief and I went to the US Embassy Emergency Action Committee meeting where all the major embassy entities got together to discuss security issues. This meeting was called to address the significant rise in attacks on Route Irish. The US military was reluctant to admit that they had lost security control of Route Irish and could not provide enough protection to ensure that vehicle traffic would not be attacked.

The Department of State senior all-source analyst working in the TOC provided an in-depth briefing on the progression of risk on Route Irish, utilizing some very scary statistics on the number of attacks and resulting injuries and deaths. When the US military, represented by a colonel, objected to the data and asked for source information, the room was stunned to learn the data came from, well, the US military. That sealed Route Irish's fate—the embassy declared it off limits to regular use and forced everyone under COM authority to make alternative arrangements to move personnel and material. It was a major blow to the military and a severe impediment to progress for a lot of the improvement projects.

The station management and support staff had several meetings, and finally the embassy decided, in December 2004, that due to the risk on Route Irish, government personnel would travel from BIAP to Baghdad via helicopter. Luckily for us, one of the main helicopter pads in Baghdad was situated in the middle of the Green Zone. It was not an easy fix, but the alternative of trying to ride the Highway of Death was worse. I felt a huge sense of relief after they closed Route Irish. After I left Iraq in 2005, US and coalition military forces increased patrols and the road became safer and more reliable.

Too little too late for some of the victims, as they say.

October 14, 2004

The Green Zone, while more secure then the areas outside the city (the Red Zone), was hardly immune from a variety of threats and was becoming an increasingly regular target for insurgents. Besides the frequent indirect fire attacks from rockets and mortars, Iraqi insurgents were forever trying to sneak VBIEDs and SVBIEDs into the city. If they could not get in the gates of the city, they would detonate their cars among the people waiting to get in.

A significant event during my tour was a double suicide bomber attack on October 14, 2004. I was on my way back from a meeting at the CPA when I heard two almost simultaneous explosions coming from the direction of the downtown area of the Green Zone. I immediately radioed PAS.

"OPERATOR, OPERATOR, this is SLINGER, do you copy?"

"SLINGER, SLINGER, this is OPERATOR, go ahead."

Armored vehicle hit by a VBIED, Baghdad, Iraq.

"OPERATOR, there has been some type of explosion in the vicinity of the downtown section of the Green Zone. Contact the RSO TOC and find out if that was a controlled det [planned detonation by friendly forces] or some indirect fire impacts. Also begin a preliminary personnel accountability drill for any of our personnel who may be off the compound near the explosions."

"Roger that, SLINGER. Making the call now."

I immediately made my way to the PAS office to follow up on the event, with a true sense of dread. When I arrived, one of my PAS operators was just hanging up the landline telephone.

"SLINGER, looks like there were two IED explosions: one at the Green Zone Cafe and the other in the *souk*. No word yet on whether these were indirect fire."

I was very concerned, not only because we continuously faced the threat from mortars and rocket attacks, but also because I was aware of a report that an IED had been found the day before in a sandbag in front of the Green Zone Cafe, a popular restaurant several blocks from the CPA headquarters. The Green Zone Cafe and the local *souk* were both popular places for US and foreign troops to go to relax and to buy souvenirs and bootleg movie DVDs.

I had assumed that the US authorities in the area would've been doing constant threat assessments and, as a result, would have increased security at that venue. Unfortunately for the people killed and wounded that day, that hadn't happened. My PAS team quickly conducted a thorough personnel accountability exercise so I could ascertain whether any of our own had been injured, killed, or reported missing. I later learned that one of the embassy personnel injured in the attack was a friend of mine. He was a human resources officer who had transferred from an embassy in Asia to the diplomatic mission in Baghdad. He had been attending a going away party for some people at the café when the blasts erupted, and he was wounded by shrapnel and suffered a perforated eardrum.

Later in the evening I received a briefing from the RSO's office that, according to witnesses, two men carrying backpacks had entered the Green Zone Cafe around the lunch hour and drank tea for about thirty minutes. One individual left the café and an explosion was heard shortly afterward. The man who'd remained in the café detonated his bomb moments later. The blasts were nearly simultaneous, sending plumes of black smoke into the air. The one near the market left a huge crater. Ten people were killed—four of them US citizens who were working as DynCorp security personnel and the other six Iraqis. Among the total of twenty people injured in the attack, two other Americans were seriously wounded and several embassy employees had minor injuries.

The Green Zone, rimmed with cement blast walls and check-points, was often the target of attack from the outside but rarely the inside. It was the first time that insurgents had struck from within the heavily guarded compound, too close for comfort in the minds of the British and US embassies and Iraqi government offices that operated in the area.

A group loyal to Jordanian militant Abu Musab al-Zarqawi claimed responsibility for the attacks in a statement on a website. "Two lions from the Tawhid and Jihad group's Martyrdom Brigade managed to get inside…the Green Zone in the capital Baghdad…" said the claim, calling the attack in question one of the Zarqawi group's most successful operations.

Al-Zarqawi's Tawhid and Jihad group was believed to have similarly been responsible for a number of atrocities, including the beheading of British hostage Ken Bigley. As a result of the attack, the RSO's office strongly encouraged Americans living or working in the Green Zone to curtail their movements, travel in groups, carry several means of communication, and avoid the bazaar and restaurants inside the compound.

But such warnings weren't enough to prevent all tragedies.

* * *

During my Iraq tour, our compound and the surrounding compounds had to contend with a variety of indirect fire incidents, to include impacts from mortars and rockets fired by insurgent groups from outside the Green Zone. Boy, we hated those rockets! When they sent those big 122mm rockets flying your way and you heard the telltale sonic boom, you knew they'd missed you but that someone else might not have been so lucky. Surprisingly, we discovered that Saddam's bunkers were able to survive a direct hit from an exploding 122mm rocket. His military had gotten that part right.

Many of the rockets were Chinese-made and had faulty fuses that failed to cause a detonation when they impacted. Unfortunately, a 122mm rocket travels at Mach 2 (twice the speed of sound) and hits like a huge bullet, so they remain extremely lethal as kinetic weapons. Our forces tried to mitigate indirect fire with a variety of countermeasures, but none were very successful. The military had some "counter-battery" capability, rockets or mortars that would fire at the suspected location where the enemy rockets had been launched, but the effectiveness of that countermeasure waned when the Iraq insurgents started to use timer mechanisms from old washing machines to delay the launch of the rockets until they were safely out of the area.

The second month I was in country, one of the rockets struck an annex to the CPA, punching through a roof and side wall and impacting, without detonating, in an office area killing two US citizens at work in the contracts department. An ARSO was killed on October 24, 2004, when a rocket struck his trailer during a rocket attack on the US base Camp Victory, located near BIAP.

Impossible to hear about that and not think, "It could have been me."

* * *

Late in October, I got up early and was just leaving my pod on the way to the chow hall to grab my breakfast when I heard my radio chirp. It was a full hour before I was scheduled to attend the morning staff meeting.

"SLINGER. SLINGER, this is INDIAN. We have a problem," was the message that came over my radio. INDIAN was the call sign for Mark, one of my contract security officers.

"INDIAN, INDIAN, this is SLINGER. Send your traffic."

"SLINGER, I need your help at Checkpoint Twelve."

I got one of our security vehicles, radioed OPERATOR where I was going, and then drove out to Checkpoint Twelve. We had been having some problems getting a number of our local Iraqi staff (cooks, cleaners, and so forth) into the Green Zone, and I was guessing this was the reason for my visit. As I drove up to the gate, on the Green Zone side of the checkpoint, I could see Mark standing next to his vehicle. I noticed that he was wearing his ballistic vest. I hadn't brought mine, as

I assumed I would just be talking with one of the Army soldiers inside the command post within the Green Zone.

"What's up with the vest?" I asked Mark as I sipped my first coffee of the day.

"SLINGER, we have to go outside the Green Zone to speak to the Army corporal who sits with the Iraqi guards checking IDs."

"Shit! I didn't bring my vest!"

"Don't worry. We'll slip out for a few minutes and then come right back in."

"Okay, let's do it," I replied, breaking one of my own hard-and-fast rules.

We walked past the Abrams tank sitting just inside the checkpoint gate and slipped through the concrete T-barriers that made up the outer perimeter of the Green Zone. Just as we passed outside the barriers, my cell phone rang.

Before I could answer it, INDIAN said, "Don't answer that out here! The guards will think you are using the phone to set off an IED!"

We stopped, turned around, and walked back six feet to pass back toward the T-barriers. As soon as I was through, I took out and activated my cell phone and said hello.

It was the chief of the British intelligence service (MI6) unit in Iraq. "Hi, Tom. Can we make arrangements for me to visit your boss?"

Before I could answer, I was partially knocked off my feet from the concussion of an explosion that went off only feet away on the outside of the Green Zone T-barriers. My coffee went flying.

"I'm going to have to call you back," I managed and hung up.

I grabbed my radio and, with my ears ringing, called into OPERATOR. "Explosion at Checkpoint Twelve! Conduct accountability for all units outside the Greens Zone!"

An SVBIED had detonated near the first Iraqi-manned checkpoint, killing three Iraqi soldiers and wounding a number of civilians. The only reason I was alive was that I had stepped back into the Green Zone to answer my cell phone. On the lighter side, I had broadcast my explosion report on the radio's "All" channel, so when I got back to the office I faced a barrage of laughter from the rest of the security team in response to the higher-than-usual octave of my voice. I hadn't noticed it due to the ringing in my ears, but those guys never missed an opportunity to give someone the razz. I secretly vowed to never again get caught squeaking on the radio.

* * *

While the days were long, the nights could be wild, as hard to believe as that might sound. Everyone needed to blow off some steam, and they did it at the Babylon Bar. I had heard rumors before I deployed that there were some war zone romances happening in Baghdad, but I found them to be more numerous than I ever expected. Corners were always occupied by couples that had come together from the loneliness, tension, and sense of constant threat, or perhaps such passions were rooted in nothing more than wanting one last hurrah, just in case. To keep things from getting out of hand, either my deputy or I would keep an eye on the bar. I also assigned security officers to patrol the bar every Thursday night to prevent incidents or deal with situations before they got out of hand, or at least to mitigate the situation. Station management held me directly responsible for any incidents, as I had assured them that I had the resources and willpower to keep that vital part of our morale within acceptable parameters. Personally, I liked to grab a beer or two and relax, and knowing that my deputy and my security officers were covering things allowed me that luxury. Plus, I had made a friend.

"The usual?" Nathan asked me.

"Yep," I replied, taking a seat at the bar.

Nathan was a former Marine from Denver who worked as a mechanic in our motor pool and liked to play part-time bartender. He made terrible mixed drinks but was more than capable of cracking open a beer.

"Here ya go," he said, sliding the beer to me.

"Thanks," I said.

I sat and sipped my beer and hoped she would come. I looked around, scanning the crowd.

"You waiting for Lara?" Nathan asked.

I almost choked. "Ummm, maybe."

"She'll be here," he said with a smile.

And he was right. I was only partially through the beer when there she was. Lara worked as a contractor in the embassy's badge office. She was a short Hispanic woman who also happened to be a former US Marine. She waved at me from across the bar, and I couldn't stop myself from grinning. She came and took the seat next to me.

"How was your day?" she asked.

"No one died," I replied. "Yours?"

"Ugh, they just gave us a new form for the badges and people are having a shit fit. Nothing new, in other words."

Although I knew I was in the middle of a war zone, I was enjoying my budding romance. It had been a long time since I had felt this way about someone, and the fact that I could wander over to Lara's office on my way to the embassy meant I could see her pretty regularly, without hiding the truth of who I was or what I was doing the way it was with civilians. Lara and her coworker liked our bar, and it was easy for me to invite her over on a regular basis. She was a life of the party type, with a huge grin and a booming laugh.

I'll always remember the different characters I met around the bar and on the embassy compound. The revolving cast included South Africans working projects to remove land mines, contractors from DynCorp and Brown & Root, Department of State Diplomatic Security Service officers, as well as Americans working in the CPA, which would later morph into the US Embassy. Everyone was there to do a job in a hostile environment, cherishing those few minutes a week when they could let their hair down with a drink and have a laugh.

One Thursday evening, as everyone was preparing to hit the bar, a US military helicopter was flying low over our compound when it either was "painted" by the radar from a surface-to-air missile or had some sort of an electrical malfunction. The helicopter went into action, setting off its missile defense system, which instantly fired a stream of flares out the back of the aircraft. These flares were designed to fool any heat-seeking missile, allowing the helicopter to zigzag its way out of the area.

I was just passing through the housing area when I heard the unmistakable sound of the flares igniting, and I looked up just in time to witness them raining down into our compound. As bad luck would have it, several landed in the tops of some of the palm trees that dotted the grounds of our compound. After a month straight of 120+ degree heat, the palm trees had fronds as dry as tinder.

Poof!

Up in smoke they went and, as they burned, fronds began to be jettisoned, the sap exploding from the heat, which sent flaming palm fronds raining down on our housing pods. This was a serious problem, since these pods had wooden roofs and were as dry as the palm fronds themselves. I remembered that another US compound had previously lost five housing pods in less than twenty minutes to a fire in the south of Iraq, so I knew we were facing an emergency.

"OPERATOR, OPERATOR, this is SLINGER. We have a fire situation in the housing pod area near the Babylon Bar. Contact Baghdad Fire and Rescue and get them over here immediately. In the meantime, I need all unassigned Villa security personnel to report to me at the patio area of the bar."

"SLINGER, SLINGER, this is OPERATOR. Calling Baghdad Fire and Rescue now. Will alert security personnel to report to your location."

I ran for the trailer where the Villa groundskeeper's office was located, hoping that some of them were still on duty. Luckily two of them were in the office finishing up some paperwork when I bounded in.

"I need help immediately. We have a fire in several of the palm trees and while we wait for the fire department we need to use your gardening hoses to get some water onto the housing pods to keep them from lighting up!"

The groundskeepers were all over it, and in less than four minutes the three of us were running around like madmen, spraying as much water as we could on the pods directly under the two burning palm trees. My security personnel showed up, and I advised one of them to go to our gate and escort the fire trucks to our location.

While all this was happening, there were several Agency personnel who had begun their Thursday night partying early, and when they saw the burning palm trees they knew they were in for a show. Scooting their patio chairs to the edge so they could follow all the action, they became our cheerleading squad.

After an issue with getting their truck through our gate, the Baghdad Fire and Rescue team finally arrived and in no time they put out the flaming torches those palm trees had become, and hosed down the area underneath to ensure that no smoldering palm fronds could start a fire. The firemen immediately spotted our patio and the spectators imbibing alcoholic beverages. They made a point to ask if they could come back after their shift and share in our festivities, but alas that was strictly against procedure. So, instead, they were given a pile of "pogey bait" (military speak for candies, cookies, and other sweets) as reward for their services, along with bragging rights for having saved the party at the CIA camp.

* * *

My PAS office had a direct telephone line into the TOC, and I was a frequent visitor to their office as well the RSO's office. Combining the threat information provided by the TOC with our own threat assessments allowed me to keep my management informed. On a daily basis, I provided this threat data to our operational elements so they had an idea what they were facing when they ventured out of the confines of the Green Zone. This type of close coordination between the RSO office and my security elements helped prevent misunderstandings and de-conflict activities that may have caused some "blue-on-blue" incidents between the embassy security elements and mine. Later in my tour, I permanently assigned a security officer from my office to the TOC for immediate and accurate coordination during critical incidents, such as indirect fire attacks as well as possible major insurgent activity, to ensure both parties had the latest threat information.

That's just one illustration of how important the relationship was to keeping personnel safe in such a war-torn environment. Another example was the close working relationship I had with the Assistance Regional Security Officer (ARSO) who was in charge of Ambassador James F. Jeffrey's protective detail. I got to know that ARSO, Joey L., very well and we'd often talk shop after work over a beer. We were kindred spirits, realizing that given the extremely fluid threat environment along with the huge bureaucracies in place, the only way to capitalize on real threat intelligence was to keep the communications lines open between the key elements, two of which were sitting at the bar.

With my background in protective operations, I knew exactly what kind of information Joey needed to help keep his protectee, the ambassador, safe. We also knew that if we just relied on the established bureaucracy, it was highly likely that actionable threat information would either not reach him in time or would end up being garbled by the long chain of people who would get it before it reached the operational element that would need the information. It was because of these discussions that I realized, during high-threat situations where people's lives were on the line, the coordination of information between the operational elements was paramount and the bureaucracy would have to sit back and wait.

Joey and I exchanged cell phone numbers and I promised that I would contact him directly if anything came my way that I thought he needed to know ASAP. He made the same promise to me. It was not a violation of any rules, as long as we did the required paperwork. I began to implement that type of real "need to know" into my work across the board, and that became another of the leadership lessons I learned in Iraq: if at all possible, keep it at the lowest working level and make sure the people who really need the information get the information.

One day, my PAS office learned that an Iraqi insurgent and his crew were in the process of placing IEDs in a road to specifically get the ambassador, a.k.a. Big Fish. I knew the RSO TOC had been tracking an insurgent bomb maker whom we'd nicknamed "the Worm." Based on the information we had learned, we could only conclude the IED was in place and that the insurgents were waiting on the arrival of Big Fish. Having coordinated earlier in the week with Joey, I knew the ambassador had a motorcade movement to a meeting in the Red Zone scheduled for virtually right that minute.

I ran outside my office to get a clear cell phone signal and frantically began to dial Joey's cell, hoping I would get through and that he'd answer. Thankfully, Joey picked up on the second ring.

"Tom, what's up?"

"Joey, the *Worms* are out! You have to cancel your movement!"

Joey instantly understood what I meant, and he yelled to the driver of the ambassador's vehicle to stop the car just before they crossed the bridge into the Red Zone. I gave Joey all the information we had, and he had a pretty good idea where the bad guys were waiting to hit the motorcade.

I later found out that when Joey stopped the motorcade and informed Ambassador Jeffrey that their movement was canceled, the ambassador said, only half jokingly, "Joey if you are wrong about this, you're fired."

What I didn't know at the time was that General George Casey, the commander of the Multi-National Force–Iraq, was traveling with the ambassador for a critical meeting with an Iraqi minister. US military elements had been dispatched along the ambassador's motorcade route and they found that the area near the venue, which normally was bustling with locals, was deserted. They also spotted several local Iraqis with a video camera fleeing the scene. As part of the insurgents' propaganda efforts, videotapes of successful attacks had proven to be very effective.

An explosive ordnance disposal (EOD) unit was dispatched, and they found several IEDs buried along the roadway where the ambassador's motorcade was set to travel. Only a few minutes had separated us from disaster. Needless to say, that truly cemented my friendship with Joey, and I like to think it got me some brownie points with the ambassador. But the important lesson there was the fact that security elements must work extremely closely, and when critical information is learned, it must be passed to the operational elements first. If we hadn't established a relationship before the incident occurred, Joey may not have trusted my information and he may have opted to continue the motorcade movement.

That is another critical leadership lesson: you need to get to know the people you'll be working with during a critical incident *before* that incident occurs. It's too late once you're in the midst of a crisis. It is a human relations thing that helps keep personality issues to a minimum when stress is at its highest. And it also saves lives.

A good thing, given what was to come.

23

Baghdad, Iraq ▪ March 2005

Mosul is considered the second largest city in Iraq, with a population of approximately three million. Modern-day Mosul consists of the twin cities of Mosul and the ancient Assyrian city of Nineveh, sitting on opposite sides of the Tigris River on the Nineveh Plains in the Nineveh Governorate, northern Iraq. It's located 400 kilometers north of Baghdad, 85 kilometers west of Erbil, and 125 kilometers south of the border with Turkey.

Mosul's history of numerous occupations and its status on a crossroads between cultures has bred a diverse population that includes Arabs, Turkmen, Kurds, Yazidis, and Shabaks. Over the years it has boasted a sizeable Christian and Jewish population, but the majority of the population remained Sunni Muslim. Historically, Mosul was a center of trade, a thriving city on the *Silk Road*. It became known for metalwork, a miniature painting style, marble, crude oil, and textile production; in fact, "muslin" gets its name from Mosul.

After World War I, Mosul was brought under temporary British administration. Ottoman Turkey and Allied nations signed the Treaty of Sèvres in 1920 that gave Kurds the right to form a state, including those from Mosul. But the Treaty of Lausanne in 1923 replaced the

272

Treaty of Scvres, leaving the fate of Mosul in the hands of the League of Nations. The current Iraq-Turkey border was defined in 1926 under the Frontier Treaty, which saw Turkey give up Mosul on the agreement that Baghdad give Ankara a 10 percent royalty on Mosul's oil deposits for twenty-five years. Mosul later became one of the several "disputed areas" that Erbil (the capital of the Kurdistan region of Iraq) and Baghdad vied for control over. As a disputed area, Mosul was included in the no-fly zone imposed over Kurdish areas in 1991.

Beginning in 2003, the presence of the 101st Airborne Division, under then Major General David Petraeus, restored order to Mosul and helped reinstitute balance among the city's diverse groups. During 2004, after the 101st was replaced by a smaller force, ethnic tensions grew, and a balance emerged whereby insurgents and Arab nationalists controlled the west side of Mosul while Kurdish political parties and militias controlled the east side. In November 2004, Mosul's police force collapsed in the face of an insurgent assault. Up to 3,200 of the city's 4,000 police officers either deserted or joined the insurgents during the attacks.

After several tough weeks of fighting, coalition forces retook the city with the help of a large number of Kurdish Peshmerga forces. In the aftermath of the Battle of Mosul, the previous stalemate was solidified with overwhelmingly Kurdish army forces operating on the east side of the city and insurgents on the west side. The biggest change was that before November 2004 the insurgents in Mosul were mostly associated with the former regime, but afterward there was an increasing presence of Al-Qaeda and Jamaat Ansar al-Sunna members. The city's Sunni Arab population that tolerated and even supported Al-Qaeda and other insurgents developed into a hub for the figurative offspring of Osama bin Laden.

I had previously visited Mosul to rendezvous with US military and embassy security personnel. Though it was heavily fortified, the insurgent uprising and the resulting Battle of Mosul had provoked a significant increase in the number attacks in the area, making it very difficult for military and State Department personnel to operate.

Mosul was several hours flight time from Baghdad. The support officers and I caught a helicopter flight from the Green Zone to BIAP, where we were going to get on a fixed-wing for the flight to the US military base just outside the city. From the helicopter, we had a bird's-eye view of the sun just coming up. Up in the air was the best place in the Green Zone to watch the sunrise, and when dawn broke the world always seemed more positive.

I got a chance to see Mosul from the air when our aircraft did a tight circle to land on the military landing strip. I recognized the dirty rolling hills and the large, flat landscape from my previous visit. I couldn't help but muse over the fact that I had seen similar landscapes in a number of war-torn countries, and the thought occurred to me that I needed to change travel agents!

After landing at the military base, we were met on the tarmac by a POC team that had been dispatched to Mosul to transport us off the base and around the city. We would have to traverse some dangerous territory, but the POC officers were well versed on the threat environment and had primary and alternative routes planned with associated safe havens identified along the way for emergency use.

I walked up to the two fully armored sedans parked to the side of the runway. Both had dark tinted windows and were dusty from riding the roads. Not bad for government rides. I was greeted by the POC team leader, call sign JACKAL, whom I'd met on a previous trip.

"SLINGER, are you ready to ride?" JACKAL asked.

"Absolutely, JACKAL. I hear things have heated up out here. How are you guys holding up?"

"Better than the military. Those poor guys got hit bad in their chow hall."

JACKAL was referring to an attack on December 22, 2004, just a month after the Battle of Mosul fighting ceased, when a suicide bomber dressed like an Iraqi soldier managed to get into the Army

Iraqi War Zone Coin and Baghdad Station Coin, given for service in this war zone.

mess tent on Forward Operating Base Marez and detonated himself, killing twenty-two people, including fourteen American soldiers.

"That definitely was a tragedy," I said, shaking my head. "I read that they have already rebuilt it and that the new chow hall is like an armored diner!"

"You heard right, SLINGER. In fact, we'll get a chance to grab some chow there later this trip. They pulled out all the stops. It's as good, if not better, than any mall food court, with the added security features to prevent a mass casualty event. Probably the safest eating establishment in all of Iraq," JACKAL boasted playfully, having clearly maintained his sense of humor, a must in our world.

I hopped into the lead car with JACKAL while the support officers climbed into the rear vehicle. We had to move through the maze of roads on the airfield to get to one of the outside gates. Flashing our lights, we were cleared for movement into the Red Zone of Mosul. We shot out onto the road and after two turns were among the population moving about the city. JACKAL and his team were seasoned veterans, having deployed to Mosul many times, and I had faith in their judgment.

JACKAL turned and looked at me from under his worn-out Dodgers hat and aviator sunglasses and said, "With the threat level so high, we need to get to a more secure location."

"Well, then let's do it," I replied.

"Let me give you another tour of our beautiful city," JACKAL said, sarcasm lacing his voice.

The base was located a half mile from the heart of Mosul city. The city was stereotypical of the region. The various neighborhoods had small markets and shops, and people moved about doing their business amid a palpable level of fear you could detect from the way they kept their heads on a swivel to persistently keep watch over their environment. Traffic consisted of older, beat-up vehicles mixed in with some newer models. We had to go through one of the more congested parts of the city to get to our base, and without any traffic lights and minimal traffic signs it was more like a version of controlled chaos. The traffic reminded me of Washington, DC at close to rush hour.

"What is it with all this?" I asked, motioning to all the cars.

"Mosul is the major trucking route from the border of Iraq," JACKAL explained. "I'm not sure how it has stayed so active. We have very little control over the insurgents here. Gunfights erupt all the time. Because of the civilian traffic, many innocent civilians end up in the crossfire."

"That's not good," I said, stating the obvious.

As we drove through the city, we passed several large mosques as well as some municipal buildings. Several miles down one of the main streets cutting across the city, we noticed that an older-model gray BMW sedan and a brown Toyota SUV had suddenly pulled out from a side street and were several cars behind us. We began to carefully watch their movements while we continued to observe the other areas around our motorcade. After several blocks and two turns, we determined we were being followed, given that both vehicles appeared to be correlating to our movements over time and distance. It was also obvious that the two vehicles were working together and most likely had some sinister intentions.

I noticed JACKAL had switched his rifle's safety selector switch from SAFE to FIRE. We went around a traffic circle, effectively reversing our direction and affording us a quick look at the people in the two suspicious vehicles. We could clearly see there were at least four Iraqis in each of the sedans, and they gave us a hard look as we passed. Technically, we call that "target fixation," as their actions showed that they were intent on closing the gap and executing an attack on our convoy.

In hostile areas, we rely on our low-profile vehicles and our lack of time and place predictability to give us an edge. But when these two suspicious vehicles increased their speed and began to weave their way through traffic in an effort to close the distance between us, we knew it was time to get aggressive. JACKAL radioed to the follow vehicle to ensure they were aware of the presence of our new "friends," and the convoy picked up speed. Immediately the enemy vehicles reacted, matching our pace and making it abundantly clear that their intentions were hostile.

We needed to do everything possible to evade our tail and not engage them in any way. Engaging with the enemy is against the principles of protection; stopping to fight would have endangered the protectees, in this case myself and the other support team members. There was no tactical advantage to engaging in a firefight in the middle of Mosul. Even more so, in Mosul any type of gunfire would attract additional insurgents, and we could quickly find ourselves seriously outnumbered and outgunned à la the events depicted in *Black Hawk Down*.

Instead, the correct response when coming upon potential attackers was to "get the hell out of Dodge." Our POC driver immediately began to use his excellent knowledge of the city to make a series of turns to frustrate the hostiles on our tail. Several times they tried to speed through the traffic to close the distance between us, but each time our POC driver cut over a lane, made a turn, and used the heavy traffic to slow them until we cut over an overpass and left them floundering at an intersection. My last glimpse of them was a view of the passengers in the lead vehicle sitting completely frustrated with a hostile glare on their faces as they realized they'd lost and we'd left them in our dust.

"Welcome back to Mosul!" JACKAL said with a laugh.

"I'd say I've got my work cut out for me here," I said as both JACKAL and the POC driver whooped it up, letting off some steam.

After the attempted attack by the insurgent version of the Welcome Wagon, the rest of my trip proved not nearly as life threatening. During our tour of the city we took a look at some of the bunkers that Saddam Hussein's Republican Guard had used as barracks. The barracks were so strongly built that they could survive the impact of a 122mm rocket. I even stayed overnight in one of them. What the bunkers did not do well was stifle the noise of several super snorers whom I had the unfortunate pleasure of sharing sleeping quarters with. Needless to say, I was glad to head back to the airport for the ride back "home" to my pod at the Villa.

In the end, I made some improvements in the emergency action plans that required more accountability of personnel and more documentation. They weren't all going to like it. There were going to be more rules and structure than they had been living with, but those were the types of things that kept people alive so there was no room for negotiation.

I bid JACKAL and his team goodbye and boarded the plane back to Baghdad. The flight time seemed shorter on the way back, and I landed at Baghdad International Airport when the sun was starting to set. I wasn't ecstatic about having to travel at night, and I'm sure my escorts weren't either. But one thing was for sure: it couldn't be any worse than the day I'd just had in Mosul.

"Howdy, SLINGER," MULE said with a wave as I exited the plane on the tarmac at BIAP.

"Good to see you, MULE," I said.

"Good trip?" he asked with a smile.

"It was another adventure. Do you know how Louis L'Amour, the famous Western novelist, defined an adventure? A life-threatening event you survive!"

"Let's hope the helo flight home doesn't qualify as one of those," he replied.

"Let's hope, indeed. I could use a beer. Or three," I told him as I walked over to the helicopter and buckled up for the short flight from BIAP to Baghdad.

I sat quietly as we safely made our way back to the Green Zone, glad to be out of Mosul, keenly aware that the old saying about leaving the frying pan for the fire had never seemed more applicable.

* * *

The threat level rose by the day in Iraq, and the Agency mission was directly impacted. The ability to safely conduct operations in that war zone became a critical factor, and the POC played a vital role in protecting our people and enabling them to accomplish their mission.

Originally, POC operators were all staff employees. After 9/11, the POC had to respond to the uptick in requirements that forced the operators to spend most of their time on deployments to war zones and away from their families. But we soon found out that with wartime operations in both Iraq and Afghanistan, there was no way we could keep up with the demand, so the Agency started hiring contractors to fill the gap. The POC contractors were subject to a strict vetting process that included competency testing. They had to be able to adapt to the unique way we operated, which was low profile. We also had a formula that worked very well, a good staff-to-contractor ratio. Adequate span of control was an essential part of good leadership. This allowed for sufficient management oversight while still leveraging the expertise and experience of the contractor workforce.

Staff POC team leaders provided operational and tactical control over the team members, while I, as head of security, had overall accountability and program management control over all POC personnel (as well as all other security elements). The contractors became a key factor in the success of the POC (translate that into lives saved, people uninjured, and missions accomplished).

Several other factors contributed to the enormous success of protective operations in Iraq, Afghanistan, and other warlike zones. Operationally, a major factor was the ability to move under the radar and out of sight from the kind of watchful eyes that were always looking for their next target in such a high-threat environment. Government and civilian protective details in the war zones typically followed a commonsense rule that it's best to blend into your environment.

Following low-profile protection principles worked exceptionally well in those types of environments, and the principles were not unique to the POC. There were other protection details in the war zones that followed the same protocols. One company that conducted low-profile protective movements was Edinburgh Risk and Security Management (ERSM). Known locally as just Edinburgh Risk, the company became infamous in Iraq after videotape surfaced on the internet from a dash camera in one of three vehicles that was part of a motorcade ambushed by some formidable insurgent forces. Their after-action report was very detailed about their low-profile protective protocols. It was also detailed about the mistakes they made and the lessons they learned from the deadly ambush.

Per their report, on April 20, 2005, eight members of ERSM as a part of Operation Apollo (supporting the Independent Election Commission of Iraq), were assigned the task of driving from the Green Zone to Baghdad International Airport to pick up several colleagues returning from leave. The journey would take them along the twelve-kilometer Route Irish, still the only direct road from the Green Zone to BIAP and at that time still considered to be the most dangerous stretch of road in the entire world. We had previously shut the route down for official traffic in favor of helicopters, but it was still open to elements that did not fall under the Department of State's Chief of Mission authority, including private security companies. As a result, the road remained the scene of almost daily attacks by VBIEDs, IEDs, and small arms fire.

Besides insurgent attacks, the ERSM team was also concerned with the possibility of blue-on-blue incidents. Due to the fact that the team was operating in low-profile vehicles to blend in with the surrounding local traffic, they were right to be concerned about being felled by friendly fire.

The ERSM team, like other protective teams, used video cameras to record their routes, as much a navigation training tool as anything else. The protective details often used routes on dirt roads in the middle of the desert, driving along the sides of canals and through farm fields to avoid detection and lessen the chances of encountering an IED or ambush. Many of the routes weren't on a map, so learning them was a matter of trial and error. When a new route had been established, the video footage was used to refresh protective personnel's memories before a trip, as well as to train new personnel.

The ERSM motorcade was made up of three low-profile vehicles: two unarmored BMW sedans, one with a manual transmission, both carrying three contractors, and a level B6 (rifle round resistant) armored Mercedes sedan with two men. Most protective details carried 5.56mm automatic rifles, but some used locally procured AK-47s, RPKs, and PKM belt-fed machine guns, largely dependent upon the security company's resources. The ERSM team was armed with 5.56mm rifles, 9mm MP5 submachine guns, and Glock 19 handguns. The rear gunner of the motorcade was armed with an M249 squad automatic weapon (SAW), the equivalent of a light machine gun. The other rear gunner was armed with an RPK (a larger version of the AK-47) and an M249 SAW. All typical weapons to shoulder in low-profile motorcades.

When the ERSM motorcade exited the Green Zone via Checkpoint Twelve and moved onto Route Irish on the day of the attack, the mission commander, seated in the right front seat of the third car, issued commands and danger area warnings to the motorcade. It was standard procedure during high-risk movements, identifying potential threats and areas of concern and relaying the information to the rest of the motorcade. Specific areas of concern included overpasses and pedestrian bridges, as insurgents liked to drop grenades and IEDs from those structures onto motorcades passing underneath.

Camouflage is a low-profile motorcade's biggest tactical advantage, and to obtain maximum concealment it must blend into and become part of the surrounding traffic; to look like civilians, in other words. The motorcade should never intentionally do anything to draw attention to itself, but there are times when camouflage fails and a motorcade is noticed, regardless of all the precautions taken.

One constant danger is having the military or another protective security detail (PSD) mistake you for a group of insurgents and shoot at you. For identification, many PSD vehicles carried small laminated American flags tucked away under the right front passenger seat sun visor, and some teams also used large American flags for identification at longer distances.

Normally, the markers would remain hidden until approaching checkpoints or while traveling on strictly controlled military highways, like MSRs Tampa, Irish, and so on, when the laminated flags would be propped up in the windshield of each car. By displaying the flags and slowly approaching any checkpoints or roadblocks, the teams reduced the chances of any blue–on–blue incidents.

Several times during the movement toward BIAP, the ERSM's lead vehicle made numerous semi-aggressive moves to clear traffic lanes or block vehicles momentarily from entering onto the highway, allowing the other motorcade vehicles to maintain their formation (intervals and spacing) without any local traffic becoming mixed into the group. While these were tactically sound actions for high-profile motorcades, such moves inevitably draw too much attention and should never be used while operating in a low-profile configuration.

When the motorcade reached the last overpass before the checkpoint to BIAP, it found the military had established a roadblock and closed the highway to deal with the aftermath of an IED explosion. The detail was hesitant to get closer than two to three hundred yards from the roadblock to avoid a possible blue-on-blue event. The motorcade remained static for approximately forty minutes, during which the rear gunner fired several warning shots to keep civilian traffic clear. This obviously didn't constitute low profile, as the shots clearly showed that the group of vehicles was a motorcade.

The motorcade chose to remain static for so long that the driver of Vehicle One, whose leg tired from holding down the clutch, put the manual transmission vehicle in neutral and set the emergency brake. The problem with this was that you must remember to release the emergency brake and put the vehicle in gear when it's time to go. Unfortunately, the driver of Vehicle One didn't remember.

Even if he had, it still takes time to depress the clutch, release the emergency brake, shift into gear, and accelerate. When under attack, you want to be able to respond as fast as possible. Each member of a protective detail has an assigned responsibility and for the drivers, their key responsibility is the operation of the vehicle.

The ERSM vehicle did not notice that an SUV had pulled up nearby on the frontage road. During that period, no one in Iraq was driving SUVs except PSD teams and certain military motorcades. So, an SUV sitting just off the most dangerous strip of highway in the world should have set off alarm bells.

Based on reports, the insurgents in the SUV were probably armed with two Russian PKM belt-fed machine guns that they then used to strafe the motorcade. With their first burst of fire they hit all three vehicles, killing one driver almost instantly and wounding three other men, two critically. Vehicle One's driver believed it was another of Vehicle Three's warning bursts, and only when he felt rounds begin to impact his vehicle did he realize they were under attack. He tried to use the other big tactical advantage of low-profile motorcades: speed. He hit the accelerator and the engine raced, but the car didn't move because it was in neutral with the emergency brake engaged. Under the enormous stress of the attack, he believed the vehicle had been disabled by gunfire, so he opened his door and bailed out.

Standard operating procedure when taking fire is to flee the scene, so the ERSM team attempted to drive out of the kill zone, but due to several driver errors they were unable to do so. With Vehicle Three's driver slumped lifeless and rounds impacting the vehicle, the mission commander exited the vehicle and took cover behind it. Another option would have been to take control of the vehicle from the passenger seat and attempt to drive it out of the kill zone, but he had chosen to exit instead. Stopped motorcade vehicles are commonly known as bullet magnets, so the number one priority after exiting a vehicle under fire is to move away from it as quickly as possible, especially if it is an unarmored vehicle.

An ambush is a loud, chaotic, and terrifying experience, with the environment evolving from one moment to the next. There is a tremendous amount of information to process in an extremely short period of time. This is where proper training, rehearsals, and mindset are the keys to reacting effectively. The technical term for the tactic/ techniques you perform in reaction to an ambush is called an "immediate action." In this case, several of the ERSM team reacted tactically and threw smoke grenades to obscure the vision of the attackers while other team members attended to the wounded.

According to the video taken from the dash-mounted camera in Vehicle Three, the initial contact lasted thirty-two seconds and resulted in three ERSM operators being rendered combat ineffective due to enemy fire and all three vehicles disabled either through damage and/ or driver errors and wounds. The enemy forces fired on the motorcade for one minute and ten seconds before they fled the scene.

284

Coalition forces, located some three hundred meters away, responded and took command of the scene. They evacuated the wounded ERSM team members to Camp Victory, where the wounded received medical treatment, but three ultimately died.

Even when properly trained and prepared, things can and will still go terribly wrong. Prussian military strategist and German field marshal Helmuth von Moltke once noted, "No operation extends with any certainty beyond the first encounter with the main body of the enemy." This quote has been simplified down to "no plan survives contact with the enemy." Standard operating procedures and immediate action drills must be kept simple and easy to execute, and practiced regularly. Additionally, protective teams must maintain a high degree of flexibility and the ability to improvise.

That ERSM tragedy reinforced the fact that principles of low-profile protective operations work well, but when the principles are violated things can go very wrong. The most important lesson is that the best way to survive an ambush is to avoid it altogether. Protection details that use a low-profile configuration must commit totally to the concept of camouflage, and in the event the camouflage fails and they're attacked, they must break contact immediately, preferably by driving away. If you're forced to bail out of the vehicles, tactically move away from the vehicles as quickly as you can.

* * *

The POC was constantly adapting to our enemy's actions as well as learning from other people's mistakes. This, coupled with our commitment to following low-profile protective operations protocols, was why we were so successful. Operationally, the POC proved to be one of the greatest assets in Iraq for enabling our personnel to get out and collect intelligence. The professionalism of the POC, both staff and contractor, and their ability to safely move Agency personnel in country was a huge factor in the success of our mission. Our personnel relied upon the POC to keep them safe and get them home alive.

While my tour in Iraq was one of the most satisfying of my career, even someone with my background and experience could only live under that kind of constant stress for so long. So, after a year away and one too many close calls, it was time to go home.

24

Washington, DC ▪ July 2005

I settled in back at the headquarters building in Langley while I waited for another assignment to open up. It was going to be my real first desk job in several years, and I knew it would be an adjustment.

After having been away so long, and in war zones, I figured that some of the people back in HQ would just assume I would come back wearing cargo pants or BDUs (battle dress uniforms), so I made sure to swing through Thailand on my way home to pick up a number of top-of-the-line custom suits, shirts, and accessories. I knew from the look on several people's faces they were shocked at my bespoke appearance. Just like any other war zone (and HQ was a war zone), I knew I needed to blend in, so my new clothes were a hit.

Since I had just come from Iraq and had significant on-the-ground experience in a variety of Middle East locations, I was given the job as the temporary Deputy Chief of Security in the Near East (NE) Division. I put my experience to good use providing security policy guidance to senior NE Division managers and personnel and ensured effective and timely security support for NE personnel assigned to headquarters as well as in NE stations and bases overseas.

As part of my new duties, I would brief senior NE managers on sensitive personnel and counterintelligence cases and assisted senior Office of Security managers. I also assisted regular employees with overall security guidance regarding security clearance processing, contact reporting, travel security awareness, outside activities, financial disclosure, security incidents, personal security, and emergency evacuation programs. I worked with Office of Security managers, other Agency components, and other intelligence community members in support of the secure establishment and maintenance of overseas facilities, personnel, and information.

I was very interested in helping prepare our personnel for their assignments to the war zones, so I also became one of the instructors for the Iraqi Familiarization Course. It was an in-depth course on how to prepare for deployment to the Iraqi war zone. We covered everything from the different cultural aspects of the country to proper decorum and dress codes. We even provided guidance on personal preparations such as wills, beneficiary designation, and pre-trip packing. Significant others were given information on how to help their loved ones prepare for their deployment and provided with instructions on how to get in touch with them while they were deployed.

I had a chance to catch up with all my friends as well as spend some time back in Milwaukee seeing family. It was strange being back home in the United States, but I enjoyed being busy at work in my new deskbound role, hitting the gym, and going out for beers with some of my buddies. Time flew by as I waited for a position to open where I could continue to utilize my skills in an appropriate manner, and I was already getting antsy to do so.

Baghdad, Iraq ▪ November 2005

On November 18, 2005, I was asked to return to Baghdad to lead the US Secret Service (USSS) advance team for a secret visit to Iraq by Vice President Dick Cheney. The Agency had been approached by the USSS for assistance, and somehow the request got to Near East Division. The Chief of Security for NE decided I was the best person to help the USSS with all the required security support and keep VP Cheney's visit confidential, since I'd recently returned from Iraq where I had served as the Chief of Security and helped coordinate President Bush's visit in Manila.

Of course, I was happy to do it, although I never really thought I'd be going back to Iraq for any reason, much less to help the vice president. To start off the preparations for the visit I attended several meetings with the VP's protection detail. They told me the general parameters of the trip, who he was to meet with, where he would go, and some ideas of how they wanted to move between venues. The schedule was still tentative, and a lot of coordination was needed. A VIP visit like that has hundreds of moving pieces.

I woke up early on December 11, my return day to Baghdad. It was a cold and cloudy day. I was a bit nervous about the trip with so much at stake. Since I basically was representing the CIA, I felt the weight of that responsibility on my shoulders. But it was an opportunity to serve my country in a way I had never done before. Not that I hadn't assisted the USSS in the past. In Manila, I had coordinated with their advance teams in preparation for President Bush's visit and worked with the actual detail during his visit.

I got my luggage ready and headed off to CIA Headquarters to catch a ride from one of our motor pool drivers to Andrews Air Force Base, where I would meet up with the rest of the USSS advance team and board their Air Force aircraft for the flight to Baghdad. I remember thinking I could really get used to having someone chauffeur me around and put me on airplanes, something I had done for others when I was with the POC as well as the CIA director's protective detail.

The advance team consisted of a variety of personnel, including White House communications staff, the USSS agents who were the advance team for the vice president's trip, and several US military liaison officers. We were crowded into a small waiting area near the hangar where our ride, a USAF C-17 aircraft, was being readied for the long flight to Baghdad.

The C-17 was by no means a luxury plane. It was military issue and capable of rapid strategic delivery of troops and cargo to operating bases and deployment areas, a tactical plane used often because of its inherent flexibility. But I figured it would be better than being stuck in the middle seat in coach.

Once aboard the aircraft I realized it was truly in cargo-carrying mode, since within the hold was a large Chevy Suburban with several major modifications in place for its use as a mobile communications unit. Conditions were austere in the workhorse aircraft, with seating consisting of web sling seats hanging off the walls. It was debatable, then, whether that mode of travel was actually preferable to that dreaded middle seat. The takeoff was definitely not commercial air-craft style, as the C-17 is a souped-up version of a cargo plane with very little resemblance to the workhorse it replaced, the C-130 Her-cules! The C-17 can take off on a short runway and has so much acceleration I felt like a passenger in a drag racer. After climbing to its cruising altitude, the ride smoothed out and I moved around in my sling seat, trying to get comfortable.

The trip was noisier than a commercial flight and, unlike a com-mercial plane, there was little or no heating system. I soon realized that it was going to be a cold trip. Before long, my feet were numb from the cold and I was shivering. I'd never flown on a C-17 before so I was unprepared, having failed to bring a blanket or layered clothing. No choice but to just gut it out. Finally, I started to doze, fantasizing about that coach seat stuffed between two large passengers.

Somewhere over the Atlantic, the C-17 did a midair refuel. I had heard this was a unique experience, but I slept through the whole thing. About three quarters of the way through the trip, I woke up to hear an announcement over the public-address system that we had filled the sewage tanks, so the bathroom would no longer be available, making the last several hours unexpectedly unpleasant.

US Secret Service Challenge Coin given for services provided to Vice President Cheney during his visit to Iraq in December 2005.

After the eighteen-hour flight, we finally arrived at Baghdad International Airport at four thirty in the morning local time. The aircraft taxied to a remote section of BIAP and dropped the rear cargo ramp. The slightly cool, crisp, and dry winter air of Iraq hit me as I walked down the ramp to be greeted by some of the Agency logistical personnel who would be assisting our advance party. I made my way to the air operations center to greet the chief of our logistical hub, a man I had worked with for several months before I'd finished my tour at the Villa in Baghdad.

After a much-needed restroom stop, I headed to the chow hall where I got my first cup of hot coffee and met up with the BIAP security officer. We were old friends, and she was incredibly well connected with both embassy and military personnel at BIAP. She had brought me a radio and quickly got me up to speed on the local threat conditions and any relevant changes that had occurred since my departure from Iraq. I then headed to the armorer, where I was kitted up with a holster, mag pouches, Glock 19 pistol, and spare magazines.

I was back in my Iraq work attire. I spoke with the senior USSS advance agent and told him that we needed to set up a meeting with the embassy RSO, the senior US government security officer in country. Luckily I had worked with him before. The RSO worked out of the embassy compound in Baghdad, and I made a call to his office, but due to the early hour got his voice mail. I left a message asking for a 9:00 a.m. meeting to discuss an urgent issue.

I later learned that the RSO, upon listening to my voice message, was very curious why a former CIA Security Chief would ask for an urgent meeting. He didn't have to contemplate the mystery long, because at about 8:00 a.m. he was summoned to the ambassador's office where he was told about the vice president's secret visit.

After making the call to the RSO, I arranged for two of the senior USSS advance agents and I to take a helicopter from BIAP to Landing Zone (LZ) Washington, which was directly across from the US Embassy compound. The early-morning view from the window of the helicopter showed me the scenery had not changed since my last flight over Route Irish and the outer city area of Baghdad. Upon arrival at LZ Washington, we made a short walk across the street into the embassy compound and then made our way to the Villa. I brought my USSS companions to our chow hall and treated them to a nice breakfast before we took a walk through the compound to the RSO's office for the meeting.

The meeting was an effort to combine the CIA's protective operations resources, namely the POC, with both the embassy's Diplomatic Security Service resources and those of the US military. From that moment on, the visit was an Agency, DOS Dip/Sec, and DoD collaborative effort. I coordinated the use of several POC teams to provide security services to the USSS team. Vice President Cheney was to ride in an armored limousine provided by the ambassador while USSS agents were to ride in advance and follow vehicles that were armored and driven by the POC due to their intimate knowledge of the Baghdad landscape. Several POC teams were used to take USSS advance agents to venues that the vice president was planning to visit.

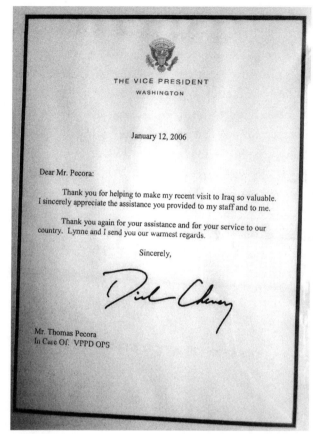

THE VICE PRESIDENT
WASHINGTON

January 12, 2006

Dear Mr. Pecora:

Thank you for helping to make my recent visit to Iraq so valuable. I sincerely appreciate the assistance you provided to my staff and to me.

Thank you again for your assistance and for your service to our country. Lynne and I send you our warmest regards.

Sincerely,

Dick Cheney

Mr. Thomas Pecora
In Care Of. VPPD OPS

Appreciation letter from Vice President Cheney for helping lead his US Secret Service Advance Team in Baghad, Iraq, December 2005.

Everything was meticulously planned, and locations were scouted prior to Vice President Cheney's arrival.

The vice president arrived in Iraq on Sunday, December 18, 2005, and every aspect of his trip proceeded flawlessly. While he was in Baghdad, I was given an opportunity to meet him. Several of us stood in line, and as the VP walked past he shook our hands, thanking us for supporting his visit. No one told him that I was a CIA security officer and, from what I learned later, that was probably a good thing, given that at the time he wasn't exactly a fan of the CIA director who happened, of course, to be my boss!

After Vice President Cheney was safely out of the country, I caught another USAF C-17 aircraft ride back to the US, but this time I planned ahead and brought a nice sleeping bag to keep me, and my feet, warm. When I returned stateside, I received a CIA Exceptional Performance Award and two Letters of Appreciation from the White House—one from the White House Communications Agency and the other a personal letter from Vice President Cheney himself thanking me for my assistance. A short time later I received an autographed photo of me shaking hands with him, definitely suitable for framing.

But I wasn't going to have a lot of time to look at it, since it wasn't long before I was sent back into the field in a zone that gave hot a whole new meaning.

25

South Asia • July 2006

In 2006, I had just started to enjoy my time back in DC and hoped to spend some time with my daughter when I became one of a number of Agency officers surged into South Asia as part of the US government's efforts to combat Al-Qaeda and find Osama bin Laden. I was given a directed assignment as Chief of Security in one of the South Asian countries, the same type of position I had filled in Southeast Asia before; but by no means was it the region where I wanted to work. I swallowed my disappointment, packed my bags, and left to support yet another group of third world countries.

As a Chief of Security in the region, I was responsible for assisting several Agency and other US government elements with the security of their operations and the protection of personnel, information, and facilities through appropriate threat-based risk analysis and the application of security processes, procedures, and equipment. I planned, implemented, and maintained countrywide integrated security programs in the fast-paced high terrorism and critical threat environments of South Asia ensuring the safety, security and accountability for all Agency personnel within the region.

South Asia had a long history of conflict, and I was going smack dab into the middle of one of its most violent moments. I knew that going in. I also received some pretty good briefings on all the complex pieces at play, which just made my job that much more difficult since sometimes too much information is worse than not enough. As Jose Rodriquez stated in his book *Hard Measures: How Aggressive CIA Actions After 9/11 Saved American Lives*, "As stressful as the lives of CTC personnel back in Langley were, that was nothing compared to the burden on officers on the front lines in Afghanistan, Pakistan, and hellholes around the world."

According to David Kilcullen, in his book, *The Accidental Guerrilla*, "during the 1980s, in the midst of the Soviet-Afghan War, the United States, the Pakistani intelligence service (the Inter-Services Intelligence Directorate, ISI), and groups like those supported by the young Saudi militant Osama bin Laden were running separate networks for the mujahidin from safe houses in different parts of Peshawar, then and now, a stronghold of insurgency and tribal warfare."

Al-Qaeda's presence was a long-standing phenomenon in the region. The Soviet invasion of Afghanistan in 1979 eventually brought up to twenty-five thousand Arabs to Afghanistan to fight on the side of the mujahideen. These included Osama bin Laden and the Maktab Khadamāt al-Mujāhidīn al-'Arab (Afghan Services Bureau), which he supported and eventually led, subsequently establishing the nucleus for Al-Qaeda. Apart from a few years in Saudi Arabia and Sudan in the 1990s, the Al-Qaeda leadership had been based in the Afghan-Pakistan frontier region for a generation, and the Arab *takfiri* (an "impure Muslim") presence in the Federally Administered Tribal Areas (FATA) in northwestern Pakistan had been nearly continuous. During the same time period, the Taliban originated in Afghan refugee camps in or near the FATA and grew through a network of tribal connections as well as support from ISI under successive Pakistani regimes, establishing a strong presence in the same areas.

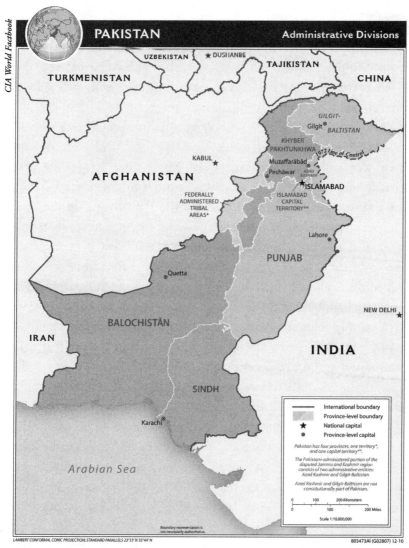

Map of Pakistan and Afghanistan.

Over that time, both Al-Qaeda and the Taliban as well as Al-Qaeda–allied foreign fighters that included Chechens, Uzbeks, Uighurs, and others, had burrowed deeply into tribal society through activities such as intermarriage with local tribes, co-opting of local

leaders, purchase and operation of businesses and other services, char-
ity activities, sponsorship or partnership with madrasas, and settling
of local disputes. Thus, by the turn of the twenty-first century, the
takfiri presence in the FATA was well established, with strong local
allies embedded into the fabric of local society.

The Karlani hill tribes of the Pashtun ethnic group were a harsh
people. Most men carried a rifle from boyhood, and women were
rarely seen and never heard in public. Fierce pride, unyielding self-
reliance, and exacting reciprocity (the Pashto word for revenge, *badal*,
can also mean exchange) were key assets in the struggle for life. The
hill tribes regarded warfare and pillaging as forms of extreme sport and
tribal solidarity, the code of Pashtunwali and sharia law being the only
standards that counted. The harshness with which men treated women
and adults exploited children was often astonishing and revolting to
outsiders, highlighting the insular nature of those people and illustrat-
ing a coming collision of cultures diametrically opposed to each other.

In July 2002, under strong pressure to support the international
community in the war on terrorism, the government of Pervez Musharraf deployed the Pakistani army into the Tirah Valley in upper
Khyber Province. The army's primary mission was to deal with Al-
Qaeda and Taliban remnants who had fled into Pakistan following
the fall of the Taliban regime and the escape of Al-Qaeda senior leaders after the Battle of Tora Bora (in the Spīn Ghar mountain range),
which had occurred in December 2001 on the Afghan side of the
frontier, about ten kilometers from the FATA. Following negotiations
with reluctant tribal leaders, the Pakistani army also entered North
Waziristan, and later South Waziristan, in a similar effort to mop up
Al-Qaeda and Taliban remnants.

Attempts to force the tribes to surrender foreign militants to the
government backfired badly, as did the heavy-handed military tactics,
so that by early 2004 the tribes were in open revolt across key parts of
the FATA in the largest tribal uprising since the Great Frontier War
more than a century earlier. Heavy fighting first erupted near Wana

in South Waziristan, leading to a major pitched battle in March 2004 between the Pakistani army and up to four hundred tribal fighters.

That meant the Pakistani army had broken the government's end of the deal in attempting, at the behest of *kafir* (unbelievers/non-Muslims) foreigners no less, to force the tribes to break two key tenets of Pashtunwali: *melmastia* (hospitality to a guest) and *nanawatei* (protection of a defeated combatant seeking refuge). Tribal honor and Islamic principle alike, especially the Koranic injunction against siding with any infidel against any fellow Muslim, combined to ensure that the tribal leaders would utterly reject the demands. The Pakistani army, remember, had first broken the deal, not the tribes, so why then should the tribes have remained quiet? By the end of 2004, the tribes were in a full, though undeclared, frontier revolt against the government. By early 2005, heavy army casualties in the FATA had forced the government to alter its strategy from confrontation to negotiation.

Al-Qaeda and other extremists moved into an already disrupted social framework in the FATA during and after the Soviet-Afghan war, worsening an existing problem of poor governance and societal weakness. A *Washington Post* article published in September 2007 stated that "counterterrorism officials were slow to grasp the resurrection of al-Qaeda Central. For years, many U.S. and European intelligence officials characterized it as a spent force, limited to providing inspiration for loosely affiliated regional networks. Bombings in Europe and the Middle East were blamed on homegrown cells of militants, operating independently of bin Laden."

On June 24, 2003, President Bush declared Al-Qaeda's leadership largely defunct. At a Camp David summit, Bush praised Pakistan's General Pervez Musharraf, crediting his country with apprehending more than five hundred members of Al-Qaeda and the Taliban. "Thanks to President Musharraf's leadership, on the Al-Qaeda front we've dismantled the chief operators," Bush said. Although bin Laden was still at large, his lieutenants "no longer posed a threat to the United States or Pakistan," the president added.

Six months later, Musharraf was nearly killed in an assassination attempt by Al-Qaeda operatives. Shortly afterward, a group of Al-Qaeda leaders held a summit of their own in the Pakistani region of Waziristan, where they plotted fresh attacks thousands of miles away, including targets in London and financial institutions in the United States, according to Pakistani officials.

Many US, Pakistani, and European intelligence officials by then agreed that Al-Qaeda's ability to launch operations around the globe hadn't diminished after the invasion of Afghanistan nearly as much as previously thought. Further investigation showed, for example, that Al-Qaeda's leadership, with bin Laden's direct blessing, made the decision to activate sleeper cells in Saudi Arabia in 2003, prompting a wave of car bombings and assassination attempts that the Saudi government has only recently brought under control.

From hideouts in Pakistan, according to court testimony and interviews, bin Laden's deputies ordered attacks on a Tunisian synagogue in 2002, a British consulate and bank in Istanbul in 2003, and the London transit system in 2005. US intelligence officials also blame the Al-Qaeda brain trust for orchestrating dozens of other failed plots, including a plan to blow up transatlantic flights from Britain in August 2006.

"All this business about them being isolated or cut off is whistling past the graveyard," Michael Scheuer, a former CIA analyst who led the Agency's unit assigned to track bin Laden, told the *Washington Post* in September of 2007. "We're looking at an organization that is extraordinarily adept at succession planning. They were built to survive, like the Afghans were against the Russians." Otherwise, the search for Al-Qaeda's leaders in Pakistan had hit a wall. Scheuer said information concerning their whereabouts had grown scarcer and less reliable. By his account, Pakistani security officials hadn't come across a single clue as to bin Laden's potential location in the tribal areas. Occasionally, they received tips regarding Ayman al-Zawahiri and others, according to Scheuer, but only several weeks after the trail had run cold.

In July 2007, US intelligence agencies published a report concluding that Al-Qaeda had regrouped in remote northwestern Pakistan, aided by a 2005 decision by the Pakistani government to declare a truce with Taliban forces and withdraw troops from the tribal area of Waziristan. Latif Afridi, a Pashtun tribal elder, said that many places along Pakistan's border with Afghanistan had been effectively taken over by foreign militants, mostly Uzbeks, Tajiks, Chechens, and Arabs. Although they weren't all associated with Al-Qaeda, bin Laden's network had been able to rely on them for protection.

"We have Al Qaeda, we have Taliban, we have foreigners, and we have Pakistani-trained militant groups that have been banned," Afridi said in an interview in Peshawar. "They're running the show."

Pakistani and US intelligence officials both reported that the number of militant training camps had surged along the border. But unlike Al-Qaeda's fixed camps in Afghanistan before 2001, they consisted of small groups that gathered for a few days for firearms or bomb-making practice before disbanding, making them hard to detect. The truce between the Taliban and the Pakistani military collapsed in North Waziristan in July and in South Waziristan a month later. Since then, Pakistani forces had reentered the tribal areas and resumed clashes with the Taliban and other militants.

According to an article by the *Guardian* in November of 2006, the Pakistani intelligence service was suspected of being complicit with the Taliban. Afghanistan president, Hamid Karzai, said Pakistan was up to its decades-old policy of dirty tricks and meddling in Afghan affairs.

Western military officials as well as the Rand Corporation, an American think-tank, believed the ISI was providing training, money, and sensitive information to the Taliban. Pakistan's history of instability and untrustworthiness is illustrated by the event on November 21, 1979, when a mob in the Pakistani capital, Islamabad, burned the US Embassy to the ground, killing a US Marine. The five-hour siege began as an organized student protest triggered by a radio report from the Iranian leader, Ayatollah Khomeini, saying Americans were behind the occupation of Islam's holiest site, the Great Mosque in Mecca, Saudi Arabia, on November 20, 1979.

And that was just the beginning.

Nearly a generation later, on January 23, 2002, American journalist Daniel Pearl was kidnapped and murdered in Karachi. Pearl was investigating alleged connections between a radical Pakistani cleric and Richard Reid, who had attempted to detonate a bomb hidden in his shoe on a transatlantic flight in December 2001. Evidence showed that Pearl was abducted and then killed by Khalid Sheikh Mohammed (KSM), the self-described mastermind of the 9/11 attacks. KSM, who remains incarcerated at the US detention center at Guantanamo Bay, Cuba, admitted at a military hearing in 2007 that he had killed Pearl.

On March 17, 2002, in Islamabad, an unknown assailant exploded three grenades inside a church near the US Embassy. Five people were killed, including a US Embassy employee and her daughter. More than forty persons, including thirteen Americans, were injured.

On May 8, 2002, nine French nationals and five Pakistanis, including a suspected suicide bomber, were killed and thirty-four more injured in a bomb explosion inside a bus opposite the Sheraton Hotel, Karachi.

On June 14, 2002, also in Karachi, another suicide bomber detonated a large truck bomb fifty feet from the US Consulate. The blast killed twelve persons and injured more than fifty, including a US Marine, and knocked down a twelve-foot section of the facility's concrete-reinforced perimeter wall.

On February 28, 2003, two Pakistani policemen were shot dead outside the United States Consulate in Karachi, the same place where twelve people were killed by a truck bomb eight months earlier.

On May 26, 2004, two car bombs exploded within twenty minutes of each other outside the Pakistan-American Cultural Center and near the US consul general's residence in Karachi, killing two men and injuring more than twenty-seven people, mainly policemen and journalists.

On October 28, 2004, an explosion occurred inside the lobby of the Marriott Hotel in Islamabad. The Pakistani government was quick to report that the blast was the result of a short circuit in the hotel's electrical system and that there was no sign of militant activity. However, the facts on the ground indicated the blast was more likely caused by a sophisticated improvised explosive device, having caused severe damage to the hotel lobby and destroyed the X-ray machine at the security station. Nearly all windows on the ground floor of the hotel were shattered by the blast. Flying glass caused a number of injuries; protective Mylar film was reportedly covering at least some of the windows and might have decreased the total number of casualties. Eight people were wounded in the blast, including one US diplomat and two Marriott hotel employees.

On May 27, 2005, at least twenty-five people, including a suspected suicide bomber, were killed and approximately a hundred others sustained injuries during a powerful explosion at the Bari Imam shrine of the Shia sect located in the vicinity of the diplomatic enclave in Islamabad.

On March 2, 2006, a US diplomat, his Pakistani driver, and an Army Ranger official were killed and fifty-four people injured in a suicide car bombing near the US Consulate in Karachi, a day before President George W. Bush came to Pakistan for a visit.

Also on March 2, 2006, in Karachi, a suicide bomber detonated a vehicle filled with explosives outside the US Consulate as an armored consulate vehicle passed by, killing a US diplomat and his driver.

That gives you a clearer picture of the maelstrom that was ongoing in Pakistan, something I would have to confront firsthand as a security officer surged to the region. And just when you think things can't get any worse....

26

Islamabad, Pakistan • July 2006

I can tell you that things had not gotten better since June 2003 when President Bush had declared Al-Qaeda "defunct." An article was published in the *Christian Science Monitor* describing how it was for US personnel working at the embassy in Islamabad. Titled "The U.S. Embassy in Pakistan: Fortress Against Terror Threats," the article described how Pakistan might well have been the most dangerous posting in the world for American diplomats.

The routine attacks and constant threats—intelligence officials and diplomatic security staff often analyzed as many as five a day turned the U.S. installations there into virtual fortresses. The sprawling compound in Islamabad was surrounded by thick brick ramparts topped with razor wire and reinforced by steel pillars to keep a vehicle from smashing through. Staff members were trained to check their cars for bombs and their residences for suspicious behavior. The embassy staff drilled routinely, practicing scenarios that ranged from car bombs to a sudden attack by an angry mob.

I was lucky that a friend of mine who I'd previously worked with at headquarters was also "drafted" onto the South Asia team. Dave Burkstrom was a Directorate of Operations (DO) Targeting Officer.

Targeting Officers are integral to the planning and implementation of DO foreign intelligence collection, counterintelligence, and covert action operations. They combine specialized training, advanced analytical skills, the most sophisticated analytical tools available, and in-depth knowledge and experience in DO operational tradecraft. They help find people, relationships, and organizations having access to the information needed to address the most critical US foreign intelligence requirements and find opportunities to disrupt terrorist attacks, illegal arms trade, drug networks, cyber threats, and counterintelligence threats.

As part of my duties, I directed a security staff composed of staff security officers and personnel accountability section officers, and we were responsible for providing security support for hundreds of officers working in multiple locations. I coordinated all emergency management planning and response, to include personnel accountability, emergency action, and evacuation to ensure the safety and security of all Agency personnel in the various countries.

As one of the senior security officers in the region, I also enjoyed overall cognizance over POC teams working at several sites. The POC country team leader managed the day-to-day operations of the POC, coordinating with the individual team leaders at every location where the POC was operating.

My days were filled with the sound of beeping radios, ringing phones, and constant updates from the field. There were times when I felt that even if I had cloned myself ten times over I would still be shorthanded.

If that wasn't enough, as in Iraq, I had to travel to different locations where I mainly focused on security policies and processes, updating emergency action plans and accountability procedures, and assessing physical security needs. Sometimes I would travel with a security technician who'd install cameras, locks, and other security hardware.

For the bases that were not located in major cities, I'd have to make do with whatever transportation was available. For example, when I was in Pakistan and had to travel outside the major cities, the only available transportation was via Pakistani military helicopters, specifically Russian-built Mi-17s. The ones flying in Pakistan had seen better days, but they were easy to maintain and thankfully not too difficult to fly, given that the Pakistani pilots were not very good. We nicknamed the pilots "Seagulls," because you had to virtually throw a rock at them to make them fly. They were so limited in their skills that we were grounded in any sort of bad weather or at night.

To get a ride on the helicopters the Pakistanis required that we try to blend in, so we had to dress like the locals. When moving around the interior of Pakistan, I wore local attire, the *shalwar kameez*—which consisted of string-tied, loose-fitting pants and baggy shirts. We had a local tailor make ours so we could add belt loops for our duty belts. We always wore jeans or some type of battle dress uniform/tactical pants under the baggy pants, as we still needed to travel with our sidearms and long guns. We topped off the look with a local hat. With my dark skin tone, the only thing missing was a mustache or beard and I would've been able to double for a Pakistani man.

Unlike our embassy in Afghanistan, the US Embassy in Islamabad had a very nice club with a restaurant and a bar, where most people congregated after work hours. When people went out "on the economy," a catchphrase for going out into the local areas, there were a variety of restaurants but no bars. Besides eating there was always shopping, and the biggest things selling in Pakistan were the rugs that could be had for a decent price, if you were a good haggler. Every couple of weeks, the embassy would invite local craftsmen onto the compound to sell their wares.

There were also good deals to be had for clothing. The Pakistani tailor shops, while not Savile Row, could custom-tailor suits, shirts, and dresses. I liked the leather shops, where you could get a custom-sized leather jacket for about one hundred dollars, a virtual steal. One other shop of note was the one we nicknamed the "North Fake" store, because it specialized in knockoff North Face clothing. Word had got out to the point that when US government officials visited Islamabad, they'd inevitably request to go shop for a rug and to visit the North Fake store.

The embassy softball field was decent, and there was a softball league with games scheduled on the weekends. These were just for fun, as most of the personnel assigned to the embassy were not highly skilled at the sport. It broke up the monotony of work and gave them something to do to let off a little steam. There was also a swimming pool, weight room, and a running track. To keep in shape and deal with the stress of the job, many officers made good use of both the weight room and the track.

I corresponded regularly with the RSOs in the area, especially the one in Islamabad. I even attended his weekly meetings when I was in town to keep in sync with threat reporting. In my role I also functioned as a focal point for a number of other government agencies such as the FBI (in the diplomatic world, they were called legal attachés), the defense attaché's office (the US military's representative at the embassy), and the Homeland Security office. Due to the possible threat of being overrun again by Pakistani protestors, I assisted the RSO in Islamabad with creating an embassy defense plan that laid out how the armed elements within the embassy would work under the RSO if an attack occurred.

Because South Asia, especially Pakistan, was a popular spot for VIP visits, I assisted the various locations by helping them coordinate protective operations support for the large number of visiting VIPs that included the vice president, the Director of National Intelligence (DNI), the directors of the CIA, FBI, and NSA, as well as Senate and congressional delegations. These visits required intense coordination between all the embassy security elements and, on many occasions, the POC teams played a pivotal role in the visits due to their superior knowledge of the terrain, their ability to move around relatively unnoticed, and the fact that we had some of the best armored cars in the region.

CIA Director's Challenge Coin for providing protective operations support to his visit to Islamabad, Pakistan.

Due to the size of some of the delegations, I personally worked side by side with my POC personnel, providing protective operations support to the CIA director's visit, including conducting site advances and surveys, as well as driving one of the motorcade vehicles myself. I have to admit it was always fun to be back working in the field! In recognition of one of my POC country team leader's superb leadership and operational abilities, I nominated him for a Directorate of Support Leadership Award.

In this world, credit goes where credit is due.

* * *

Mid-afternoon on January 26, 2007, I was in the office working on the normal status reports and administrative paperwork that fills the gap between real work and minutia. My telephone rang and, from the other end of the line, the RSO in Islamabad notified me that there had been some sort of explosion at the Marriott Hotel. He had no other details, but promised me an update as soon as he got more. I assured him that I would do the same if I got any info.

The Marriott Hotel was one of two major hotels in Islamabad and was located in one of the nicer neighborhoods, close to some of the major Pakistani government buildings. It was one of the hotels that catered to media that were always around trying to dig up stories on the various conflicts in Pakistan but, in many ways, reporters were an endangered species in South Asia, especially in Pakistan. Many had already been killed, including Daniel Pearl, and I had no idea how those people could endure in those environments with just a microphone to protect themselves.

The Marriott Hotel chain had been a major terrorist target for many years, as it seemed to represent the Western world. And this particular hotel was no different. It had already been targeted by terrorists in 2001 when an improvised explosive device detonated in the lobby, and it appeared the Marriot had gotten hit again.

After getting off the phone with the RSO, I immediately notified my PAS units and had them begin an accountability drill through select security elements so that we could acquire more hands-on intelligence. I went and briefed my senior management and then it was back to the PAS office to monitor, document, and advise as required.

Meanwhile, the details were falling into place. At approximately 2:37 p.m. local time, a suicide bomber attempted to gain access to the Islamabad Marriott Hotel through a side entrance instead of taking a more direct approach through the front lobby that was better guarded, since the hotel had been alerted important visitors were expected to be arriving. The Indian High Commission was scheduled to hold a Republic Day function at the hotel that would have brought a number of Indian dignitaries to the location.

The bomber was trying to break his way into the lightly trafficked side entrance when one of the local Marriott parking lot security officers saw him. The officer rushed over to the side of the building and confronted the bomber. A struggle ensued and the bomber detonated his vest, killing the guard and injuring at least six people.

Though a lot less impactful thanks to the brave actions of the officer, the incident still hit close to home, as there were more than fifty US Embassy personnel staying in the hotel at the time.

That Marriott parking lot security guard who'd saved the day made the equivalent of about thirty-five cents an hour, and he left a pregnant wife and two children behind. I used that as a lesson during my security briefings: be nice to the local guards, as they may be the only thing between you and a suicide bomber.

When I was finally wrapping up my reports, I noticed a note that had been placed on my desk.

Call home asap!

It had been sitting on my desk all day. One of my PAS officers had been meaning to bring it to me but hadn't gotten to it amid the frenetic response to the bombing. Jennie, the department receptionist, came walking up to me just as I was sitting down.

"Hey, Tom. How are things at the Marriott?" she asked, fiddling with the Post-it Note between her fingers.

"Okay. Only one casualty besides the bomber. Everyone else will make it," I told her.

"That's good. I know things are crazy busy here and it is bad timing, but your stepbrother called *again*. He sounded *really* upset," Jennie said. "You should probably call him."

"Thanks, Jennie," I said, taking the note from her nervous hands.

Jennie didn't leave. I tried to gesture her away with a gentle head twitch, but she stood in place. She gestured back toward the phone. I picked up the receiver. She smiled at me and turned and walked away. I guess Jennie won that round. I dialed my stepbrother's cell phone.

It rang and rang.

"Hello?" my stepbrother Dave greeted finally.

"Hi, Dave. It's Tom."

"Tom…"

"Is something wrong? Everything okay? I was told you called several times. I'm sorry I didn't get back to you, but we were dealing with…"

"Tom, you need to come home," Dave interrupted. "Richard [my stepfather] has been diagnosed with terminal cancer and he doesn't have much time."

I felt my stomach sink. "Dave, I'll be on the first flight available." Things had gone from bad to worse.

27

Milwaukee, Wisconsin ▪ January 2007

I was in Milwaukee two days later. My stepdad Richard had helped raise me from the time I was twelve years old. He was as much of a father to me as my biological father. I caught a cab from the airport and arrived at the family home, where I'd lived my entire life until I moved to Washington to join the Agency.

Going up the front walk was surprisingly difficult. To have come that far so fast and then to have trouble walking the last few steps.... I knew it was my not wanting to face the fact that Richard was dying.

I was surprised it was my stepbrother Dave, himself, who answered the door. Over a cup of coffee, he filled me in on the prognosis and the general plan. Hospice care had already been arranged, but they weren't round the clock—yet. Dave had been in town for a week, and it looked like the burden was getting to him. Richard was still ambulatory with a little help, and he was sleeping in his room upstairs. I went up to see him and he was awake. The walls in the old house were so thin that he'd heard me downstairs.

"Hi, Tom. How are you doing," my stepfather asked, his voice sounding slightly raspy but still strong.

312

"I'm okay." I wanted to ask him how he was doing but stopped short, since his answer could only be bad for both of us. "Dave told me the news," I continued instead. "I'm just glad I'm here."

"Me too. Take a seat."

That day, things took a turn for the worse. Richard couldn't make it down the stairs on his own, and he grew weaker and weaker. Hospice nurses did their usual incredible job helping everyone. We watched some television. Talked about what was on the news. I watched him sleep, a lot. I got a few calls from my friends in Milwaukee once the news went out that I was in town, but I didn't see any of them.

Even though I knew I'd made it home while he was still coherent and had some energy, I also knew that my time was running out. I'd promised to try and get back to South Asia as soon as possible, since there was no replacement or even a temporary officer available and the threat level was through the roof. The safety of everyone there was my responsibility until the day my tour ended, and I couldn't help them from Milwaukee. Nor could I help my stepfather.

"You should go back now," Dave said. "I have all the help I need, and you were here when I really needed the support. They need you back there more than I do, more than Dad does."

The morning I left, Richard was sitting up in a chair by the front windows, waiting for one of his old buddies to stop by. My cab pulled up and when I gave him a hug, he whispered to me, "Come home when you can."

Those were the last words he said to me.

South Asia • January 2007

I didn't think the region could ever be any more of a shit show than it was before I left, but escalation across the board awaited me upon my return. It was as if the devil himself was in South Asia stirring the pot. Besides all of the US military activities in Afghanistan, the threat level in Pakistan remained extremely high as local insurgents were blowing themselves up within Islamabad in an effort to kill off rival groups and select politicians. Being in the wrong place at the wrong time was a serious issue.

In February 2007, a suicide bomber detonated his explosives in a parking area outside the Islamabad International Airport, injuring five people. A few months later, at least seventeen people were killed and fifty injured as a suicide bomber blew himself up outside the venue of the district bar council convention in Islamabad, killing mostly political workers waiting for the arrival of Pakistan's chief justice, who was to address a lawyer's convention. That's just to name two of many incidents.

Meanwhile, US relations with our Pakistani counterparts from the Inter-Services Intelligence (ISI) showed increasing strain as trust continued to deteriorate. "The loyalties of the ISI will probably always be suspect from an American perspective," Jose Rodriguez wrote in the previously cited *Hard Measures*. "How much ISI officers knew about Bin Ladin's [sic] whereabouts had always been hotly debated."

Fast-forwarding to 2012, the movie *Zero Dark Thirty* portrayed a lot of CIA activities in Pakistan. Let's just say I found it was very helpful for non-CIA people to understand the events that led to the final assault on bin Laden's compound in Pakistan. In a statement to CIA employees, Acting Director Michael Morell wrote, "The hunt for Osama Bin Ladin was a decade-long effort that depended on the selfless commitment of hundreds of officers. The filmmakers attributed the actions of our entire Agency—and the broader Intelligence Community—to just a few individuals. This may make for more compelling entertainment, but it does not reflect the facts. The success of the 01 May 2011 operation was a team effort—and a very large team at that."

Back in the region, I had just gotten through a very long day. After reviewing reports about a series of suicide bombings and political shootings in Islamabad, I finally left my PAS office and made my way back to my desk. I fell into my office chair. It felt good just to sit down. It felt like I hadn't sat down in almost sixteen hours. My feet hurt, my body ached, and I was exhausted, but I still had to finish up writing the incident reports for the day. I pulled my chair into the desk and saw a sticky note stuck onto my computer:

CALL HOME.

This time I called immediately. I knew.

My stepfather Richard had passed away. I knew when I left Milwaukee that it would be the last time I was going to see him alive. I called my stepbrother Dave and he answered on the first ring. He told me I'd missed a hell of a party. Richard had all his old buddies over to the house, and they told stories until late that night. It was a great send-off. He died peacefully in his sleep a few days later. Dave had been in no rush to tell me to avoid making me feel guilty over what he knew would be my inability to fly across the world a second time in so short a period. Richard also wouldn't have wanted to risk distracting me while I was in the middle of so much danger.

I was glad I could make it back to see my stepfather before he died. I would mourn him in my own way and in my own time. At that point, the CIA was hunting the number one terrorist our world had ever known, and I was at the forefront of keeping the hunters safe. I had to focus on what I could control, not what I couldn't.

Islamabad, Pakistan • July 2007

It was early morning when word reached me that the Pakistani military and police had begun laying siege to the Lal Masjid, the Red Mosque and the madrasa (school) associated with it. The Red Mosque had been taken over by Islamic militants who advocated the imposition of *Sharia* (Islamic religious law) in Pakistan and openly called for the overthrow of the Pakistani government. The congregants of Lal Masjid had been in constant conflict with authorities in Islamabad for the past eighteen months, engaging in violent demonstrations, destruction of property, kidnapping, arson, and armed clashes with

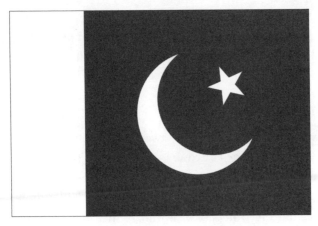

Flag of Pakistan.

the authorities. After Lal Masjid militants set fire to the Ministry of Environment building and attacked the Pakistani Army Rangers guarding it, the military finally responded and the siege of the Lal Masjid complex began.

Due to an acute housing shortage on the US Embassy compound, embassy employees had been living in rented houses and guesthouses all over the city of Islamabad. Several of the residences were close to the Lal Masjid complex, and it became immediately apparent that we needed to help the embassy evacuate those people to safer locations. After gathering as much information as possible about Pakistani troop placement and activities, security elements conducted both a map review and actual route reconnaissance to determine the best course of action. All of the affected personnel were contacted and given orders to get ready to move and then, with as little fanfare as possible (read low profile), RSO and POC teams swooped in and got all of the US Embassy people out. They used specific routes out of the area to avoid contact with itchy-fingered Pakistani troops manning roadblocks and conducting house-to-house searches.

The Lal Masjid complex was besieged for eight days while negotiations continued between the militants and Pakistani authorities. Once negotiations failed, the complex was stormed and captured by the Pakistan Army's Special Service Group. The government reported that the operation resulted in 154 deaths, and 50 militants were captured (other estimates were higher). It also prompted pro-Taliban rebels along the Afghan border to nullify a ten-month-old peace agreement with the Pakistani government, triggering the third phase of the Waziristan War, which marked another surge in militancy and violence in Pakistan and resulted in more than 3,000 casualties.

I felt like I was on a merry-go-round that just kept spinning faster and faster.

September 2007

Another event of significance was the declaration of martial law in Islamabad that resulted in all cellular and landline telephone service being cut. US Embassy operations ground to a halt. Personnel were restricted to their residences, except for those with specific intelligence and operational assignments, that is. We had to ramp up to gather intelligence on the situation in Islamabad and across the country. Having worked in a variety of harsh environments, I was experienced with the trials and tribulations that came with breakdown of communications equipment and networks.

As the explosive ordnance disposal experts used to quote, "One is none, and two is one." Meaning that if you rely on only one piece of equipment, you're in trouble. Upon my arrival in the region back in 2006, I had assessed the emergency communications equipment we were using and quickly realized that we had begun to rely solely on cellular and landline telephones. While relatively reliable, the devices are also completely controlled by the local governments and, as history has shown, in an emergency the cellular system would quickly become inundated if the population panicked and flooded the system with calls and text messages. This phenomenon has been experienced in far more modern countries than Pakistan, even New York City on 9/11, for obvious reasons.

I had immediately begun to explore options for our locations. To my delight, I discovered that in many locations we had handheld push-to-talk (PTT) radio systems—what we as kids called walkie-talkies! But in some locations, such as Islamabad, they were in disrepair. I arranged for repairs to the repeater system and upgrading of the base station, then had additional radios purchased. The process took more than six months, but it was well worth the effort because the system was available when it was needed most, providing a means for us to communicate from the moment martial law was declared and the Pakistani government shut down all landline telephones and cellular networks. Security officers and diplomatic personnel were able to communicate and collect information using the handheld PTT radios they were issued in anticipation of just that type of action by the host government.

A week later, meanwhile, marked the official end of my tour as Chief of Security. From South Asia I flew directly to Bangkok, Thailand, to visit my cousin who was living and working there. We hit the beach and I began my decompression cycle, slowly getting rid of the stress that came with working in a position of serious responsibility in a high-threat environment.

During those types of tours, you have to stay focused on the mission and keep your mind off nonessential issues. Compartmentalizing was a skill I'd learned early in my career and, while it was extremely useful, it came with a price. It was after my tour in South Asia had concluded that I realized how much I had sacrificed to protect the Agency people in the region—going as far as to let the mission overshadow my familial responsibilities, something that made me begin to question the priorities the job imposed upon me.

Although I have no regrets whatsoever about my service, at a certain point you need to put yourself and your family first. It took me years to understand what an Agency psychologist meant when she told me, "It's not your job to save them all."

That hadn't stopped me from trying, but it was time to go home.

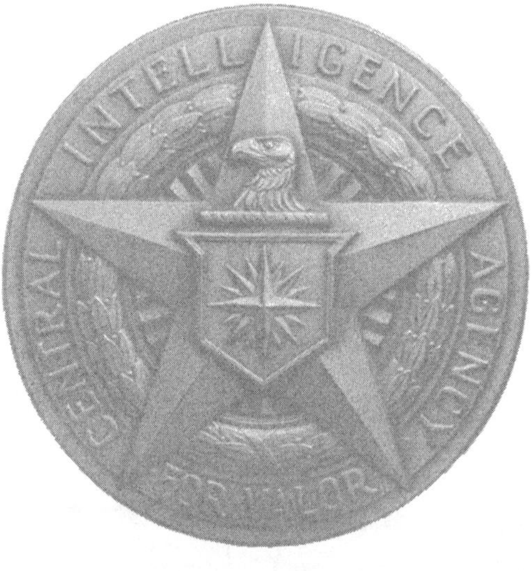

PART FIVE

THE HOME FRONT

28

National Reconnaissance Office ▪ July 2008

After I left South Asia, I reported back to CIA HQS where I applied for and was selected to be the director of security for a National Reconnaissance Office (NRO) Mission Ground Station (MGS). The NRO is one of fourteen members of the United States intelligence community. Headquartered in Chantilly, Virginia, the agency develops and operates unique and innovative overhead reconnaissance systems and conducts intelligence-related activities for US national security. It was established in 1960 and was classified from its inception in 1961 until it was declassified to the public in 1992. It remains a lesser-known agency, while maintaining responsibility for designing, building, launching, and maintaining America's intelligence satellites. Its motto is *Supra Et Ultra*: "Above and Beyond." The director of the NRO reports to the secretary of defense, who, in concert with the Director of National Intelligence (DNI), has ultimate management and operational responsibility.

The NRO maintains Mission Ground Stations in several locations within the United States and also maintains a presence at facilities in Australia and the United Kingdom. A hybrid organization consisting of some three thousand personnel, the NRO is jointly staffed by members of the armed services, the Central Intelligence Agency, and Department of Defense civilian personnel.

An example of some of the critical support that the NRO provides the US military was illustrated during a speech on April 21, 2010, by Ms. Betty Sapp. In her capacity as NRO director, she described an incident to the House Armed Services Committee Subcommittee on Strategic Forces that occurred on March 2010, when a helicopter from the 101st Airborne Aviation Brigade went down in a remote location near a forward operating base (FOB) in Zabul Province, Afghanistan. With no available organic ISR (intelligence, surveillance, and reconnaissance) assets due to the FOB's remote location, weather, and other tasking priorities, the brigade's intelligence staff requested immediate imagery assistance from a combined NRO/National Geo-spatial-Intelligence Agency (NGA) cell. This cell was able to rapidly provide multiple images of the area, which enabled the brigade to quickly assess the situation and secure a new perimeter around the crash site. Key imagery intelligence was provided to the operations and rescue teams within minutes, with the end result being the safe rescue of fourteen wounded soldiers and the crash site secured and protected. One of the intelligence officers from the brigade relayed to the NRO the following after this mission: "I wanted to pass on my sincere thanks for your support that night. An aircraft down is one of the worst things we can experience as a unit and your timely imagery support was pivotal to our rescue teams."

After spending several months at the NRO headquarters in Chantilly, getting to know the vocabulary and unique security issues associated with the agency, I left for my new job.

* * *

I was excited about taking on the domestic assignment with the NRO for a number of reasons. First, it was nice to be back in the United States. Second, the NRO Mission Ground Station where I was to

Logo for the National Reconnaissance Office (NRO).

work was located in a great location, and the people in the area were some of the nicest I have met outside of my hometown of Milwaukee. It was also in a state that generally valued physical fitness, with residents across the board heavily involved in fitness, outdoor activities, and healthy lifestyles.

I felt the assignment had enough challenges that I wouldn't feel deskbound all day. Yet, at the same time I was on domestic soil, so I didn't have to worry about being blown up just for going out and grabbing a cup of coffee; quite a relief from the lifestyle I'd grown accustomed to over so many years in the field.

I chose to live in the downtown area so that I'd have a nice reverse commute of about thirty minutes with little traffic in the morning, but at night the commute would be closer to fifty. I was fine with the driving, as unlike when I drove to work in the war zones, I didn't have to worry about a terrorist trying to blow me up or shoot me. The time in the car also allowed me to decompress from all of the issues at the office.

Typically, when I was on assignment I had to have my guard up at all times, as complacency in a war zone is potentially deadly. People living in the United States enjoy a level of safety almost incomprehensible for most people on the planet. In the US, most people simply don't realize what has to happen in the background so that they can sedately drive to work, take their kids to school, and go out for dinner with hardly a thought about their safety. There has to be someone on that "wall" 24/7, and, in my new assignment, I was taking advantage of the fact that there were people other than me making that possible—police officers, EMTs, firefighters, and other public servants who keep us safe and help when tragedy strikes.

That isn't how the rest of the world operates; in fact, I've spent an enormous amount of time in countries with police who are as dangerous as the criminals they're supposed to be working against. Public security apparatuses were often underfunded, undertrained, and barely able to respond adequately to a hard rainstorm.

Even when off duty in the stateside NRO position, it took a lot of effort for me to adjust to being home. I had to consciously work on relaxing and dialing back my awareness level, keeping it from revving into the red. Locally, Mission Ground Stations were called Aerospace Data Facilities (ADFs), and these ADFs were often the main tenant on a US government site or military base. MGSs were responsible for the command and control of reconnaissance satellites involved in the collection of intelligence information and the dissemination of that intelligence to other US government agencies.

Three months into my tour, my position was renamed to Chief of Security.

The first thing you see when you visit a MGS/ADF site are the large radomes, structures that cover the satellite dishes to protect them from the elements and that resemble large golf balls. The ADF to which I was assigned featured a large compound with several buildings, along with the radomes, and was located on a US military base. Military "security police" forces provided security for the base as well as the outer perimeter of the ADF.

At the ADF, I led a large staff charged with providing security management for what was the NRO's largest mission ground station supporting complex operational, physical, and personnel security and safety programs for several thousand employees and a multibillion-dollar facility with an exorbitant annual security budget.

The security division consisted of four branches with a large workforce that included staff officers from the NRO, NSA, NGA, and US military, as well as industrial contractors. This included a contractor guard force that provided 24/7 access control and emergency medical response. Seventy percent of the ADF workforce was composed of contractors who were dedicated to supporting operations while managing multiple competing priorities, tasking and programming initiatives from senior officials in the various intelligence and military agencies.

After a week in the position, I was informed that I was the Workplace Violence Assessment Team (WVAT) chair. I had no idea what that entailed and had to make a visit to the human resources office to find out what responsibilities were associated with the position. It turned out that I was responsible for investigating allegations of workplace violence/hostile workplace and implementing appropriate actions in accordance with approved NRO policies.

Looking at the policy documents associated with the new posting, I quickly realized that I was not in a good position to do the job, given that there were a total of two pages of guidance and procedures on the complex issue, not to mention the liability for actions that I would be forced to take to protect the workforce. I did some research, consulted with other agencies, and then revamped the Workplace Violence Prevention Program (WVPP) policies and procedures, actions that were fully supported by the site management as well as relevant officials back at NRO headquarters. Then, in reaction to the terrorist attacks in Mumbai, India, in 2008 and at Fort Hood, Texas, in 2009, I began an effort to modernize the NRO's emergency response to an armed threat incident (active shooter) by sponsoring a training class with an expert in workplace violence and the active shooter phenomena. I don't think I've ever quite gotten over being on duty when Mir Amal Kasi attacked our personnel outside CIA Headquarters in Langley, and that was as close as I'd ever get to slaying that particular dragon.

The deep dive into the active shooter phenomena reinforced another one of my leadership principles: creating strong cross-functional relationships. Specifically, this principle focuses on the need to proactively develop relationships across organizations to enhance cooperation. This is critical prior to an incident; indeed, it's much better to get to know someone before you are in the middle of a crisis.

In 2008, the ADF I was assigned to received recognition from the Director of National Intelligence with the 2008 DNI National Intelligence Award for Collaborative Leadership in a clear statement of the ADF's excellence. Specifically, to quote the award, "The Aerospace Data Facility has established itself as the Intelligence Community leader for guiding and institutionalizing a culture of collaboration and information sharing between these IC agencies, Department of Defense personnel, foreign mission partners and a global customer set."

That climate of collaboration was one of my biggest challenges, as I was responsible for providing security support for the more than forty thousand annual visitors as well as protective operations support to multiple protective details from the intelligence community leadership and US military leadership, including the chairman of the Joint Chiefs of Staff, during their site visits.

The visits required extremely close coordination with the security elements for the various organizations and the associated support work to ensure their visits were not only secure but seamless. My protective operations background was put to good use, since I was more than familiar with the requirements of the protection details for those guests.

Although we were not in Afghanistan or Iraq, the senior-level leaders still required well-thought-out protective plans and support that took into account any local threats. This meant close coordination with US military security elements at the base, as there was a very strict policy of no admittance without prior notice and coordination. I also had to constantly be sure that I was up to speed on any possible local threats, to include protest groups, criminal elements, and even the weather. My security team made it exceedingly easy for all visitors, but especially VIPs, to visit our site—instilling confidence that we had their back, something I was very much used to.

* * *

The security team achieved NRO senior leadership attention when it won *ADF Team of the Year* in recognition of the close working relationship between the contractor and government staff along with the resulting improvements to security services site-wide.

I'm convinced that the award was the result of the hard work of my predecessor, who laid the groundwork that enabled me to begin to establish a better working relationship with all the contract companies that were a part of my workforce. I was successful in motivating high levels of performance from those people just by showing my appreciation for their hard work. I took every opportunity to announce the great job people were doing at the site, and then followed up with a letter to the individual as well as a letter/email to the most senior person I knew in their home organization. I also made sure that my upper management knew who was behind every successful project, every crisis handled, and every good deed done. Only by acknowledging the success of my subordinates could I truly show the appreciation I felt for the hard work they did.

The backside of this was to take responsibility for any failings that occured as a result of honest mistakes with no attribution to the employee. The buck always stops with the boss. That is an example of yet another leadership principle I learned over the years: show appreciation.

The only way to succeed in such a complicated environment was by working closely with host government security and intelligence organizations, applying many of the same principles learned in the field to my work back in the homeland. That allowed the development of new security and law enforcement partnerships to significantly improve insight into potential terrorist and counterintelligence threats to the facility. I made sure I attended the monthly US military security meetings, coordinating closely with the two military investigative agencies, the Air Force Office of Special Investigations (OSI) and the Naval Criminal Investigative Service (NCIS). I also worked closely with the FBI as a member of the Joint Terrorism Task Force. This was another example of the importance of the leadership principle of developing cross-functional horizontal relationships.

Due to my large staff at the ADF and my role as a member of the support staff leadership team, I worked closely with the human resources department to provide leadership training and personality assessment testing for junior officers, especially through the use of the Myers-Briggs Type Indicator, to help them determine personality preferences and maximize their effectiveness. It was the first chance I had to take advantage of some of those advanced human resources services. I found that the personality tests, especially the Myers-Briggs, were invaluable for determining personality type and inclinations. By knowing what your personality preferences were, along with the inherent strengths and weaknesses of those preferences, you were better able to capitalize on your abilities, mitigate your weaknesses, and understand how to work with other people's preferences. This had a huge impact on my security team, and it is why I consider the use of the personality tests an essential part of the leadership process and yet another of my leadership principles: know thyself.

Some of the things I was proud of accomplishing while at the ADF included developing/implementing a five-year strategic plan, creating a site-specific customer service training course for support personnel, and launching a first-ever customer service survey to assess customers' perceptions of the level of service provided to them. In many ways I felt that my tour at the ADF was one of the most fulfilling management positions of my career due to the support I received from senior leadership.

* * *

In February 2009, I learned my biological father was having some health issues. He had been living with Parkinson's disease for the past seventeen years, and it had finally begun taking its toll. He eventually had to get off all the Parkinson's medication, which left him physically disabled. He ended up having to go into a nursing home to get the care he needed. My stepmother was there every day to visit him at what my dad called "the Prison Camp." Throughout the ordeal, he kept his sense of humor, amusing the nursing staff with his jokes. I remember visiting him one morning.

"Hi, Dad. How are you doing? Did you get your breakfast?"

"You don't work—you don't eat!" my father responded.

A joke from the old days; he had one for almost any occasion. My brothers and I laugh and tell people that our warped sense of humor is genetic—we got it from our father.

My father's condition worsened; then the dementia really kicked in and he mostly lapsed into silence. I was able to visit him several times over the course of three months, and was in Milwaukee for a week before he passed away. It was a devastating blow to my stepmother and very rough on my brothers and me. I returned to work heavyhearted but content with the fact that I'd seen so much of him before he passed.

You may think that with all the stress and danger I'd experienced, I'd be somehow hardened to tragedy and loss, so numbed by all my service that I couldn't feel pain anymore. I actually believe the opposite is closer to the truth. Witnessing the loss of lives and fearing you may be next heightened my appreciation for the sanctity and value of human life. I realized how truly important our loved ones are, because you never know how long you'll have them. I think death actually hit me harder then, given that my respect for life was so high.

I'd lost my father and my stepfather in a relatively short span, something that whatever success I'd achieved in my latest posting couldn't compensate for. I thought I'd broken Thomas Wolfe's oft-repeated axiom that "you can't go home again." Come to find out, while I *could*, death kept chasing me down.

September 10, 2009

The worldwide threat level rises each year on the anniversary of 9/11. On that day, no matter where I am, I take extra precautions to keep my people safe. That year, at my new posting I worked closely with US military security and other base elements as well as my own ADF security personnel to raise awareness levels and implement some enhanced security procedures.

While in the middle of a normal workday, I was approached by a senior manager at the ADF about a possible threat. According to sources in the Washington, DC, area, there was an individual under investigation by the FBI for having terrorist contacts in Pakistan and who was suspected of being self-radicalized. The next day, September 11, 2009, I received some additional open press reporting about a possible terrorist plot, but because it was the anniversary of the attack on the World Trade Center, those generalized threats were hardly unexpected. Due to the lack of any intelligence received through approved official channels, neither the base nor the ADF could act to initiate enhanced force protection protocols. With no specific threat data, I could only discuss standard precautions with base and ADF senior management. I also tasked my ADF security personnel to be especially diligent during that period. Nothing occurred and the time passed peacefully, but always better to be safe than sorry.

Then, on September 19, some disturbing news broke. A suspected terrorist named Najibullah Zazi had been arrested. According to press reports, he had purchased large quantities of components necessary to produce TATP (an explosive) and proceeded to construct a bomb in a hotel room. Bomb-making residue was found in the room that Zazi used, and he later confessed that he planned to set off the bombs in Manhattan subway lines as soon as they were ready.

I pursued the information with the Air Force Office of Special Investigations at our base as well as the local FBI office. Zazi could have decided to pursue an attack on our military base. Again I had to use my training and experience to do all I could to protect my personnel and the ADF site. Moving back to the US did not remove me from the threat of terrorism.

Terrorism, it seemed, had followed me home.

Indeed, my two years at the NRO illustrated something I already knew: that terrorists don't just hide in the armpits of hell; they can pop up in any country, in any city of the world. The war on terror is worldwide. The terrorism of the past, where our enemy fought for political control over their own land, has morphed into a global jihad where the goal is to take over the entire world and force everyone to accept their religion and their way of life, or be killed. It is a war that isn't going to stop and can't be easily won, if at all.

And I was still on the front lines.

29

Washington, DC ▪ 2010

After completing my assignment with the NRO, I took advantage of the Agency's "Leave Without Pay" program and took a six-month sabbatical to go back to Milwaukee where I helped my stepmother with some of the issues that were lingering from my father's passing. I also took some extended overseas vacation time, living in Thailand for several months learning some Thai language and attending a Wing Chun Kung Fu training camp. I then traveled to several Asian countries including the Philippines, Laos, and Cambodia. It was a mental health break from the consecutive high-stress tours I had experienced starting back in 2004.

During that time, I planned several visits to see my daughter Kirsty, each of which was waylaid by both of our schedules. She was growing up fast, in college at that point, and I was struck by the fear that I'd lost touch with my daughter. With no danger-fraught posting to distract me, I found myself fixating on the losses I'd suffered: my mother, father, stepfather, and now, I hated to think, my daughter, though due to entirely different circumstances called life. I resolved to do something about that, to not let our relationship slip through my fingers, but I needed to find the right opportunity and not just the resolve.

I went back to Washington, DC, with the batteries recharged and ready to tackle the rest of my career. Upon my return to CIA Headquarters, I was assigned to the Anti-Terrorism Force Protection (ATFP) office as a Special Counter-Terrorism Projects Manager. I was tasked with assisting the ATFP program manager in assessing the effectiveness of measures taken to prevent or mitigate hostile action against Agency personnel, facilities, and other resources. Specifically, I provided guidance on how to ensure that adequate security countermeasures were included in the planning, design, and execution of facility and compound construction and renovation projects in both war zone and non-war zone locations.

With my extensive war zone experience and background in personnel recovery and crisis management, I created and provided a briefing on crisis and emergency management for senior leadership bound for the war zones. I was also asked to be one of the instructors for a training course for security officers bound for the war zones teaching antiterrorism force protection principles, crisis management, and emergency management planning.

It was a really fun part of my duties, as I worked with a great group of instructors and our students were very motivated and receptive to our instruction. Many of them were junior security officers who needed as much structured guidance as we could give them, considering their pending assignments to war zones and other hostile regions of the world. I knew where they were going, because I'd been there. Figuratively as well as literally.

I felt a heavy sense of responsibility for those security officers, and I also knew that there was no way I could give them everything they would need to succeed in the chaos that was the field. I could only hope that we were providing them with the right and most applicable principles to guide their decision-making, and some atmospherics so that they could keep the right perspective when things got crazy. And they were going to get crazy—I could be sure of that much. They were going to be the tip of the spear and would be supporting our personnel in some of the most dangerous environments in the world. CIA management would expect them to step up and handle crisis situations and document them correctly so that HQS would know what happened, how it happened, and what the people on the ground were doing about it.

All of that is easier said than done, and the "Monday morning quarterbacking" remained a constant part of the job. Acquiring mentally thick skin was a necessity to keep functioning when you were second-guessed, but it just comes with the territory. Having survived my own tours, I knew the pitfalls as well as the immense satisfaction of being part of the team that got shit done. There is no greater feeling than to be in the field working issues that you knew were going to be briefed to senior leadership, even possibly to the president; and I hoped the students I was tasked with training would take the same attitude I had.

* * *

During that tour, there were several significant attacks on US embassies and consulates across the world. I was even involved in helping some of our officers in the field walk through their emergency plans. The situations highlighted a lack of preparation at some locations and caused us to reevaluate our emergency action plans. As a result of a review of those issues, I was asked to work on revamping emergency action plans on a global scale. This ended up being one of the most significant projects of my career, during which I created templates (personnel accountability, crisis management, emergency destruction, and emergency evacuation) to be used as general guides for the creation of station- and base-specific emergency management plans. The templates were designed to be useful for anyone, from the novice junior support officer up to senior security officers. I also provided extensive examples to facilitate matters and make it as much of a cut-and-paste process as possible, thus reducing the amount of effort to the bare minimum while ensuring continuity/consistency within the reports. The templates were then distributed worldwide and are now the standard for Agency crisis management.

While no true field guy likes a headquarters assignment, I was lucky to be in a position where I could put to great use all of my hard-earned experience and expertise and make a difference helping outbound senior management and security officers prepare for the huge challenge of war zone environments. In terms of seeing coworkers and friends in the big building, it was good to be back in Washington. I got a chance to live more of the nine-to-five lifestyle without all the politics that come with a command position like I had in the NRO.

But it was not all roses; I thought I'd be able to work on some other important issues, but time in the position meant I was subject to the mounds of paperwork, paperwork, and more paperwork that comes from an assignment within the "House of Flying Daggers.

Washington, DC ▪ July 2011

After several months with the ATFP office, I applied for and was selected to be the Deputy Chief of Security for the Counterterrorism Center (CTC). As CTC was one of the central players in the fight against terrorism, this was near to the top of the food chain within my career field at the CIA. As the deputy, I was tasked with supervising a large multidisciplinary security staff providing operational, policy, and procedural guidance to senior management on security issues, to include crisis management, personnel security processing, and information security management.

One interesting part of the job was the fact that I became directly involved in the strategic planning for the drawdown of the US military in Afghanistan and the subsequent changes to US intelligence and military operations.

Due to the critical focus of the US government on terrorism, I felt the weight of the position and all the responsibility that comes with having to provide effective, timely security support for CIA personnel at headquarters as well as at stations and bases overseas directly tasked with addressing the threat. During the tour I managed several multimillion-dollar force protection and security projects that directly impacted the security of our personnel in the field. I was in frequent meetings with senior CTC and Office of Security management on a variety of security issues. Due to the large population within CTC, I was involved in a significant amount of personnel security management issues assisting senior leadership and the human resources department with personnel security processing.

It might sound strange, but a lot of my real-world experience was actually put to use dealing with the personnel problems that we had in CTC. In many cases, I provided some important background information on what it was like for the officers serving overseas both in traditional non-war zone locations as well as in the hot spots. I tried to find the reasons for their issues and the best ways to deal with them and still keep them in the ranks. Anyone who served, especially in the war zones, deserved a second chance, if possible, and dependent upon the severity of the issue.

Instead of ending up more callous from my years fighting the evil hordes, I found that I had more empathy. Maybe it was all my life experiences tempering the standard black and white of the rules and regulations. Either way, I was glad I didn't work in the personnel security field early in my career. Instead, I used my experiences as lessons for the young security officers I managed.

One lesson that I had learned the hard way was sometimes it was easier to go sideways into the boat rather than head-on. Specifically, many of the younger folks were struggling with the more traditional environment at the Agency, and they resorted to what had always worked for them in the past, which meant hitting the internet or their peers for answers. The problem with this method is there are things you don't know you don't know, and the internet and your equally inexperienced peers are not going to be able to figure it out.

I began to secretly train my subordinates using various ploys. My favorite was the "I can't use my office so I have to work in the bullpen with you folks" excuse to spend the day in the cubicle farm that my staff worked in. I would then make telephone calls to other offices, mainly to personnel at the lowest level, to get certain issues fixed. On the telephone, I would not tell them I was a senior security officer. Instead, I would act as if I was just one of my staff and ask the person on the phone if they could help me. I knew my staff was listening and could clearly hear how I did not throw my weight around, how I politely asked for help. If the person I was speaking to could not help me, I would ask if they could suggest someone or another office who could. I would ask if I could use their name (giving them recognition) as a reference when I contacted the other person or office. I would often follow up with a thank-you letter from my office to the individual's boss to let them know how much assistance I received from their officer. This made it more likely that I would get help from them again if I called.

The strategy allowed me to demonstrate several of my preferred leadership principles. Specifically, I would show a humble ego and ask others for assistance. I would try to create strong cross-functional relationships and solve organizational problems/issues at the lowest level. Lastly, the thank-you letter I sent to their management showed appreciation.

While it was not "tip of the spear" stuff, I felt that the leadership training was very important for the future success of our younger officers, and it made the workplace much nicer. As the saying goes, "You get more bees with honey than you do with vinegar."

Initially, I enjoyed the pace in CTC and put up with the bureaucracy, but after a while I realized that, other than training the younger officers, I was moving farther and farther from the action. I could also see senior management looking to move me into more administrative leadership positions. While that might be a rewarding post for some people, something they'd built their entire careers toward, it would

Appreciation plaque for serving in the Counter-Terrorism Center (CTC).

take me into territory where my skills and experience wouldn't be as valuable.

I guess that was the moment when I realized my career was winding down. I had done every action job that I wanted to do at the CIA, and the handwriting on the wall said I was bound for strictly managerial roles in the future. That left me with some serious soul-searching to do.

* * *

In May 2012, I attended Kirsty's graduation at the University of Kent in Canterbury, England. Watching her get her diploma and talking about what she wanted to do for her career made me feel that my life had come full circle. I was so proud of my daughter and wanted so badly to make up for the fact that I had missed so much of her life. I wouldn't take back a single minute of service to my country and all the good I believed I had done in my various postings. Call it the classic zero-sum game, since all I'd achieved had come with a price.

Now, though, I was beginning to understand that there was more to life than the mission, that maybe I could have a life of my own and that life could include more time with my daughter.

Then, half a world away, Benghazi happened.

30

Washington, DC ▪ September 18, 2012

The week after the attack on the US Consulate in Benghazi, I met Bill at a local bar to catch up. The news channels were buzzing over the attack and the tragic loss of life by both State Department personnel and the Agency. Bill asked me what I knew about the attack. I responded that I didn't know much more than what was on the news, except for the fact that the word from our security personnel who had visited the consulate several weeks ago was that they had discussed the insufficient security measures with the Regional Security Officer in Benghazi and that the RSO had told them requests had been made for additional security resources. It was obvious from the reporting that the State Department had not responded to the requests, and that the result had been the loss of a standing ambassador.

When the consulate came under attack, the CIA annex security personnel had responded and saved the lives of the remaining State Department employees. Unfortunately, this action exposed the CIA annex building, and the terrorists then turned their firepower on that facility with the result being the loss of several security officers as well as one ARSO.

The situation wasn't unfamiliar to me, as I had seen various government interests underestimate the threat, politicize the issues, and resist the implementation of needed security measures. The United States was subjected to an unexpected mental reset when we got one between the eyes on 9/11. That caused us to rethink our security protocols in what became a true paradigm shift. For example, pre-9/11, if an aircraft was hijacked, standard recommended protocols for passengers and security personnel was to sit back and let the authorities negotiate with the hijackers. Post-9/11, no one will idly sit and wait. They simply won't take a chance that their plane will be used to kill innocent people. They will attack, as did the passengers on the ill-fated United Flight 93.

Unfortunately, humans, especially in large bureaucracies, soon forget the pain and begin to let their less honorable aspects take over: greed, avarice, envy, and denial. When these combine, death is not an uncommon result. Look at Daniel Pearl, the *Wall Street Journal* reporter whose drive to get "the story" overrode his common sense and the very pointed security recommendations made to him by a Diplomatic Security Service officer. This DSS agent was the last person Daniel spoke to, and the last words that Daniel heard were, "Don't leave the restaurant!"

In the case of Benghazi, while that honest assessment occurred on the ground level, the chain of command didn't heed the warnings and didn't respond to the repeated requests for more security support. As someone who has learned that the chain of command is a critical element in an effective organization, I knew that responsibility runs up and down the chain. At the end of the day, in the US military, the buck clearly stops with a senior command element. And it looks like that realization had to be learned the hardest of ways by the Department of State.

The saddest part of that tragedy is no one can really say if the DOS management learned a lesson from it. Who ultimately took responsibility? When the secretary of defense did not heed the requests for additional armor in Somalia in 1993 and lives were needlessly lost in the Battle of Mogadishu, he was fired. This sent a clear message to

Retirement photo on the CIA official seal in the entrance area of the Headquarters Building.

the US military that the buck stops at the top, and you will be held responsible.

Fast-forward to Benghazi: Secretary of State Hillary Clinton did not heed repeated requests for additional security support and, in the end, lives were needlessly lost, but no one was fired. The oblique finger pointing, deflections, the lies, left no doubt in the public's mind that the buck did not stop at the top—it just got lost in the bureaucracy. A sad day for the brave men and women of the Department of State who risk their lives in hellholes across the world trying to accomplish difficult tasks. How much more difficult is it when they do not know if they can count on their management to protect them?

I glanced in the mirror behind the bar and realized the two guys with the thousand-yard stares were Bill and me. We had gotten lost in the memory of the ambush we'd barely survived in Mogadishu so many years ago.

"Bill, how many lives does a cat get?"

"Tom, I don't know, but if I were you I wouldn't push my luck!"

That was a sobering thought, eye opening even as far as my future was concerned.

"Are you okay, Tom?" Bill asked me. "You're looking pretty grim there."

"Bill," I replied, "I'm just tired of the fight. I've spent more than two decades in combat with terrorism, and these people are still determined to kill us. There's no negotiating with them. It's a duel to the death, win or die, just like it was when we started. Did we really make a difference? Were all the sacrifices we made worth all of the life we missed?"

Bill grabbed me by the shoulder and looked me in the eye. "Arrive alive, baby! Nobody died on our watch and, by God, you're damn right that means something!"

* * *

I went back to the grind of being a senior security manager in head-quarters, except for a favor I did for a friend who desperately wanted to spend the Christmas and New Year's holidays with his family. The kicker was he was posted in Kabul, Afghanistan. I agreed to replace him despite the threat reporting that the bad guys were not behaving as expected. Usually they go up to their caves in the mountains to wait out the winter, but not that winter. They were increasingly active, making it the most dangerous holiday I ever spent overseas.

After returning from my three-week TDY in Afghanistan, I decided it was time to do something different, to hand the baton off to the younger security officers, and for me to try and use my skills and experience somewhere else. I had done my duty, fulfilled all my obligations, and come September—based on age and time in service—I would be eligible to retire with full benefits.

On October 31, 2013, I officially retired from the CIA. In many ways it was fitting to retire on Halloween, since I'd worn so many

The United States of America

Central Intelligence Agency

Citation

THOMAS PECORA

is hereby awarded the

CAREER INTELLIGENCE MEDAL

in recognition of over twenty-four years of exemplary service to the Central Intelligence Agency. Throughout his career, Mr. Pecora was an innovative and driven Security Officer who consistently demonstrated excellent performance, outstanding initiative, and dedication to the Agency mission. He served with distinction in the Directors Area, National Clandestine Service, and Office of Security in positions of increasing responsibilities and mission impact. He took the dangerous assignments and provided support required of those positions and then established written procedures for the protection of programs and people that leave an enduring legacy. Mr. Pecora's exceptional contributions and courage under fire reflect great credit upon him, the Office of Security, the Central Intelligence Agency, and the Federal Service.

Career Intelligence Medal given for twenty-four years of exemplary service to the CIA.

costumes during my career. Background Investigator, Security Duty Officer, Protective Operations Cadre officer, Counter-Terrorism Unit member, Counterterrorism Training Officer, Area Security Officer, Special Projects Manager, and Chief and Deputy Chief of Security. It was time to try on a new one: civilian security consultant. My security colleagues threw me a superb unofficial retirement party attended by many of my closest friends. We reminisced and laughed about the crazy circumstances we had found ourselves in over the years. How we used to say, "You have to love it when it sucks." As we joked about how much *fun* we had in the war zones, I knew that the only thing I would really miss were my friends.

It was only after the party that I came face-to-face with the fact that my career was over. I had spent so much of life *in it* that I never really contemplated what it would be like when I was *out of it*. I guess I was going to find out.

"When you make difficult decisions," Jose Rodriguez wrote of his own retirement in *Hard Measures*, "you must do so with the hope but not the expectation that in the end your actions will be validated and vindicated. The easiest thing in the world is to make no tough decisions. I could have had a much more placid and profitable life in recent years if I had elected to make no tough choices. Those who 'go along to get along' rarely suffer negative consequences."

It was a bright sunny day when I drove out of the CIA Headquarters compound and hit the highway, heading to Milwaukee to start a new life. I had arrived twenty-four years earlier a much different person, and was leaving with no regrets.

After you retire, you receive a US flag that was flown over the CIA Headquarters building, a medallion that represents your number of years of service, and a certificate of appreciation signed by the Director of Central Intelligence thanking you for your service. Months later, a committee of your peers reviews your career and, depending upon the impact of your service, you may get an additional award. In my case, I was awarded one of the highest of all in the form of the Career

Intelligence Medal for a cumulative record of exemplary service that reflected exceptional achievements that substantially contributed to the mission of the Agency. The award citation reads:

> *Throughout his career, Mr. Pecora was an innovative and driven Security Officer who consistently demonstrated excellent performance, outstanding initiative, and dedication to the Agency mission. He served with distinction in positions of increasing responsibilities and mission impact. He took the dangerous assignments and provided support required of those positions and then established written procedures for the protection of programs and people that leave an enduring legacy. Mr. Pecora's exceptional contributions and courage under fire reflected great credit upon him, the Office of Security, the CIA, and the Federal Service.*

A month later I left the United States for London, where I was going to begin to make up for all that lost time with my daughter. Call it a different kind of adventure, and I wouldn't have it any other way.

EPILOGUE

London, England ▪ August, 2017

Over the next few years, in addition to getting to know my daughter better, I traveled extensively throughout Asia before going back home to Milwaukee. I'd barely gotten my bags unpacked when I got the news that Kirsty had fallen in love with a young Englishman and was set to get married. In August of 2017, I was slated to walk my daughter down the aisle.

Call it making up for lost time, given she was almost a teenager when I'd first met her.

It was to be a traditional English wedding with all the trimmings, to include morning coats with tails and top hats for the men. The church featured old English architecture nestled among worn-down gravestones sitting within a small, battered stone wall. A local pub sat just across the street, making it easier for patrons to quench their thirst after the Sunday sermon.

The reception venue was a quaint manor house on a large estate surrounded by working farm fields and some livestock. The Tudor-style structure was full of character, including beautifully worn wood floors, while the two main banquet halls boasted more modern construction with tent-like materials hiding their corrugated steel roofs and glass doors. The smaller hall was to be our vessel for the wedding

347

reception, including the "Breakfast Meal," specially named since it's the first the bride and groom enjoy as a married couple. Later during the evening, a barbeque was prepared to feed the additional guests who came to the less formal dance part of the occasion.

The fourteen American relatives as well as some of the local English ones took a red double-decker bus from the church to the reception, enjoying the scenery of the English countryside afforded from the top deck of the bus. The sixty or so people who arrived at the reception were greeted to a tasteful Disney motif including a wedding cake topped by Mickey and Minnie Mouse playing their role as bride and groom. A stuffed Cheshire Cat would sneak from place to place during the festivities, helped by the sly machinations of the reception staff. We were later gifted to a double rainbow before night fell, along with a mini fireworks display.

Before the traditional father of the bride walk down the church aisle, I was treated to a solo ride with my daughter to the church in a custom-made wedding car. I took the moment to present Kirsty with a small token of my affection in the form of a Pandora bracelet charm with "DAUGHTER" written on it as a reminder that while big things were in play, one thing would still stay the same. I waited until the father of the bride speech was behind me before finally fetching myself a well-earned beer, and began to mentally prepare for the last of my duties in the form of the father-daughter dance!

I didn't know until the moment we linked arms how much that dance meant to me and how proud I was of Kirsty. I made sure to twirl us slowly around the dance floor to ensure people could get the required photos. Her dress lit up as it passed over the pinhole lighting in the floor that radiated an almost supernatural glow. The song felt like it lasted a second, mostly because a part of me never wanted it to end. I'd chosen it myself, from my own heart, and later heard from Kirsty's mother Allison how much she'd enjoyed my choice for the sentiment and message it conveyed.

Father and daughter at her wedding in England.

That song was "Landslide" by Fleetwood Mac, in large part because of the appropriateness of the stanza that references the fact that we're all getting older, that you can't stop time.

I watched the evening pass in magical form as my daughter and her new husband, my son-in-law, made their way around the room chatting and laughing with their new collective friends and family. The day could not have gone more smoothly and I was remarkably content, and a bit drunk, as I waved off the final guests in their taxis, grabbed a Krispy Kreme donut, and headed up to my room in the manor guest wing.

The birds singing and the bright sunshine woke me early the following morning, which I greeted with a nasty hangover from imbibing a few too many beers. After cleaning up, I hit the downstairs breakfast area and found I was the first in, so I grabbed a coffee and contently waited for the other immediate family who'd also stayed overnight at the manor house. It was a short wait, as everyone seemed to come in at once. After assisting with some of the packing up of gifts, cards, and wedding decorations, I was given a ride to a local hotel, where I dropped off my stuff and immediately headed to the Reading train station to do a one-day tourist romp through Windsor Castle and its surrounding sights.

My England trip ended with a visit to Canterbury Cathedral and a local haunted pub built in the 1400s. Then it was back to the US to my new house in Milwaukee, where I was looking forward to the next phase of my life, digging new roots in old soil. It might not be as exciting or fulfilling as my twenty-four years as a special operator, but that's okay.

Because, as the song says, I'm getting older, too.

APPENDIX

LEADERSHIP OPERATING PRINCIPLES

After a twenty-four-year career in the Central Intelligence Agency, people have asked what key elements were influential in making my career successful and helping me move up the ladder, taking positions with more and more responsibility and managing larger, more complex programs. I have thought about that, and it boils down to six principles that I've already touched upon briefly.

1. Maintain a humble ego.

- Do not let your ego get in the way of finding solutions, new concepts, and improvements. You do not have all the answers!

- Accept that people—managers, peers, staff, and so on—are your best resource, and you need to interact with them to be successful.

- Ask for help: from managers, peers, and direct reports.

- Focus on success as the end product, not who did the work.

In the Security Duty Office, "customer service" was a critical element to accomplishing the mission. This element is very difficult if you wear your ego on your sleeve. You must put yourself into the mindset that helping people get what they need is the goal. As a general principle, asking for help when you don't know the answer, especially from personnel outside of your area or with a lower rank, is often the best way to get the job done in the most efficient manner possible.

In Iraq, that principle was especially important as I often needed the optic from ground-level personnel who, if they could not help me themselves, often knew who could. In life-threatening environments, respectfully asking for assistance is not seen as a weakness but a strength.

2. Know thyself.

- Understand your preferences in working with others (i.e. your internal software) by taking self-assessments: Meyers-Briggs Type Indicator, Firo-B, TKI, and Psychometrics 360.

- Flex your preferences as needed when working with other people to maximize your influence, effectiveness, and results.

- Develop this understanding of yourself early so you can create the best possible career.

While serving in the SDO as the Chief of Security and as the Director/Chief of Security at an NRO facility, I worked with a wide variety of personnel from a number of agencies and organizations. Learning to understand your own personal "operating system" will make a huge difference when you are exposed to a variety of people wired differently than you. It also allows you to depersonalize an issue if it is a matter of personality rather than a matter of intent. Understanding different personality types, including your own, also gives you insight in how best to present your ideas and what methods would be most efficient to get group consensus.

3. Create strong cross-functional horizontal relationships.

- Proactively develop relationships across the organization to enhance cooperation, communication, knowledge/data sharing, sharing of resources, and networking.

- Invite stakeholders to your staff meetings, have lunches and regular one-on-one meetings, share knowledge/data, and attend department/company events to network and create strong relationships.

While conducting background investigations, I quickly realized that I could leverage the knowledge and experience of people by establishing strong relationships with them. I had to collect information from a variety of sources within and without an organization, from senior managers to administrative assistants, from coworkers to neighbors, and I learned it was especially important to have solid relationships in place prior to a crisis because it is a bad time to start introductions during an emergency!

I started a process, in all of my staff meetings, where we would go around the room asking if anybody had any suggestions for improvement to our unit, any issues that needed to be addressed, or any problems that needed to be solved. I would write down everything that was said and do my best to implement at least one of the suggestions or address one of the problems identified. I would then report what was done and give credit to the individual who provided the information. I could break through some serious barriers that way, and I began to truly tap into the knowledge, expertise, and experience of my officers.

After 9/11, I used my connections among my peers to keep an eye on how other locations were dealing with their threat issues. I also frequently leveraged my peers within other organizations to work around bureaucratic problems.

4. **Solve organizational problems/issues at the lowest level.**
   - Proactively identify organizational problems/issues at your level and find solutions at the lowest vertical and horizontal level.
   - When required, raise critical problems/issues vertically with co-created solutions with your cross-functional stakeholders.

While I was in Iraq, I often went to the lowest ranking military member I could find to get help with problems that they were familiar with. Often just letting them know that you could use their help was enough to open the door. Not only did they frequently have the answers I needed, if they didn't they almost variably knew someone who did.

In CTC, I always started looking for a solution at the lowest level by contacting the office that was responsible for the issue and asking the working-level officers for assistance. Only when they could not solve the problem or were not cooperative did I kick up the food chain.

5. Nurture positive passion.

- A positive passion mindset recognizes that we learn, grow, and develop in our work, projects, and assignments even when they are challenging or when setbacks occur.

- Express your passion for your work, projects, and assignments. Even when you face challenging projects, have a positive manner.

- Seek new roles, jobs, or organizations if you do not have passion about your work, projects, or assignments.

When I was running background investigations, I made it a point of telling my management how excited I was to have an opportunity to attend the Special Protective Operations Cadre training. While attending SPOC training, I was the guy on the range who would run down (not walk) to set the targets back up, as this would give us more training time. I showed sincere interest in the coursework, asked questions, and listened intently. These are types of actions that show passion and are much more believable then mere words.

As my career progressed, I attempted several times to get into the Counter-Terrorism Unit, and I made sure to let everyone know that I was willing to do whatever it took to make it happen. This is a variation of the "cat" principle: "It never hurts to ask for what you want," especially if you do it with a sincere smile on your face!

6. **Show appreciation.**
   - Both managers and employees should express their appreciation when their peers, leaders, clients, vendors, or staff do very good work.
   - Utilize email, texts, face-to-face/video conferences, staff meetings, or one-to-one meetings to express appreciation, and always make sure the employee's direct manager knows as well.
   - Appreciation creates more engaged employees and a positive culture that produces higher productivity!

I asked the POC management if we could show our appreciation for all of the part-time POC members by drafting up a letter for each of them that was customized to specifically mention the trips they took and the sacrifices (holidays, nights, weekends, birthdays, and so forth) they made. These letters would go to the recipients as well as the personnel office for use during their performance evaluations.

At NRO, I took every opportunity to announce the great work people were doing on site and then followed this up with a letter to the individual as well as a letter/email to the most senior person I knew in their home organization. I also made sure that my upper management knew who was behind every successful project, every crisis handled, and every good deed done. Only by acknowledging the success of my subordinates could I truly show the appreciation I felt for the hard work they did.

As leaders, we must take responsibility for any shortcomings that happen as a result of honest mistakes with no attribution to the employee. The buck always stops with the boss!

ACKNOWLEDGMENTS

To Michael Milbier, who helped me develop my leadership/operating principles model and to David Mahon, a true security professional and leader who inspires people by his example.